P9-EML-548

EVERY ONE A WITNESS
THE PLANTAGENET AGE

ALSO BY A. F. SCOTT

MEANING AND STYLE
POETRY AND APPRECIATION
MODERN ESSAYS (three series)
TOPIC AND OPINIONS (three series)
THE SPOKEN WORD (two series)
SPEAKING OF THE FAMOUS
VITAL THEMES TODAY
THE CRAFT OF PROSE
CURRENT LITERARY TERMS
(A Dictionary of their Origin and Use)
ANGLO-BENGALI SCHOOL FINAL ENGLISH
COMPOSITION AND TRANSLATION
(with Professor Dharanimohan Mukherjee)
NEW HORIZONS, in ten books (with N. K. Aggarwala)
(Macmillan)

ENGLISH COMPOSITION (Books I-IV)
POEMS FOR PLEASURE (Books I-III)
THOUGHT AND EXPRESSION
PLAIN ENGLISH (Books I-V)
THE POET'S CRAFT
(Cambridge University Press)

ILLUSTRATED ENGLISH (Books I-VIII)
(Max Parrish)

NEW READING, in sixteen books
(The Reader's Digest Association)

ODHAMS YOUNG PEOPLE'S ENCYCLOPAEDIA
(four books, section on English Literature)

CLOSE READINGS
(Heinemann)

TABARIN TALES (Books I-VI)
(Geoffrey Chapman)
EVERY ONE A WITNESS: THE GEORGIAN AGE
EVERY ONE A WITNESS: THE STUART AGE
WITCH, SPIRIT, DEVIL
(White Lion Publishers, London)

WHO'S WHO IN CHAUCER
(Elm Tree Books, Hamish Hamilton)

EVERY ONE
A WITNESS

The Plantagenet Age

COMMENTARIES OF AN ERA

A. F. SCOTT

WHITE LION PUBLISHERS LIMITED
London, New York, Sydney and Toronto

ST. PHILIPS COLLEGE LIBRARY

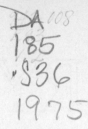

DA 108
185
·S36
1975

Copyright © Scott & Finlay Ltd., 1975

First published in the United Kingdom
by White Lion Publishers, 1975

ISBN 7274 0040 1

Made and printed in
Great Britain
for White Lion Publishers Limited
138 Park Lane, London W1Y 3DD
by
R. Kingshott & Co. Ltd.,
Deadbrook Lane, Aldershot, Hampshire

CONTENTS

54046

LIST OF ILLUSTRATIONS

The Author and publisher acknowledge with thanks permission to reproduce the illustrations listed below.

viii

ACKNOWLEDGEMENTS

The author and publishers are grateful to the authorities named for permission to use copyright material. Furthermore, the publishers have tried to trace the owners of all copyright material, and apologise for any omissions. Should these be made known to us proper acknowledgements will be made in future editions.

To my daughters
Jennifer and Christine

Men's eyes were made to look, and let them gaze.
                                          Shakespeare

        . . . beneath whose eyes,
  All period, power, and enterprize
    Commences, reigns, and ends.
              Christopher Smart

Royalty

Neither Henry II nor Richard was popular in his own day;
Historians have seen their deeds in a brighter light, but it is only
now that John's reign is being seen as a period of consolidation,
and one of utilisation and improvement on the administrative
structures built by his father. Thus John of Salisbury could
nickname John 'Proteous'—referring to his underhand negotiations
—and William of Newburgh, writing in Richard's reign, can say of
Henry's reputation 'The experience of present evils has revived
the memory of his good deeds, and the man who in his own
lifetime was hated by nearly all men is now declared to have been
an excellent and beneficent prince .'
The 'Lion of Chivalry' portrait of Richard was indeed sketched
during his reign, as witness the remarks of Richard, Canon of
Holy Trinity in Aldgate, but the true picture was more often that
revealed by Gerald of Wales who saw him as a man who 'cared
for no success that was was not reached by a path cut by his own
sword and stained with the blood of his adversaries.' Indeed,
the Itinerarium Pergrinorum, (the Journey of the Crusaders) is
untypical in indulging in flowery, rhetorical descriptions of his
Apollo-like valour and behaviour.
   A contemporary picture of John is much harder to obtain. The
great biographers had died by about the turn of the century.

HENRY II
You may know then that our king is still ruddy, except as old age
and whitening hair have changed his colour a little. He is of
medium stature so that among small men he does not seem large,
nor yet among large men does he seem small. His head is spherical,
as if the abode of great wisdom and the special sanctuary of lofty
intelligence. The size of his head is in proportion to the neck
and the whole body. His eyes are full, guileless and dove-like
when he is at peace, gleaming like fire when his temper is
aroused, and in bursts of passion they flash like lightning. As to
his hair, he is in no danger of baldness, but his head has been

1

closely shaved. He has a broad, square, lion-like face. His feet are arched and he has the legs of a horseman. His broad chest and muscular arms show him to be a strong, bold, active man. His hands show by their coarseness that he is careless and pays little attention to his person, for he never wears gloves except when he goes hawking . . . Although his legs are bruised and livid from hard riding, he never sits down except when on horseback or at meals . . . He always has his weapons in his hands when not engaged in consultation or at his books. When his cares and anxieties allow him to breathe, he occupies himself with reading, or in a circle of clerks tries to solve some knotty question . . .

Peter of Blois, *Epistolae*

HENRY II

Henry II, king of England, was a man of reddish, freckled complexion with a large round head, grey eyes which glowed fiercely and grew bloodshot in anger, a fiery countenance and a harsh, cracked voice. His neck was somewhat thrust forward from his shoulders, his chest was broad and square, his arms strong and powerful. His frame was stocky with a pronounced tendency to corpulence, due rather to nature than to indulgence, which he tempered by exercise. For in eating and drinking he was moderate and sparing, and in all things frugal in the degree permissible to a prince. To restrain and moderate by exercise the injustice done him by nature and to mitigate his physical defects by virtue of the mind, he taxed his body with excessive hardship thus, as it were, fomenting civil war in his own person.

In times of war, which frequently threatened, he gave himself scarcely a modicum of quiet to deal with those matters of business which were left over, and in times of peace, he allowed himself neither tranquillity nor repose. He was addicted to the chase beyond measure; at crack of dawn he was off on horseback, traversing waste lands, penetrating forests and climbing mountain-tops, and so he passed restless days. At evening on his return home he was rarely seen to sit down either before or after supper. After such great and wearisome exertions he would wear out the whole court by continual standing. But since 'above everything moderation is beneficial in life', and no remedy is good by itself alone, the swelling of his feet and legs, aggravated by injuries sustained in spurring his refractory horses, brought on other bodily ailments, and without doubt old age the mother and handmaid of many evils.

In stature he was of middle height, and in this he was matched by none of his sons, for the two eldest were a little above the average, while the two youngest stopped short of it. Except when troubled in mind or moved to anger, he was a prince of great eloquence, and what is remarkable in these days, polished in letters.

He was most diligent in guarding and maintaining peace, liberal beyond comparison in almsgiving and the pecular defender of the Holy Land; a lover of humility, an oppressor of the nobility and a contemner of the proud, 'filling the hungry with good things and sending the rich empty away, exalting the humble and putting down the mighty from their seat'. By his detestable usurpations in the things pertaining to God he was highly presumptuous; out of zeal for justice, but not informed by knowledge, he joined together, or rather confounded the laws of Church and State, making them both one. As a son of the church, from whom he acquired the sceptre of royalty, he was either forgetful of his sacramental unction or ignored the fact that he had received it, devoting scarcely an hour to the divine mysteries of the sacred Host, and that very time, perchance through pressure of affairs of State, he passed more in taking counsel and in discussions than in his devotions. The revenues of vacant benefices he paid into the public treasury and as the whole lump may be spoilt by a little leaven, whilst he confiscated the revenues which Christ claims for himself, new difficulties continually arose and he was forced to pour forth his whole treasure, bestowing on the impious soldiery the moneys which should have been given to the priesthood. Through his consummate prudence he devised many changes and ordered them with foresight, but the issue of events was not always favourable and often seemed to work to a contrary end. Never did a great misfortune arise which was not brought about by familiar causes.

Gerald of Wales, Expugnatio Hibernica,
English Historical Documents II

HENRY II

This same King Henry was a man of many and large and fat almsdeeds, but in secret, lest it should be known to his left hand what his right hand gave. . . .

There is a fault which, as I have already said, he contracted from his mother's teaching: he is wasteful of time over the affairs of his people, and so it comes about that many die before they get their matters settled, or leave the court depressed and penniless, driven by hunger. Another fault is that when he makes a stay anywhere (away from home), which rarely occurs, he does not allow himself to be seen as honest men would have him do, but shuts himself up within, and is only accessible to those who seem unworthy of such ready access. There is a third fault, that he is intolerant of quiet and does not in pity refrain from troubling almost half of Christendom. In these three ways he goes wrong: in other respects he is very good, and in all amiable. There does not seem to be anyone beside him possessed of such temper and affability. Whatever way he goes out he is seized upon by the crowds and pulled hither and thither, pushed whither he would not, and surprising to say, listens to each man with patience, and though assaulted by all with shouts and pullings and rough pushings, does not challenge anyone for it, nor show any appearance of anger, and when he is hustled beyond bearing silently retreats to some place of quiet. He does nothing in a proud or overbearing fashion, is sober, modest, pious, trustworthy and careful, generous and successful, and ready to honour the deserving.

> Walter Map, *De Nugis Curialium,* translated by M. R. James,
> Crymmrodorion Record Series

RICHARD 1, RICHARD CŒUR-DE-LION

He was lofty of stature, of shapely build, his hair halfway between red and yellow, his limbs straight and supple, His arms were somewhat long and, therefore, better fitted than those of most folk to draw or wield a sword. He had, moreover, long legs in keeping with the character of his whole frame. His features showed him to be a ruler, while his manners and bearing added not a little to his general presence. He could claim the highest position and the praise, not only by reason of his noble birth, but because of his virtues. He far surpassed other men in courtesy and the greatness of his strength.

> Richard, Canon of Holy Trinity in Aldgate,
> *Itinerarium Peregrinorum et Gestis Regis Ricardi*

RICHARD I

His generosity, and his virtuous endowments, the ruler of the world should have given to the ancient times; for in this period of the world, as it waxes old, such feelings rarely exhibit themselves, and when they do they are subjects of wonder and astonishment. He had the valour of Hector, the magnanimity of Achilles, and was equal to Alexander, and not inferior to Roland in valour; nay, he outshone many illustrious characters of our own times. The liberality of a Titus was his, and, which is so rarely found in a soldier, he was gifted with the eloquence of Nestor and the prudence of Ulysses; and he shewed himself pre-eminent in the conclusion and transaction of business, as one whose knowledge was not without active goodwill to aid it, nor his goodwill wanting in knowledge. Who, if Richard were accused of presumption, would not readily excuse him, knowing him for a man who never knew defeat, impatient of an injury, and impelled irresistibly to vindicate his rights, though all he did was characterized by innate nobleness of mind? Success made him better fitted for action; fortune ever favours the bold, and though she works her pleasure on whom she will, Richard was never to be overwhelmed with adversity. He was tall of stature, graceful in figure; his hair between red and auburn; his limbs were straight and flexible; his arms rather long, and not to be matched for wielding the sword or for striking with it; and his long legs suited the rest of his frame; while his appearance was commanding, and his manners and habits suitable; and he gained the greatest celebrity, not more from his high birth than from the virtues that adorned him. But why need we take much labour in extolling the fame of so great a man? He needs no superfluous commendation, for he has a sufficient need of praise, which is the sure companion of great actions. He was far superior to all others both in moral goodness and in strength, and memorable for prowess in battles, and his mighty deeds outshone the most brillant description we could give of them. Happy, in truth, might he have been deemed had he been without rivals who envied his glorious actions, and whose only cause of enmity was his magnificence, and his being the searcher after virtue rather than the slave of vice.

Itinerary of Richard I, written in French by an eyewitness unknown, then translated into Latin by Richard, Prior of Holy Trinity, Aldgate, London

JOHN

Then the king heaved deep sighs, began to feel the utmost irritation, started to turn in upon himself and languish . . . He started to gnash his teeth and roll his staring eyes in fury. Then he would pick up sticks and straws and gnaw them like a lunatic and sometimes he would cast them away half-chewed. His uncontrolled gestures gave indications of the melancholy, or rather of the madness, that was upon him.

Matthew Paris, *Chronica Majora*

JOHN

How the king of England by letters patent ordered the aforesaid liberties [in the Great Charter] to be observed.

After this King John sent his letters patent through all the English territories, strictly ordering all the sheriffs of the whole kingdom to make the inhabitants in their jurisdictions of every rank swear to observe the above-written laws and liberties, and also, as far as lay in their power, to annoy and harass him, the king, by taking his castles till he fulfilled all the above-mentioned terms, as contained in the Charter. After which, many nobles of the kingdom came to the king asking him for their rights of land and possessions, and the custody of the castles, which as they said, belonged to them by hereditary right; but the king delayed this matter till it was proved on the oath of liegemen, what of right was due to each; and, the more fully to effect this, he fixed the 16th of August as a day for them all to come to Westminster. Nevertheless he restored to Stephen Archbishop of Canterbury the castle of Rochester and the Tower of London, which by old right belonged to his custody: and then breaking up the conference, the barons returned with the above-named charter to London.

How king John retired clandestinely to the Isle of Wight and laid plans against the barons.

After the barons, as has been stated, had gone from the conference, the king was left with scarcely seven knights out of his proper body of attendants. Whilst lying sleepless that night in Windsor Castle, his thoughts alarmed him much, and before daylight he fled by stealth to the Isle of Wight, and there in great agony of mind devised plans to be revenged on the barons. At length, after divers meditations, he determined, with the assistance of the apostle Peter, to seek revenge on his enemies with two swords, the spiritual and temporal, so that if he could not succeed with the one, he might for certain accomplish his purpose with the other. To strike at them with the spiritual sword, he sent Pandulph the Pope's subdeacon with other messengers to the court of Rome, to counteract, by the apostolic authority, the intentions of the barons. He also sent . . . with his own seal, to all the transmarine territories to procure supplies of troops in those parts, promising them lands, ample possessions, and no small sum of money. . . .

Roger of Wendover, *Flowers of History*, translated by J. A. Giles, Bohn's Antiquarian Library

JOHN

He was a great Prince certainly but hardly a happy one, and, like Marius, he experienced ups and downs of fortune . . . Ireland, Scotland and Wales all bowed to his nod—a situation which, as is well known, none of his predecessors had achieved—and he would have thought himself as happy and successful as he could have wished, had he not been despoiled of his continental possessions and suffered the Church's curse.

Annals of Barnwell Priory in 'Memoriale Walteri de Coventria' edited by W. Stubbs (Rolls Series 1872-3)

HENRY III

He was, however, of moderate stature, of compact body, with the lid of one eye rather drooping, so that it concealed part of the blackness of the pupil; robust in strength, but impulsive in action . . .

Nicholas Trivet or Trevet, *Annales Sex Regum Angliæ*

EDWARD I

Edward, king of the English, the first-born of Henry III and Eleanor, daughter of the Count of Provence, was thirty-three years and five months old on the day when his father died and he succeeded to the kingdom. He was a man of tried prudence in the transaction of affairs, devoted from his earliest years to the practice of arms. Hence he had won that fame as a knight in diverse lands which gave him a transcendent place among christian princes. He was handsome, and so tall that he stood head and shoulders above most people. His hair, light and silvery when he was a boy, turned very dark in manhood, and, as he grew old, became as white as a swan. He had a broad brow and symmetrical features, except that a droop of the left eyelid recalled his father's appearance. He was persuasive and ready in speech, in spite of his lisp. His long arms with their powerful and agile play enabled him to become a swordsman second to none; his chest projected beyond his belly, and his long shanks gave him his firm seat in the saddle and his mastery over the most spirited thoroughbred. When he was not fighting, his passions were hawking and the chase, particularly of stag, which he followed on a courser, and slew with his sword, making no use of the trap or buckstall as a hunter.

He was a very fortunate man, protected by the most high God. One day, when he was quite young, he was playing chess with a knight in a vaulted chamber, and, for no particular reason, suddenly arose and went out of the room, whereupon an enormous stone fell just where he had been sitting. On numerous occasions too he escaped from tight places, and was saved from accidents. He had that greatness of mind which is impatient of injury, heedless of danger in the pursuit of vengeance, yet easily mollified by submission. One day he was hawking by a river and noticed that one of his companions was neglecting to deal with a falcon which had fastened onto a duck among some willows. He expostulated, and when the other seemed slow to respond, lost his temper and began to threaten him. The stream was between them; no ford or bridge was nearby, and the man flippantly called attention to his immunity. Edward, thoroughly aroused, immediately plunged into the water, not knowing how deep it was, swam his horse across, and in spite of the overhanging bank forced his way out on the other side. He now pursued his companion sword in hand, but when he, despairing of escaping, turned his horse and awaited the blow with bared head Edward checked his horse, sheathed his sword and they returned amicably to deal with the falcon.

Nicholas Trivet, *Annals,* edited by T. Hog.
Translated by F. M. Powicke *Henry III and Lord Edward*

EDWARD PRINCE OF WALES, LATER EDWARD II

To Louis of Evreux, half-brother of Philip IV of France:
We are sending you a big trotting palfrey, which can hardly carry, and stands still when laden; and we send you some misshapen greyhounds from Wales, which can catch a hare well if they find it asleep, and running dogs which can follow at an amble, for well we know how you love the joy of lazy dogs. And, dear cousin, if you would care for anything else from our land of Wales, we will send you some wild men, if you like, who will know well how to give young sprigs of nobility their education.

To the Earl of Lincoln:
Know, sire, that on Sunday the thirteenth of June we came to Midhurst, where we found our lord the king our father; and on Monday following, on account of certain words which were reported to him as having passed between us and the Bishop of Chester, he became so enraged with us, that he has forbidden us to be so bold as to come into his household, we or any of our following, and he has forbidden all the folk of his household and of the Exchequer to give or lend us anything for the upkeep of our household. We have remained at Midhurst to await his

1. This bronze effigy of Eleanor of Castile, the wife of Edward I, is a masterpiece by the sculptor William Torel, c. 1291-1293, Westminster Abbey.

goodwill and favour, and we shall follow him all the time as best
we can, ten or twelve leagues away from his household, so that we
may recover his good will as we greatly desire.

Wherefore we pray you especially that on your return from
Canterbury you will come to us, for we have great need of your
aid and counsel.

To Sir Walter Reynolds, Keeper of the Prince's Household:
Since we hear that Queen Marie of France and Monsire Louis her
son will soon be coming to England, and that we shall have to
meet them and keep them company while they are over here; and
it is desirable therefore to be well mounted in respect of palfreys
and well dressed in respect of robes and other matters against
their coming; we bid you to cause to be brought for our use two
fair palfreys suitable for our own riding and two saddles with
reins cut out of the best we have in the care of Gilbert of
Taunton, and the best and finest cloth that you can find for sale
in London for two or three robes for our use with the fur and
loops appurtenant; and when you have provided these things,
cause them to come to us wherever we may be as quickly as you
can.

> *Letters of Edward Prince of Wales,* 1304-1305,
> edited by Professor Hilda Johnstone for the Roxburghe Club.

EDWARD III
Before the Battle of Crecy

The king then mounted a small palfrey, having a white wand
in his hand, and attended by his two marshals on each side of
him: he rode [at] a foot's pace through all the ranks, encouraging
and intreating the army, that they would guard his honour and
defend his right. He spoke so sweetly, and with such a cheerful
countenance, that all who had been dispirited were directly
comforted by seeing and hearing him.

Whe he had thus visited all the battalions, it was near ten
o'clock: he retired to his own division, and ordered them all to
eat heartily, and drink a glass after. They ate and drank at their
ease; and having packed up pots, barrels, etc. in the carts, they
returned to their battalions, according to the marshals' orders,
and seated themselves on the ground, placing their helmets and
bows before them, that they might be the fresher when their
enemies should arrive.

> John Froissart, *Chronicles,* translated by Thomas Johnes

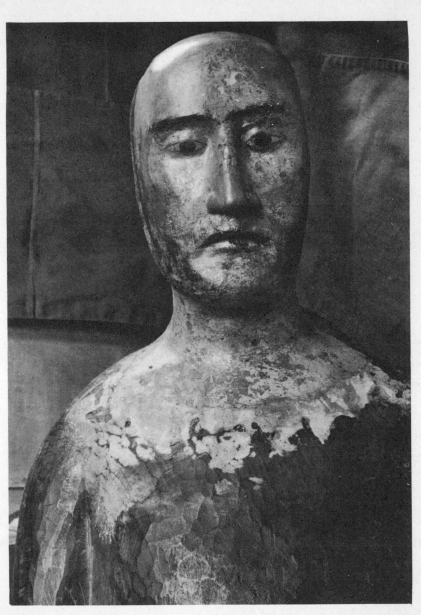

2. Edward III, wooden funeral effigy, Westminster Abbey.

QUEEN PHILIPPA
Inspection and Description of the Daughter of the Count of Hainault, Philippa by name.

The lady whom we saw has not uncomely hair, betwixt blue-black and brown. Her head is clean shaped; her forehead high and broad, and standing somewhat forward. Her face narrows between the eyes, and the lower part of her face is still more narrow and slender that the forehead. Her eyes are blackish-brown and deep. Her nose is fairly smooth and even, save that it is somewhat broad at the tip and also flattened, and yet it is no snub-nose. Her nostrils are also broad, her mouth fairly wide. Her lips somewhat full, and especially the lower lip. Her teeth which have fallen and grown again are white enough, but the rest are not so white. The lower teeth project a little beyond the upper; yet this is but little seen. Her ears and chin are comely enough. Her neck, shoulder, and all her body are well set and unmaimed; and nought is amiss so far as a man may see. Moreover, she is brown of skin all over, and much like her father; and in all things she is pleasant enough, as it seems to us. And the damsel will be of the age of nine years on St. John's day next to come, as her mother saith. She is neither too tall nor too short for such an age; she is of fair carriage, and well taught in all that becometh her rank, and highly esteemed and well beloved of her father and mother and of all her meinie, in so far as we could inquire and learn the truth.

Bishop Stapledon made this report on the prospective bride of Edward III, translated, G. G. Coulton, *Medieval Panorama*, The English Scene from Conquest to Reformation, from Register
Stapledon, 169, 1319

RICHARD II, called 'of Bordeaux'
Where he sits on his white horse, they draw back so that the good King himself may be seen by his people. How fresh-coloured his face, crowned with yellow hair, his combed locks shining under the garland; gleaming with gold in the red robe that covers too much his fair body.

Richard de Maidstone,
De concordia inter Ricardum Secundum et civitatem London

HENRY IV
The coronation of the king:
The Duke of Lancaster left the Tower this Sunday after dinner, on his return to Westminster: he was bare-headed, and had

3. Richard II, Westminster Abbey. The earliest known painting of an English King.

round his neck the order of the king of France. The Prince of Wales, six dukes, six earls, eighteen barons, accompanied him; and there were, of knights and other nobility, from eight to nine hundred horse in the procession. The duke was dressed in a jacket, after the German fashion, of cloth of gold, mounted on a white courser, with a blue garter on his left leg. He passed through the streets of London, which were all handsomely decorated with tapestries and other rich hangings: there were nine fountains in Cheapside, and other streets he passed through which perpetually ran with white and red wines. He was escorted by prodigious numbers of gentlemen with their servants in liveries and badges; and the different companies of London were led by their wardens clothed in their proper livery, and with ensigns of their trade. The whole cavalcade amounted to six thousand horse, which escorted the duke from the Tower to Westminster.

Jean Froissart, *Chronicles*

HENRY V

The most serene prince of whose appearance this attempts to treat was neither of unseemly Titan size nor stunted in poor, pigmy-like shortness. He was very well-favoured, his neck was wide, his body graceful, his limbs not over-muscled . . . He outstripped all his equals in age at running and jumping . . . in so much that, with two chosen companions, he frequently, by sheer speed of running and without any help of whatever kind, killed the swiftest fallow deer driven out in to the plain from the woodland shades.

Thomas de Elmham,
Vita et Gesta Henrici Quinti Anglorum Regis

HENRY VI

Concerning his humility . . . from his youth up he had been accustomed to wear broad-toed shoes and boots like a country-man. Also he had usually a long gown with a rounded hood after the manner of a burgess, and a tunic falling below the knees, shoes, boots, hose, everything of a dark grey colour—for he would have nothing fanciful.

Moreover, on the principal feasts of the year, but chiefly when by custom he should wear his crown, he would put on next to his skin a rough hair-shirt. . . . He was wont to dedicate holy days and Sundays wholly to hearing the divine offices, and to devout offices. . . . But the other less holy days . . . he spent, not less diligently, either in treating of the affairs of the realm

4. Henry VI, bronze lectern,
King's College, Cambridge.

with his Council, according as the necessity of the case demanded,
or in readings of the Scriptures, or in perusing writings, and
chronicles. Concerning which, a certain worthy knight, once a
right faithful chamberlain of his, Sir Richard Tunstall, bore
verbal and written testimony, saying 'In the law of the Lord
was his delight day and night'. Evidence to ,the same effect is
afforded by the bitter complaint which the Lord King himself
made to me in his chamber at Eltham, when I was there alone
with him working with him in his holy books, intent upon
wholesome admonitions and devout aspirations:—a certain most
powerful Duke of the realm having just then knocked at the
royal door, the King said, 'So do they disturb me, scarce am I
able by snatches, day or night to refresh myself with the reading
of the sacred dogmata, without somebody making a noise.'

It was his wont to use no oaths to confirm the truth of his sayings, except by uttering these words, 'Forsooth, and forsooth,' that he might make those to whom he spoke certain of what he said. Wherefore, sometimes by gently advising, sometimes by severely chiding, he restrained very many, magnates as well as commons, from great oaths; since every one who swore was abominable to him. For the King, hearing a certain great lord, his chamberlain, thoughtlessly break out swearing, seriously reproved him, saying 'Alas! while you, the master of a household, thus contrary to God's command, rap out oaths, you set the worst example to your servants and subjects, for you incite them to the like.'

> John Blakman, *On the Virtues and Miracles of Henry VI.*
> Translated by Edith Thompson from *The Wars of York and Lancaster 1450-1485,* by T. Hearne (1731 edition)

HENRY VI
In church or oratory he never indulged himself by sitting on a seat, or by walking to and fro, as is the manner of worldly men during divine service, but always with his head bare, and his royal limbs seldom erect, but continually making genuflexions before the Book, with eyes and hands raised he sought inwardly to repeat the prayers, epistles and gospels of the Mass with the celebrant . . .

> John Blakman, *De Virtutibus et Miraculis Henrici VI*

EDWARD IV
This Edward was a goodly man of personage, of stature high, of countenance and beauty comely, of sight quick, broad breasted, and well set, in every other part conformable to his body; of a pregnant wit, of stomach stout, and high of courage.

> John Hardyng, *Chronicle*

EDWARD IV
This laudatory account of Edward IV by Sir Thomas More (who gathered information from those who knew him) is designed to make darker the vices of Richard III about whom the book is written.

He was a goodly person, and very princely to behold, of heart courageous, politic in council, in adversity nothing abashed, in prosperity rather joyful than proud, in peace just and merciful, in war, sharp and fierce, in the field, bold and hardy, and

Lady Margaret Beaufort (1443-1509)

nevertheless no further than wisdom would, adventurous. Whose wars who so well consider, he shall no less commend his wisdom where he avoided, than his manhood where he vanquished. He was of attractive looks, of body mighty, strong and clean made: though in his later days with an over liberal diet, somewhat corpulent and burly, and nevertheless not uncomely. He was in his youth greatly given to fleshly wantonness; from which health of body in great prosperity and fortune, without a special grace, hardly refrains. This fault did not greatly grieve the people; for neither could one man's pleasure stretch and extend to the displeasure of very many, and was without violence, and over that in his later days lessened and well left. In which time of his later days, this realm was in quiet and prosperous condition: no fear of outside enemies, no war in hand, nor none forward, but such as no man looked for: the people towards the Prince, not in constrained fear, but in a willing and loving obedience: among themselves, the commons in good peace. The Lords, whom he knew at variance, himself in his death bed appeased. . . . And all the time of his reign, he was with his people, so benign, courteous and so familiar, that no part of his virtues was more esteemed; yet that condition in the end of his days (in which many princes by a long continued sovereignty decline to a proud bearing from debonair behaviour of their marvellous beginning) in him grew and increased: so far forth that in the summer the last that ever he saw, his highness being at Windsor in hunting, sent for the Mayor and Aldermen of London to him. For no other errand but to have them hunt and be merry with him, where he made them not so stately, but friendly and easy behaviour, and sent venison from thence so freely in the City, that nothing in many days before gained him either more hearts or more hearty favour among the common people, who often more esteem and take for greater kindness a little courtesy than a great benefit.

The History of King Richard the thirde written by Master Thomas More one of the undersheriffs of London about 1513

RICHARD III

Richard, the third son, of whom we now treat, was in wit and courage equal with either of them, in body and probity far under them both: little of stature, ill-featured of limbs, crook-backed, his left shoulder much higher than his right, hard-favoured of visage

and such as is in princes called warlike, in other men otherwise.
He was malicious, wrathful, envious, and, from before his birth,
ever forward. It is for truth reported that the Duchess his mother
had much ado in her travail that she could not be delivered of
him uncut, and that he came into the world with the feet forward
—as men be borne out of it—and (as the fame runs) also not
untoothed: either men out of hatred report above the truth or
else nature changed her course in his beginning who in the course
of his life many things unnaturally committed. No evil captain was
he in the war, as to which his disposition was more meet than for
peace. Sundry victories had he and sometimes overthrows, but
never for any lack in his own person, either of hardiness or
politic order. Free was he called of spending and somewhat above
his power liberal: with large gifts he got him unsteadfast
friendship, for which he was fain to pillage and spoil in other
places, and get him steadfast hatred.

He was close and secret, a deep dissembler, lowly of countenance,
arrogant of heart, outwardly companionable where he inwardly
hated, not hesitating to kiss whom he thought to kill, pitiless and
cruel, not for evil will always but oftener for ambition and either
for the surety or increase of his position. 'Friend' and 'foe' were to
him indifferent: where his advantage grew, he spared no man's
death whose life withstood his purpose. He slew with his own
hands—as men constantly say—King Henry the Sixth, being
prisoner in the Tower, and that without commandment or
knowledge of the King, who would undoubtedly, if he had
intended that thing, have appointed that butcherly office to some
other than his own born brother.

Some wise men also think that his drift, covertly conveyed,
lacked not in helping forth his brother of Clarence to his death,
which he resisted openly, howbeit somewhat (as men deemed)
more faintly than that were heartily minded to his welfare. . . .

He reigned two years, one month, and twenty-seven days. He
was but of a small stature, having but a deformed body, the one
shoulder was higher than the other; he had a short face and a
cruel look, which did betoken malice, guile, and deceit. And while
he did muse upon anything, standing, he would bite his underlip
continually, whereby a man might perceive his cruel nature;
within his wretched body, he strived and chaffed always within
himself; also the dagger which he bore about him, he would

RICARDVS · III · ANG · REX ·

6. Richard III.

always be chopping of it in and out. He had a sharp and pregnant wit, subtle, and to dissimulate and feign very meet. He had also a proud and cruel mind, which never went from him to the hour of his death, which he had rather suffer by the cruel sword, though all his company forsake him, than by shameful flight favour his life, which after might chance by sickness or other condign punishment shortly to perish.

Sir Thomas More, *History of Richard III*

RICHARD III

Sir Thomas More in his *History of King Richard the third* established the inaccurate picture of the man as 'little of stature, ill-featured of limbs, crook-backed . . . hard-favoured of visage'. Those who knew him mention no physical deformity; though he was small he had some admirable qualities.

As far without the certainty of a proof is the pretended deformity of his body, which is controverted by many; some peremptorily asserted he was not deformed, of which opinion was John Stow . . . who in all his enquiry could find no such note of deformity in this King . . . but hath acknowledged . . . that he hath spoke with some ancient men, who from their own sight and knowledge affirmed he was of bodily shape, comely enough, only of low stature, which is all the deformity they proportion so monstrously; neither did John Rouce, who knew him, and writ much in his description, observe any other.

Sir George Buc, *Life of Richard III*

HENRY VII

His body was slender but well built and strong; his height above average. His appearance was remarkably attractive and his face was cheerful, especially when speaking; his eyes were small and blue, his teeth few, poor and blackish; his hair was thin and white; his complexion sallow. His spirit was distinguished, wise and prudent: his mind was brave and resolute and never, even at moments of the greatest danger, deserted him. He had a most pertinacious memory. Withal he was not devoid of scholarship. In government he was shrewd and prudent, so that no one dared to get the better of him through deceit or guile. He was gracious and kind and was as attentive to his visitors as he was of access. His

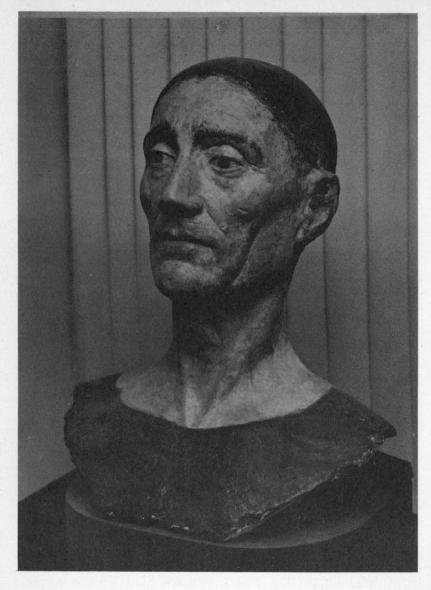

7. Henry VII, wooden funeral effigy, Westminster Abbey.

hospitality was spendidly generous; he was fond of having foreigners at his court ,and he freely conferred favours on them. But those of his subjects who were indebted to him and who did not pay him due honour or who were generous only with promises, he treated with harsh severity. . . .

Polydore Vergil, English History, 1534-1555

---

[1] 'The Historia Regum Anglicarum of William of Newburgh' in Chronicles of the Reigns of Stephen, Henry II and Richard I.
(edited by R. Howlett, Rolls Series 1884-90) i and ii p.283
[2] Giraldi Cambrensis Opera vol. viii p.247 (Rolls Series 1861-91).
[3] With the exception of Gerald of Wales, who, however, concentrated on writing his early memoirs.

Towns and Buildings

A DESCRIPTION OF LONDON, 1173

Among the noble and celebrated cities of the world that of London, the capital of the kingdom of the English, is one which extends its glory farther than all the others and sends its wealth and merchandise more widely into distant lands. Higher than all the rest does it lift its head. It is happy in the healthiness of its air; in its observance of Christian practice; in the strength of its fortifications; in its natural situation; in the honour of its citizens; and in the modesty of its matrons. It is cheerful in its sports, and the fruitful mother of noble men. Let us look into these things in turn.

If the mildness of the climate of this place softens the character of its inhabitants, it does not make them corrupt in following Venus, but rather prevents them from being fierce and bestial, making them liberal and kind.

In the church of St Paul there is the episcopal seat. Once it was metropolitan, and some think it will again become so, if the citizens return to the island, unless perhaps the archiepiscopal title of the blessed martyr, Thomas, and the presence of his body preserves that dignity for ever at Canterbury where it is at present. But as St Thomas has made both cities illustrious, London by his rising and Canterbury by his setting, each can claim advantage of the other with justice in respect of that saint. As regards the practice of Christian worship, there are in London and its suburbs thirteen greater conventual churches and, besides these, one hundred and twenty-six lesser parish churches.

It has on the east the Palatine castle [the Tower of London], very great and strong: the keep and walls rise from very deep foundations and are fixed with a mortar tempered by the blood of animals. On the west there are two castles very strongly fortified, and from these there runs a high and massive wall with seven double gates and with towers along the north at regular intervals. London was once also walled and turreted on the south, but the mighty Thames, so full of fish, has with the sea's ebb and flow washed against, loosened, and thrown down those walls in the course of time. Upstream to the west there is the royal palace [the Palace of Westminster] which is conspicuous above the river, a building incomparable in its ramparts and bulwarks. It is about two miles from the city and joined thereto by a populous suburb.

Everywhere outside the houses of those living in the suburbs, and adjacent to them, are the spacious and beautiful gardens of the citizens, and these are planted with trees. Also there are on the north side pastures and pleasant meadow lands through which flow streams wherein the turning of mill-wheels makes a cheerful sound. Very near lies a great forest with woodland pastures in which there are the lairs of wild animals: stags, fallow deer, wild boars and bulls. The tilled lands of the city are not of barren gravel, but fair Asian plains that yield luxuriant crops and fill the tillers' barns with the sheaves of Ceres.

. . . In London the three principal churches (that is to say the episcopal church of St Paul, the church of the Holy Trinity, and the church of St Martin) have famous schools by special privilege and by virtue of their ancient dignity. But through the favour of some magnate, or through the presence of teachers who are notable or famous in philosophy, there are also other schools. On feast-days the masters hold meetings for their pupils in the church whose festival it is.

By themselves in another part of the field stand the goods of the countryfolk: implements of husbandry, swine with long flanks, cows with full udders, oxen of immense size, and woolly sheep. There also stand the mares fit for plough, some big with foal, and others with brisk young colts closely following them. . . .

I do not think there is a city with a better record for church-going, doing honour to God's ordinances, keeping feast-days, giving alms and hospitality to strangers, confirming betrothals, contracting marriages, celebrating weddings, providing feasts, entertaining guests, and also, it may be added, in the care of funerals and for the burial of the dead. The only plagues of London are the immoderate drinking of fools and the frequency of fires.

To this it may be added that almost all the bishops, abbots and magnates of England are in a sense citizens and freemen of London, having their own town-houses. In them they live, and spend largely, when they are summoned to great councils by the king or by their metropolitan, or drawn thither by their private affairs.

William Fitz-Stephen, *Description of the Most Noble City of London*, prefixed to his biography of Thomas Becket

TRADE IN LONDON, Twelfth Century

Those that ply their several trades, the vendors of each several thing, the hirers out of their several sorts of labour are found every morning each in their separate quarters and each engaged upon his own peculiar task. Moreover there is in London upon the river's bank, amid the wine that is sold from ships and wine-cellars, a public cook-shop. There daily, according to the season, you may find viands, dishes roast, fried and boiled, fish great and small, the coarser flesh for the poor, the more delicate for the rich, such as venison and birds both big and little. If friends, weary with travel, should of a sudden come to any of the citizens, and it is not their pleasure to wait fasting till fresh food is brought and cooked and 'till servants bring water for hands and bread' they hasten to the river bank, and there all things desirable are ready to their hand. However great the infinitude of knights or foreigners that enter the city or are about to leave it, at whatever hour of night or day, that the former may not fast too long nor the latter depart without their dinner, they turn aside thither, if it so pleases them, and refresh themselves each after his own manner. . . .

In the suburb immediately outside one of the gates there is a smooth field, both in fact and in name [Smithfield]. On every sixth day of the week, unless it be a major feast-day on which solemn rites are prescribed, there is a much-frequented show of fine horses for sale. Thither come all the Earls, Barons and Knights who are in the City, and with them many of the citizens, whether to look on or buy. It is a joy to see the ambling palfreys, their skin full of juice, their coats a-glisten, as they pace softly, in alternation raising and putting down the feet on one side together; next to see the horses that best fit Esquires, moving more roughly, yet nimbly, as they raise and set down the opposite feet, fore and hind, first on one side and then on the other; then the younger colts of high breeding, unbroken and 'high-stepping with elastic tread,' and after them the costly destriers of graceful form and goodly stature, 'with quivering ears, high necks and plump buttocks.' As these show their paces, the buyers watch first their gentler gait, then that swifter motion, wherein their fore feet are thrown out and back together, and the hind feet also, as it were, counterwise. When a race between such trampling steeds is about to begin, or perchance between others which are likewise, after their kind, strong to carry, swift to run, a shout is raised, and horses of the baser sort are bidden to turn aside. Three boys riding these fleet-foot steeds or at times two as may be agreed, prepare themselves for the contest. Skilled to command their horses, they 'curb their untamed mouths with jagged bits', and their chief anxiety is that their rival shall not gain the lead. The horses likewise after their fashion lift up their spirits for the race; 'their limbs tremble; impatient of delay, they cannot stand still.' When the signal is given, they stretch forth their limbs, they gallop away, they rush on with obstinate speed. The riders, passionate for renown, hoping for victory, vie with one another in spurring their swift horses and lashing them forward with their switches no less than they excite them by their cries. . . .

In another place apart stand the wares of the country-folk, instruments of agriculture, long-flanked swine, cows with swollen udders, and 'woolly flocks and bodies huge of kine.' Mares stand there, meet for ploughs, sledges and two-horsed carts; the bellies of some are big with young; round others move their offspring, new-born, sprightly foals, inseparable followers.

To this city, from every nation that is under heaven, merchants rejoice to bring their trade in ships.

William FitzStephen, *A Description of London*,
translated by H. E. Butler with *A Map of London under
Henry II* by Marjorie B. Honeybourne,
Historical Association Leaflets

LONDON IN JOHN'S REIGN, 1204

Every race of men, out of every nation which is under heaven, resort thither in great numbers; every nation has introduced into that city its vices and bad manners. No one lives in it without offence: there is not a single street in it that does not abound in miserable, obscene wretches; there, in proportion as any man has exceeded in wickedness, so much is he the better.

I am not ignorant of the disposition I am exhorting; you have, in addition to your youth, an ardent disposition, a slowness of memory and a soberness of reason between extremes. I feel in myself no uneasiness about you, unless you should abide with men of corrupt lives; for from our associations our manners are formed. But let that be as it may. You will come to London. Behold! I warn you whatever of evil or perversity there is in any, whatever in all parts of the world, you will find in that city alone. Go not to the dances of panders, nor mix yourself up with the herds

8. The earliest printed view of London, showing the Tower, Old St. Paul's, London Bridge, Ludgate, and the church of the Black Friars; from the *Chronycle of Englonde*, printed by Richard Pynson in 1510.

of houses of ill-repute; avoid the dice, the theatre and the tavern. You will find more braggadocios there than in all France, while the number of flatterers is infinite. Stage players, buffoons, evildoers the number of flatterers is infiinite. Stage players, buffoons, evil-doers, musical girls, druggists, fortune-tellers, extortioners, nightly-strollers, magicians, mimics, common beggars, tatterdemalions— this whole crew has filled every house. So if you do not wish to live with the shameful, you will not dwell in London.

I am not speaking against the learned, whether monks or Jews; although, still, from their dwelling together with such evil persons, I should esteem them less perfect there than elsewhere.

Nor does my advice go far, as that you should betake yourself to no city; with my counsel you will take up your residence nowhere but in a town, though it remains to say in what.

Richard of Devizes, *Chronicles of the Crusaders*

LONDON JEWRY, 1264

Among other things I think that the slaughter of the Jews which was perpetrated at that time in London should not be passed over in silence . . . Rushing in unexpected tumult on the Jews, of whom a very great multitude dwelt with all confidence in London, little thinking that harm would happen to them, they, enticed not by the zeal of the law, but by the lust of temporal good, most cruelly slew as many as they could find in the city . . . nearly four hundred Jews of both sexes and all ranks being killed. And although they were not signed with the mark of our faith, it seemed an inhuman and impious deed to slay them without cause.

Thomas Wykes, *Chronicle*, 1264. Translated, *Annales Monastici*. Rolls Series N

WATER THROUGH PIPES, Thirteenth Century
Of the Aqueduct of the Friars-Minors at London.
The underwritten built the aqueduct. Imprimis, William, taylor to our lord King Henry III, after the conquest, gave the head of the aqueduct, at the instance of brother William Basinges, who procured all the aqueduct, and fully compleated it; but the cost and expences were administered by our illustrious lord Henry, King of England, of happy memory, abovenamed; Salekyn of Basing, a youth of an excellent disposition, Henry Frowyke, and Henry Basynges, knights. These were the principal co-operators and co-adjutors; and afterwards brother Geoffrey de Camera built the new house at the second head, and improved the former, and

searched out all the notable defects, and mended them;. and procured and did many other good things for the same. Whose principal assistants were Alan Gille, citizen of London, with his wife; the lord Henry Darcy, who gave 100 shillings for the cistern. John Tryple and others assisting, finished the work. The Friars-Minors had at London, all things computed. £110 17s. 5¼d., to whose souls God be merciful.

For knowing the Course of Passage of the Aqueduct of the Friars-Minors at London.

First, from the threshold of the door of John Sporon, the space of three foot, under the new wall of the friars, the pipe stretches as you go into the street towards Newgate; but still as it lies along the way, it holds the north side of the way, sometimes not coming near the houses, any otherwise than the lying strait requires. Under Newgate it lies 12 foot deep, and extends directly under the wall of St Sepulchre's church outward, and farther on, it bends with the bending of the street, and stretches along Lekewell; there crossing the two ways, it buts against the window of the house of John Muchtthesh, and there it bends towards Holborn-bridge; between the house of William Irotheges and the bridge, it is laid under the water [of the River Fleet] for the space of three foot, beyond the rivulet of that water, about the space of eight paces, by the wall of the bridge, beyond the breach, by the industry of the friars, where the water of the street runs down in a place that is always muddy. The first cock is hid under ground, but covered for the space of four foot with a marble stone, Thence it extends to Liweone-lane, and there it turns again strait along that lane, or street, towards the north, by the west wall of the lane, the position of it being three foot distant. At the end of that lane, on the left hand, is the second cock, almost seven foot high; and thence it extends, directly crossing the fields and hedges, to the mill of Thomas of B———, which is next to the town, where it sinks down the space of 18 foot. There, on the east side of the mill, towards the north, near the ditch, is the third cock. Thence proceeding almost the space of one furlong to the westward, inclining to the north, there appears a green trench, or furrow, lying east and west, full of briers, and winding westwards, almost eight foot wide, dividing the land of John Derkyne, which lies on the south side, from the land of ——— Basyng, which lies on the north side. In that trench, beginning at the east end 16 paces, not leaps, there from the middle part of the breadth of the trench, where the necessary mark for this purpose appears, looking to the north directly on the land of Thomas ———, for the space of 14 foot it lies hid four foot under ground. The head which is nearest, whence, for the most part, we have our water, is a little remote from the farther head. From that place it extends to the remoter head, towards the west, the little stone house whereof is seen at a distance. The water of this head is brought beyond the ditch of Thomas—on the west, a little inclining to the north, for the space of about 15 paces from the house of the head, by the way which divides the parishes of St Giles and St Andrew. This water, in the house of that head, running down to the trough, overflows, and little of it is received hence by the trough, but it floods the whole house, and is negligently lost along little rivulets, and through the cracks of the wall. The remedy must be applied by the friars, considering the loss and damage of so much expence. Afterwards brother Thomas Feltham brought a washing cistern to the porch, from the pool of the common washing place, and laid out very much in the porch, anno Domini 1300.

Item, in the year of our Lord 1420, the cistern for washing in the cloister was repaired with the money deposited by brother Robert Zengg. The total of the expense was £27 9s. 1½d.

Register of the London Grey Friars, extract translated in Sir W. Dugdale, *Monasticon Anglicanum, a History of the Abbies and other Monasteries, Hospitals, Friaries and Cathedral and Collegiate Churches,* edited by J. Caley, H. Ellis and Rev Bulkeley Bandinel

OLD ST PAUL'S, 1313

Memorandum,—that in the eighth year of King Edward the cross with the ball, all gilt, was raised upon the belfry of St Paul's; and the Bishop of London, Gilbert of Segrave, deposited many precious things in the said cross on the belfry, on the Friday next after St Michael in the following year.

In this year the cross of the belfry of Saint Paul's was taken down and repaired; and in the old cross certain relics were found, that is to say, a corporal [linen cloth], with which they sing mass, white and entire, without any defect; and in this corporal was found a part of the wood of the cross of our Lord Jesus Christ, wrought in the form of a cross; a stone of the Sepulchre of our Lord; and another stone from the place where God stood when he ascended into heaven; and another stone from Mount Calvary, where the Cross of our Lord was erected. There was also found a purse, and in this purse a piece of red sendal [fine silken material], in which were wrapped some bones of the Eleven Thousand Virgins and other relics, the names of which were unknown. These relics Master Robert of Clothdale shewed to the people during his preaching on the Sunday before the Feast of Saint Botolph [17 June]; and after the same, the relics were replaced in the Cross, and many other new ones as well, on the Day of Saint Francis [16 July].

H. T. Riley, *Liber de Antiquis Legibus,* from *Chronicles of Old London*

A LONDON GUILD, 1347

The points of the Articles touching the Hat-makers, accepted by Thomas Leggy, Mayor, and the Aldermen of the City of London, at the suit, and at the request of the folks of the said trade.

In the first place,—that six men of the most lawful and most befitting of the said trade shall be assigned and sworn to rule and watch the trade in such a manner as other trades of the said city are ruled and watched by their wardens.

Also,—that no one shall make or sell any manner of hats within the franchise of the city aforesaid, if he be not free of the same city; on pain of forfeiting to the chamber the hats which he shall have made and offered for sale.

Also,—that no one shall be made apprentice in the said trade for a less term than seven years, and that, without fraud or collusion. And he, who shall receive any apprentice in any other manner, shall lose his freedom, until he shall have bought it back again.

Also,—that no one of the said trade shall take any apprentice, if he be not himself a freeman of the said city.

Also,—that the wardens of the said trade shall make their searches for all manner of hats that are for sale within the said franchise, so often as need shall be. And that the aforesaid wardens shall have power to take all manner of hats that they shall find defective and not befitting, and to bring them before the Mayor and Aldermen of London, that so the defaults which shall be found may be punished by their award.

Also,—where some workmen in the said trade have made hats that are not befitting, in deceit of the common people, from which great scandal, shame, and loss have often arisen to the good folks of the said trade, they pray that no workmen in the said trade shall do any work by night touching the same, but only in clear daylight; that so, the aforesaid Wardens may openly inspect their work. And he who shall do otherwise, and shall be convicted thereof before the Mayor and Aldermen, shall pay to the Chamber

of the Guildhall, the first time, 40d., the second time half a
mark, and the third time he shall lose his freedom.

H. T. Riley, Memorials of London

A SHOPPING TOUR IN LONDON, Early Fifteenth Century

Then unto London I did me hie;
    Of all the land it beareth the prize.
'Hot peascods', one began to cry;
    'Strawberries ripe', others coaxingly advise.
    One bade me come near and buy some spice;
Pepper and saffron they gan me bid.
But for lack of money I might not be sped.
Then to Cheapside I went on,
    Where much people I saw for to stand.
One offered me velvet, silk, and lawn;
    Another he taketh me by the hand,
    'Here is Paris thread, the finest in the land.'
I never was used to such things indeed,
And wanting money, I might not spend.

Then went I forth by London Stone,
    Throughout all Canwick Street;
Drapers much cloth me offered anon.
    Then met I one, cried, 'Hot sheep's feet'.
    One cried, 'Mackerel'; 'Rushes green', another gan greet.
One bade me buy a hood to cover my head;
But for want of money I might not be sped.
Then I hied me into Eastcheap;
    One cried, 'Ribs of beef and many a pie!;
Pewter pots they clattered on a heap;
    There was harp, pipe and minstrelsy.
    'Yea, by Cock!' 'Nay, by Cock! some began cry;
Some sang of Jenken and Julian for their meed,
But for lack of money I might not speed.
    Then into Cornhill I took my road,
    Where was much stolen goods among;
I saw where hung my own hood,
    That I had lost among the throng;
    To buy my own hood I thought it wrong,
I knew it well as I did my creed;
But for lack of money I could not speed.

'London Lickpenny', attributed to John Lydgate in
A Chronicle of London, edited by N. H. Nicolas

SMELLS AND REFUSE, 1419

That the Streets and Lanes shall be cleansed of all impediment from dung and chips, and of all other impediment. . . .

That no Stall shall be more than two feet and a half in breadth, and that it shall be moveable and flexible

That all Streets and Lanes leading towards the Thames from the King's Highways, shall be kept clean

That no one shall throw dung into the King's Highway, or before the house of his neighbour

That each person shall make clean of filth the front of his house under penalty of half a mark

> *Liber Albus the White Book of the City of London compiled in* AD 1419 *by John Carpenter and Richard Whittington,* translated by H. T. Riley

KEEP SWINE AND LEPERS OUT OF THE CITY, 1419

If Swine shall be found in the Streets or in the Fosses [moats], or in the Suburbs, they shall be killed, and he who kills them shall have them; and he who shall wish to rear them, shall be at liberty to rear them, out of the King's Highways, in his own house

That no leper shall be in the City, or shall come there or make sojourn there. . . .

That such Pigsties as are in the Streets shall be removed; and if any Swine shall be found in the Streets, they shall be forfeited

Also, Four Men elected and sworn to take and kill such Swine as shall be found wandering about within the walls of the City, to whomsoever they may belong. . . .

The Renter of Saint Antony's [Hospital in Threadneedle Street, privileged to keep swine] sworn that he will not avow any Swine going about within the City, nor will hang bells about their necks, but only those which have been given unto them in pure alms. . . .

The Porters of the Gates of the City sworn that they will not allow Lepers to enter the City. . . .

Item, that no one who can gain his sustenance shall go about begging; and that no Lazars shall go about in the City

That the Supervisors of Lepers shall be discharged of Assizes, Juries, Summonses, Watches, etc.

Writ as to raising 100 shillings upon a tenement of the Lepers, and delivering the same unto such Lepers for their sustenance. . . .

> *Liber Albus the White Book of the City of London compiled in* AD 1419 *by John Carpenter and Richard Whittington,* translated by H. T. Riley

'LONDON LICKPENNY', c. 1450

Then to the Chepe I began me drawne,
Where mutch people I saw for to stande;
One ofred me velvet, sylke and lawne,
An other he taketh me by the hande,
'Here is Parys thred, the fynest in the land';
I never was used to such thyngs indede,
And wantyng mony I myght not spede.
Then went I forth by London stone,
Throughout all Canwyke street;
Drapers mutch cloth me offred anone . . .
Then I hyed me into Est-Chepe;
One cryes rybbes of befe, and many a pye;
Pewter pottes they clattered on a heape;
There was harpe, fyfe, and mynstrelsye . . .
The taverner took mee by the sleve,
'Sir,' sayth he, 'wyll you our wyne assay?'

Formerly attributed to John Lydgate, *Minor Poems of Lydgate,*
edited by J. O. Halliwell

THE TOWN BELL, 1154

Concerning our bell, we use it in a public place where our chief
bailiff may come as well by day as by night, to give warning to
all men living within the city and suburbs. And we do not say
that it ought to ring unless it be for some terrible fire burning
any row of houses within the said city, or for any common
contention whereby the city might be terribly moved, or for any
enemies drawing near unto the city, or if the city shall be besieged,
or any sedition shall be between any, and notice thereof given by
any unto the chief bailiff. And in these cases aforesaid, and in all
cases, all manner of men abiding within the city and suburbs and
liberties of the city, of what degree soever they be, ought to come
at any such ringing, or motion of ringing, with such weapons as
fit their degree, etc.

Customs of Hereford, *Archaeological Journal,* xxvii

TOWN HOUSES BUILT OF STONE, 1189

It should be remarked, that in ancient times the greater part of
the City was built of wood, and the houses were covered with
straw, stubble, and the like.

Hence it happened, that when a single house had caught fire,
the greater part of the City was destroyed through such conflagra-

tion; a thing that took place in the first year of the reign of King
Stephen, when, by reason of a fire that broke out at London
Bridge, the church of Saint Paul was burnt; from which spot the
conflagration extended, destroying houses and buildings, as far
as the church of Saint Clement Danes.

After this, many of the citizens, to the best of their ability,
to avoid such a peril, built stone houses upon their foundations,
covered with thick tiles, and so protected against the fury of the
flames; whence it has often been the case that, when a fire has
broken out in the City, and has destroyed many buildings, upon
reaching such houses, it has been unable to do further mischief,
and has been there extinguished; so that, through such a house
as this the houses of the neighbours have been saved from being
burnt.

Hence it is, that in the aforesaid Ordinance, called the 'Assize',
it was provided and ordained, in order that the citizens might be
encouraged to build with stone, that every one who should have
a stone-wall upon his own land sixteen feet in height, might
possess the same as freely and meritoriously as in manner already

9. Castle Rising, 1176.

10. A king discusses this building taking place in the thirteenth century. The men are using a windlass, plummet, and a form of set square.

stated; it always being the duty, that is to say, of such man's neighbour, to receive upon his own land the water falling from the house built upon such wall, and at his own cost to carry off the same; and if he shall wish to build near the wall, he is bound to make his own gutter under the eaves of the said house for receiving the water therefrom. And this, to the end that such house may remain secure and protected against the violence of fire when it comes, and so, through it, many a house may be saved and preserved unharmed by the violence of the flames.

Henry Fitzailwine's Assize of Buildings; *Liber Albus the White Book of the City of London compiled in 1419 by John Carpenter and Richard Whittington*, translated by H. T. Riley

LINCOLN CATHEDRAL, c. 1190

With wondrous art he [Hugh of Avalon, Bishop of Lincoln] built the fabric of the Cathedral [rebuilt after an earthquake]; whereunto he supplied not only his own wealth, and the labours of his servants [and the master-mason Geoffrey de Noiers], but even the sweat of his own brow; for he oftentimes bore the hod-load of hewn stone or of binding lime.

In this structure, the art equals the precious materials; for the

11. The great hall of Stokesay Castle in Shropshire, a manor-house built in the thirteenth century.

vault may be compared to a bird stretching out her broad wings to fly; planted on its firm columns, it soars to the clouds. On the other hand, the work is supported by precious columns of swarthy stone [Purbeck marble], not confined to one sole colour, nor loose of pore, but flecked with glittering stars and close-set in all its grain. This stone disdains to be tamed with steel until it have first been subdued by art; for its surface must first be softened by long grinding with sand, and its hardness is relaxed with strong vinegar. Moreover, it may suspend the mind in doubt whether it be jasper or marble; it is dull indeed for jasper, yet, for marble, of a most noble nature. Of this are formed those slender columns which stand round the great piers, even as a bevy of maidens stand marshalled for a dance.

Metrical Life of St Hugh, edited by J. F. Dimock

CANTERBURY AND OTHER TOWNS IN JOHN'S REIGN, 1204

Canterbury

Therefore if you should land near Canterbury, you will have to lose your way, if even you should pass through it. It is an assemblage of the vilest, entirely devoted to their—I know not whom, but who has been lately canonized, and had been the Archbishop of Canterbury, as everywhere they die in the open day in the streets for want of bread and employment.

Rochester and Chichester

Rochester and Chichester are mere villages, and they possess nothing for which they should be called cities, but the sees of their bishops.

Oxford

Oxford scarcely, I will not say, satisfies but sustains its clerks.

Exeter

Exeter supports men and beasts with the same grain.

Bath

Bath is placed, or rather buried, in the lowest parts of the valleys, in a very dense atmosphere and sulphury vapour, as if it were at the gates of Hell.

Worcester, Chester, Hereford

Nor yet will you select your habitation in the Northern cities, nor in Worcester, Chester, Hereford, on account of the desperate Welshmen.

York

York abounds in Scots, vile and faithless men, or rather rascals.

Ely

The town of Ely is always putrefied by the surrounding marshes.

Durham, Norwich, Lincoln

In Durham, Norwich and Lincoln, there are very few of your disposition among the powerful; you will never hear anyone speak French.

Bristol

At Bristol there is nobody who is not, or has not been, a soap-maker, and every Frenchman esteems soap-makers as he does night-men.

Country Towns

After the cities, every market, village or town, has but rude and rustic inhabitants. Moreover, at all times, account the Cornish people for such as you know our Flemish are accounted in France.

Winchester

This is in those parts the Jerusalem of the Jews, in it alone they enjoy perpetual peace; it is the school of those who desire to live well and prosper. Here they become men, here there is bread and wine enough for nothing. There are therein monks of such compassion and gentleness, clergy of such understanding and frankness, citizens of such civility and good faith, ladies of such beauty and modesty, that little hinders but I should go there and become a Christian with such Christians. To that city I direct you, the city of cities. The mother of all, the best above all.

Richard of Devizes, *Chronicles of the Crusaders*

BUILDING BY HENRY III, 1249-1250
1249 Woodstock

Orders to crenellate the queen's chamber with freestone, and to raise the chimney of that chamber to the height of 8 feet; to panel the lower chamber and make the privy chamber in the fashion of that chamber where Bartholomew Pecche used to sleep; to build a chamber at the gateway of Evereswell, 40 feet long and 22 feet wide, with a wardrobe, privy chamber, and fireplace. Also to repair Rosamund's chamber, unroofed by the wind; and to make a door to the queen's chamber, and a door to the old larder. Also to repair the bays of both our fish-stews and the causeway of the lower stew near the enclosure; to put 2 windows of white glass in the gable of the hall, and in the chamber of Edward our son, and 2 windows barred with iron in the old larder. To make leaden spouts round the alures [walks] of the same Edward's chamber; to repair all the buildings of each court where necessary; to bar the windows of the porch with iron; to build a house for

12. Medieval builders and stonemasons. They use a plumbline to check the upright, a windlass, a pulley; the man on the ladder is using a drill, two others on the ground prepare the stone.

our napery; and to pull down the rooms of William our chaplain and rebuild them between the hall and the queen's stable, making a garden on the site of the said rooms.

1250 Westminster Abbey

Relaxation for one year's enjoined penance to penitents who assist the fabric of the church of wonderful beauty now being built by the King at Westminster.

1250 Clarendon

Orders to make a baptistry in the chapel of All Saints there, and to put on the chapel a bell-turret with two bells, and to make a crucifix with two images on each side of wood, and an image of Blessed Mary with her Child. And let the queen's chamber be decently paved. And in the queen's hall let there be made a window towards the garden, well barred with iron; and two windows in the queen's chapel, one on each side of the altar, which are to be divided down the middle so that they may be opened and shut when necessary. . . . And make a bench round our great garden beside the wall, and whitewash the wall above it. In Alexander's chamber let there be made a wardrobe with a privy chamber, and roof those buildings well. Make a garden below our chamber on the north; also a window in our wardrobe; and lengthen our chandlery by four or five couples.

Translations from Public Record Office, Liberate Rolls and from the *Calendar of Papal Registers* by L. F. Salzman *Building in England down to* 1540

TOWN AND FOREST, 1253

The jury say, upon oath that the forest of Leicester was so great and thick and wide that a man could scarce go by the wood-ways for the multitude of dead wood and wind-fallen boughs; and then, by assent and will of the Earl and his council, it was granted that all might fetch dead wood at six cartloads for a penny, and a horse-load every week for a half-penny [a year], and a man's load weekly for a farthing.

Leicester records, Charles Bémont, *Simon de Montfort*

TOWN AND FIRE, 1302

Thomas Bat came before John le Blund, Mayor of London, and the Aldermen, and bound himself, and all his rents, lands, and tenements, to keep the City of London indemnified from peril of fire and other losses which might arise from his houses covered with thatch, in the Parish of St Laurence Candelwykstrete; and he agreed that he would have the said houses covered with tiles about the Feast of Pentecost then next ensuing. And in case he should not do the same, he granted that the Mayor, Sheriffs, and bailiffs, of London, should cause the said houses to be roofed with tiles out of the issues of his rents aforesaid.

H. T. Riley, *Memorials of London*

POPULATION OF SOME ENGLISH TOWNS AND COUNTIES IN THE REIGN OF RICHARD II

Figures are taken from the Poll Tax Returns in 1377 and 1381.

TOWNS	1377	1381
Bath	1,902	1,739
Bury St Edmunds	570	297

13. The construction of a timber-framed building in the fifteenth century.

Bristol	2,445	1,334
Cambridge	6,345	5,662
Canterbury	2,574	2,123
Chichester	869	787
Colchester	2,995	1,609
Coventry	4,817	3,974
Exeter	1,560	1,420
Gloucester	2,239	1,446
Hull	1,557	1,124
Lincoln	3,412	2,196
London	23,314	20,397
Newcastle-on-Tyne	2,647	1,819
Northampton	1,477	1,518
Oxford	2,357	2,005
Shrewsbury	2,082	1,618
Southampton	1,152	1,051
Worcester	1,557	932
York	7,248	4,015
COUNTIES	*1377*	*1381*
Bedfordshire	20,339	14,895
Cornwall	34,274	12,056
Devonshire	45,635	20,656
Cumberland	11,841	4,748
Dorsetshire	34,241	19,507
Essex	47,962	30,748
Hampshire	33,241	22,018
Huntingdonshire	14,169	11,299
Kent	56,557	43,838
Lancashire	23,880	8,371
Middlesex	11,243	9,937
Norfolk	88,797	66,719
Northamptonshire	40,225	27,997
Rutland	5,994	5,993
Shropshire	23,574	13,041
Staffordshire	21,465	15,993
Suffolk	58,610	44,635
Surrey	18,039	12,684
Westmoreland	7,389	3,859

Poll Tax Returns, as quoted in Powell,
The Rising in East Anglia in 1381

TOWN SANITATION, 1388

For that so much Dung and Filth of the Garbage and Intrails as well of Beasts killed, as of other Corruptions, be cast and put in Ditches, Rivers and other Waters, and also within many other Places, within, about and nigh unto divers Cities, Boroughs, and Towns of the Realm, and the suburbs of them, that the air is greatly corrupt and infect, and many Maladies and other intoler-able Diseases do daily happen, as well to the Inhabitants, and those that are conversant in the said Cities, Boroughs, Towns and Suburbs, as to others repairing and travelling thither, to the great Annoyance, Damage and Peril of the Inhabitants, Dwellers, Repairers and Travellers aforesaid: It is accorded and assented, That Proclamation be made as well in the City of London, as in other Cities, Boroughs, and Towns through the Realm of England, where it shall be needful, as well within Franchises as without, that all they which do cast and lay all such Annoyances, Dung, Garbages, Intrails, and other Ordure in Ditches, Rivers, Waters, and other Places aforesaid, shall cause them utterly to be removed, avoided, and carried away betwixt this and the Feast of St Michael next ensuing after the end of this present Parliament, every one upon Pain to lose and forfeit to ur Lord the King £20.

> Statutes of the Realm (1810-1828), Vol. II translation
> G. G. Coulton, *Social Life in Britain from the Conquest*
> *to the Reformation*

NO TOWN WANDERING IN THE DARK, 1398

Memorandum: that on Maundy Thursday in the twenty-first year of the reign of King Richard II, in the presence of the mayor and community of the town, it was ordered and agreed that no man of whatever condition dwelling within the borough of Wycombe is to go out wandering in the town after ten o'clock at night, unless he has some reasonable cause for his wandering; and if anybody should be found so wandering after the hour aforesaid, he is at once to be taken and imprisoned by the town officers, and kept in prison until he shall be released by the mayor or his deputy and the community.

Item: it was ordained the same day and year that nobody may play at dice in the town under pain of imprisonment; and also he who as host has received him shall pay to the community 4od.

> *The first ledger book of High Wycombe*,
> edited by R. W. Greaves, Bucks. Record Society

14. A town scene in the fifteenth century showing goods displayed on the open stall, a table; and through an open door one can see goods being made.

THE SCOTTISH COUNTRYSIDE, Fourteenth Century

Scotia, also, has tracts of land bordering on the sea, pretty level and rich, with green meadows, and fertile and productive fields of corn and barley, and well adapted for growing beans, pease and all other produce; destitute, however, of wine and oil, though by no means so of honey and wax. But in the upland districts, and along the highlands, the fields are less productive, except only in oats and barley. The country is, there, very hideous, interspersed with moors and marshy fields, muddy and dirty; it is, however, full of pasturage grass for cattle, and comely with verdure in the glens, along the water-courses. This region abounds in wool-bearing sheep, and in horses, and its soil is grassy, feeds cattle and wild beasts, is rich in milk and wool, and manifold in its wealth of fish, in sea, river and lake. . . .

John Fordun, *Chronicles of the People of Scotland,*
translated by F .J. H. Skene, *Historians of Scotland*

CHRISTMASTIDE, 1405

We do command and charge you . . . that you do order good and sufficient watch of folks, properly armed and arrayed, to be kept in your Ward every night during this solemn Feast of Christmas; going always, and passing, through all the streets and lanes in your said Ward, in manner as heretofore has been wont to be done. And that no persons shall go in the said city, or the suburbs thereof, with visors or false faces, on the pain that awaits the same. And that on the outside of every house that is upon the high streets and lanes of the said city, every night during the solemn Feast aforesaid, a lantern shall be hung, with a lighted candle therein, the same to burn so long as it may last; on pain of paying fourpence to the Chamber of the Guildhall, every time that default in such light shall be made. And this you are in no manner to omit.

H. T. Riley, *Memorials of London*

VIEWS OF ENGLAND IN THE FIFTEENTH CENTURY

The riches of England are greater than those of any other country in Europe, as I have been told by the oldest and most experienced merchants, and also as I myself can vouch, from what I have seen. This is owing in the first place, to the great fertility of the soil, which is such, that, with the exception of wine, they import nothing from abroad for their subsistence. Next, the sale of their valuable tin brings in a large sum of money to the kingdom; but still more do they derive from their extraordinary abundance of wool, which bears such a high price and reputation throughout Europe. And in order to keep the gold and silver in the country, when once it has entered, they have made a law, which has been in operation for a long time now, that no money, nor gold nor silver plate should be carried out of England under a very heavy penalty. And every one who makes a tour in the island will soon become aware of this great wealth, as will have been the case with your Magnificence, for there is no small innkeeper, however poor and humble he may be, who does not serve his table with silver dishes and drinking cups; and no one, who has not in his house silver plate to the amount of at least £100 sterling, which is equivalent to 500 golden crowns with us, is considered by the English to be a person of any consequence. But above all are their riches displayed in the church treasures; for there is not a parish church in the kingdom so mean as not to possess crucifixes, candle-sticks, censers, patens and cups of silver; nor is there a convent of mendicant friars so poor, as not to have all these same articles in silver, besides many other ornaments worthy of a cathedral church in the same metal. Your Magnificence may therefore imagine what the decorations of those enormously rich Benedictine, Carthusian and Cistercian monasteries must be. These are, indeed, more like baronial palaces than religious houses. . . .

Italian Relation of England. Translation Camden Society Editor

FLOODS IN THE FENS, Fifteenth Century

Throughout the whole of this county, and in Hoyland especially, there was scarcely a house or building, but what the streams of water made their way and flowed through it. Nor must you suppose that this happened hurriedly and in a cursory manner only: but continuously, during a whole month, the waters either stood there without flowing off, or else, being agitated by strong gusts of wind, swelled and increased still more and more day after day. Nor on this occasion did the embankments offer any effectual resistance, but on the contrary, though materials had been brought from other quarters for the purpose of strengthening them, they proved of very little service for that purpose; and however diligently the work might have been attended to in the day time, as the waters swelled and rose, the spot under repair was completely laid bare during the night. Then was there grief and lamentation among all, and outcries and tumult among the Hoylanders.

Ingulph, Continuator, translated in H. C. Darby,
The Medieval Fenland, Cambridge

15. The house of Thomas Paycocke, c. 1500, Coggleshall, Essex.

ENGLISH TOWNS THROUGH ITALIAN EYES, 1500

There are scarcely any towns of importance in the kingdom, excepting these two: Bristol, a seaport to the west, and Boraco [Eboracum] otherwise York which is on the borders of Scotland; besides London to the south. Eboracum was in ancient times the principal city of the island, and was adorned with many buildings by the Romans, in their elegant style, but having been sacked and burnt in the reign of King William the Conqueror, she never afterwards could recover her former splendour; so that, at present, all the beauty of this island is confined to London; which, although sixty miles distant from the sea, possesses all the advantages to be desired in a maritime town; being situated on the river Thames, which is very much affected by the tide, for many miles (I do not know the exact number) above it: and London is so much benefited by this ebb and flow of the river, that vessels of 100 tons burden can come up to the city, and ships of any size to within five miles of it; yet the water in this river is fresh for twenty miles below London. Although this city has no buildings in the Italian style, but of timber or brick like the French, the Londoners live comfortably, and, it appears to me, that there are not fewer inhabitants than at Florence or Rome. It abounds with every article of luxury, as well as with the necessaries of life: but the most remarkable thing in London is the wonderful quantity of wrought silver. I do not allude to that in private houses (though the landlord of the house in which the Milanese ambassador lived, had plate to the amount of 100 crowns), but to the shops of London. In one single street, named the Strand, leading to St Paul's there are fifty-two goldsmiths' shops, so rich and full of silver vessels, great and small, that in all the shops in Milan, Rome, Venice and Florence put together, I do not think there would be found so many of the magnificence that are to be seen in London. And these vessels are all either salt cellars, or drinking cups, or basins to hold water for the hands; for they eat off that fine tin [pewter] which is little inferior to silver. These great riches of London are not occasioned by its inhabitants being noblemen or gentlemen; being all, on the contrary, persons of low degree, and artificers who have congregated there from all parts of the island, and from Flanders, and from every other place. No one can be mayor or alderman of London, who has not been an apprentice in his youth; that is, who has not passed the seven or nine years in that hard service described before. Still, the citizens of London are thought quite as highly of there, as the Venetian gentlemen are at Venice, as I think your Magnificence may have perceived. The city is divided into several wards, each of which has six officers; but superior to these are twenty-four gentlemen who they call aldermen, which in their language signifies old or experienced men; and, of these aldermen, one is elected every year by themselves, to be a magistrate named the mayor, who is in no less estimation with the Londoners, than the person of our most serene lord [the Doge] is with us, or than the Gonfaloniero at Florence; and the day on which he enters upon his office, he is obliged to give a sumptuous entertainment to all the principal people in London, as well as to foreigners of distinction; and I, being one of the guests, together with your Magnificence, carefully observed every room and hall, and the court, where the company were all seated, and was of opinion that there must have been 1000 or more persons at table. The dinner lasted four hours or more; but it is true that the dishes were not served with that assiduity and frequency that is the custom with us in Italy; there being long pauses between each course, the company conversing the while. A no less magnificent banquet is given when two other officers named sheriffs are appointed; to which I went, being anxious to see every thing well; your Magnificence also was invited but did not go in consequence of the invitation having come from the Lord Privy Seal. At this feast, I observed the infinite profusion of victuals, and of plate, which was for the most part gilt; and amongst other things, I noticed how punctiliously they sat in their order, and the extraordinary silence of every one, insomuch that I could have imagined it one of those public repasts of the Lacedemonians that I have read of.

Italian Relation of England. Translation, Camden Society Editor

Family

BEDS, Twelfth Century
In the bedchamber let a curtain go around the walls decently, or a scenic canopy, for the avoiding of flies and spiders. . . . A tapestry should hang appropriately. Near the bed let there be placed a chair to which a stool may be added, and a bench nearby the bed. On the bed itself should be placed a feather mattress to which a bolster is attached. A quilted pad of striped cloth should cover this on which a cushion for the head can be placed. Then sheets of muslin, ordinary cotton, or at least pure linen, should be laid. Next a coverlet of green cloth or of coarse wool, of which the fur lining is badger, cat, beaver, or sable, should be put—all this if there is lacking purple or down. A perch should be nearby on which can rest a hawk. . . . From another pole let there hang clothing . . . and let there be also a chambermaid whose face may charm and render tranquil the chamber, who, when she finds time to do so may knit or unknit silk thread, or make knots of orpryes [gold lace], or may sew linen garments and woollen clothes, or may mend. Let her have gloves with the finger tips removed; she should have a leather case protecting the finger from needle pricks, which is vulgarly called a 'thimble'. She must have scissors and a spool of thread and various sizes of needles— small and thin for embroidery, others not so thick for feather stitching, moderately fine ones for ordinary sewing, bigger ones for the knitting of a cloak, still larger ones for threading laces.

U. T. Holmes, Jr., *Daily Living in the Twelfth Century,
based on the Observations of Alexander Neckham*

HAIR AND TEETH, 1188
The men and women [of Wales] cut their hair close round to the ears and eyes. The women, after the manner of the Parthians, cover their heads with a large white veil, folded together in the form of a crown.

Both sexes exceed any other nation in attention to their teeth, which they render like ivory, by constantly rubbing them with

16. A gentleman dresses comfortably by the fire; c. 1320.

green hazel and wiping with a woollen cloth. For their better preservation they abstain from hot meats, and eat only such as are cold, warm, or temperate. The men shave all their beard except the moustaches (*gernoboda*). This custom is not recent but was observed in ancient and remote ages, as we find in the works of Julius Caesar, who says 'The Britons shave every part of their body except their head and upper lip;' and to render themselves more active, and avoid the fate of Absalom in their excursions through the woods, they are accustomed to cut even the hair from their heads; so that this nation more than any other shaves off all pilosity [hairiness]. Julius also adds, that the Britons, previous to an engagement, anointed their faces with a nitrous ointment, which gave them so ghastly and shining an appearance, that the enemy could scarcely bear to look at them, particularly if the rays of the sun were reflected on them.

> *Gerald of Wales, Description of Wales,*
> translated by Sir R. C. Hoare

THE WELSH AS HOSTS, Late Twelfth Century

No one of this nation ever begs; for the houses of all are common to all; and they consider liberality and hospitality amongst the first virtues. So much does hospitality here rejoice in communication, that it is neither offered nor requested by travellers, who, on entering a house, only deliver up their arms. When water is offered to them, if they suffer their feet to be washed, they are received as guests: for the offer of water to wash the feet is with this nation an hospitable invitation But if they refuse the proffered service, they only wish for morning refreshment, not lodging. The young men move about in troops and families under the direction of a chosen leader. Attached only to arms and ease, and ever ready to stand forth in defence of their country, they have free admittance into every house as if it were their own.

Those who arrive in the morning are entertained till evening with the conversation of young women, and the music of the harp; for each house has its young women and harps allotted to this purpose. . . . The kitchen does not supply many dishes, nor high-seasoned incitements to eating. The house is not furnished with tables, cloths or napkins. . . . They place dishes before them [guests] all at once rushes and fresh grass, in large platters or trenchers. They also make use of a thin and broad cake of bread, baked every day . . . and they sometimes add chopped meat, with broth. . . . While the family is engaged in waiting on the guests, the host and hostess stand up, paying unremitting attention to everything, and take no food till all the company are satisfied; that in case of any deficiency, it may fall upon them. A bed made of rushes, and covered with a coarse kind of cloth manufactured in the country, called *brychan* [blanket] is then placed along the side of the room, and they all in common lie down to sleep; nor is their dress at night different from that by day, for at all seasons they defend themselves from the cold only by a thin cloak and tunic. The fire continues to burn by night as well as by day, at their feet, and they receive much comfort from the natural heat of the persons lying near them; but when the under side begins to be tired with the hardness of the bed, or the upper one to suffer from cold, they immediately leap up, and go to the fire, which soon relieves them from both inconveniences; and then returning to their couch, they expose alternately their sides to the cold, and to the hardness of the bed. . . .

The heads of different families, in order to excite the laughter of their guests, and gain credit by their sayings, make use of great facetiousness in their conversation; at one time uttering their jokes in a light, easy manner, at another time, under the disguise of equivocation, passing the severest censures. . . .

Gerald the Welshman, Description of Wales,

translated by Sir R. C. Hoare

DOGS, Late Twelfth Century

A greyhound belonging to the aforesaid Owen (a twelfth century Welsh prince, murdered by his brother), large, beautiful and curiously spotted with a variety of colours, received seven wounds from arrows and lances, in the defence of his master, and on his part did much injury to the enemy and assassins. When this wounds were healed, he was sent to king Henry II by William Earl of Gloucester, in testimony of so great and extraordinary a deed. A dog, of all animals, is most attached to man, and most easily distinguishes him; sometimes when deprived of his master, he refuses to live, and in his master's defence is bold enough to brave death; ready therefore, to die, either with or for his master. I shall take this opportunity of mentioning what from experience and ocular testimony I have observed respecting the nature of dogs. A dog is in general sagacious, but particularly with respect to his master; for when he has for some time lost him in a crowd, he depends more upon his nose than upon his eyes; and, in endeavouring to find him, he first looks about, and then applies his nose, for greater certainty to his clothes, as if nature had placed all the powers of infallibility in that feature. The tongue of a dog possesses a medicinal quality; the wolf's on the contrary, a poisonous: the dog heals his wounds by licking them, the wolf, by a similar practice, infects them; and the dog, if he has received a wound in his neck or head, or any part of his body where he cannot apply his tongue, ingeniously makes use of his hinder foot as a conveyance of the healing qualities to the parts affected.

Gerald of Wales, *Itinerary of Archbishop Baldwin through Wales,* translated by Sir R. C. Hoare

MARRIAGE, 1220

Further we enjoin that marriages be decently celebrated, with reverence, not with laughter and ribaldry, not in taverns or at public drinkings and feastings. Let no man place a ring made of rushes or of any worthless or precious material on the hand of a woman in jest that he may more easily gain her favours lest in thinking to jest the bond of marriage be tied. Henceforth let no pledge of contracting marriage be given save in the presence of a priest and of three or four respectable persons summoned for the purpose. . . .

Constitutions of Richard de Marisco, Bishop of Durham, at the Council of Durham, 1220

17. Knights courting in a ladies' pleasure ground.

A THIRTEENTH-CENTURY MANOR HOUSE, 1256

Robert le Moyne, Treasurer of St Paul's received from the Dean and Chapter of that church 'a sufficient and handsome hall well ceiled with oak. On the western side is a worthy bed, on the ground a stone chimney, a wardrobe [a W.C.], and a certain other small chamber; at the eastern end is a pantry and a buttery. Between the hall and the chapel is a side room. There is a suitable chapel covered with tiles, a portable altar and a small cross. There are four tables on trestles in the hall.

Likewise, too, there is a good kitchen well covered with tiles, with a furnace and ovens, one large, the other small, for cakes, two tables, and alongside the kitchen a small house for baking. A new granary, too, covered with oak shingles, and a building in which the dairy is contained, though it is divided. Likewise a chamber suited for clergymen and a necessary chamber. Also a henhouse. These are within the inner gate.

Likewise, outside of that gate are an old house for servants, a good stable, long and divided, and to the east of the principal building, beyond the smaller stable, a solar [usually an upper room] for the use of the servants. Also a building in which is contained a bed; also two barns, one for wheat and one for oats. These buildings are enclosed with a moat, a wall and a hedge. Also beyond the middle gate there is a good barn, and a stable for cows and another for oxen, these are old and dilapidated. Also beyond the outer gate is a pigstye.'

Historical MSS. Commission Reports 9, I, quoted in Robinson's *Readings in European History,* Vol. I.

PREPARATIONS FOR THE UPRISING OF QUEEN PHILIPPA AFTER THE BIRTH OF HER ELDEST SON, 15 JUNE 1330

Edward, by the Grace of God King of England . . . to the treasurer and chamberlains of our Exchequer, greeting. We are sending you enclosed herein a schedule containing many things which will be needed for the uprising of Philippa, Queen of England, our beloved consort, from childbirth. So we command and charge you that you cause payment to be made without delay from our treasure for the provision and purchase of all these things, to our beloved clerk, Master William la Zouche, clerk of Our Great Wardrobe, of all such moneys as shall be needed. And for our honour and that of our said Consort, you should take order as soon as you can, without any excuse, for payment to be made, lest through your fault the things be not ready on the said day of uprising.

Given under our seal at Woodstock, the nineteenth of June in the fourth year of our reign.

The Schedule. One robe of red velvet of three garments, to wit coat, surcoat, and mantle, with facings of pure miniver, 6 pieces.

For the churching of my Lady, a coat and hood of cloth of gold, with facings of miniver, 5 pieces.

For the great banquet, a robe embroidered with gold, of five garments, with facings of pure miniver.

For the evening, a robe of silken cloth worked with fine gold, of 3 garments, coat, surcoat, and mantle, with pure fur, 6 pieces.

A coverlet of scarlet cloth with facing of miniver, for the great cradle for the infant, and a kerchief.

Item, a cloth for the Queen's Chapel of crimson sendal of Tripoli, 6 pieces.

Item, a coverlet of scarlet for the said Queen, with the facing of pure miniver, and a kerchief for my Lady.

Item, bear in mind the cloths of gold for hanging the great chamber; and fueling for the said chamber.

Item, for dames and demoiselles of the chamber, 7½ furs of "popr'," 10 furs of 'grow', one fur and a half of miniver.

Item for dames and demoiselles of the chamber, eight hoods of miniver and one hood of miniver of 40 skins.

Item, two coffers for the infant's chamber.

Exchequer of Receipt, Warrants for issues.

WIVES

And son, if ye would have a wife, take her not for her money, but inquire wisely of all her life, and give good heed that she be meek, courteous and prudent, even though she be poor; and such an one will do you more good service in time of need, than a richer.

And if your wife be meek and good, and serve you well and pleasantly, look ye be not so mad as to charge her too grievously, but rule her with a fair hand and easy, and cherish her for her good deeds. For a thing unskilfully overdone makes needless grief to grow, and it is better to have a meal's meat of homely fare with peace and quiet, than an hundred dishes with grudging and much care. And therefore learn this well that if you want a wife to your ease, take her never the more for the riches she may have, though she might endow you with lands.

And ye shall not displease your wife, nor call her by no villainous names, for it is a shame to you to miscall a woman; and in so doing, ye are not wise, but if ye defame your own wife, no wonder that another should do so! Soft and fair will tame alike hart and hind, buck and doe.

On the other hand, be not too busy to fight and chide, if thy wife come to you at any time with complaint of man or child; and be not avenged till you know the truth, for you might make a stir in the dark, and afterwards it should rue you both.

'The Wise Man and his Son' in The Babees' Book Medieval Manners for the Young done into modern English from Dr Furnivall's Texts by Edith Rickert

BOYS, Thirteenth Century

Boys have bad habits. . . . They care nothing about the future at all and love games and vanities. They refuse to attend to what is profitable and useful. They value trifles as if they were important and regard important matters as if they were trifles or nothing at all. They like what is bad for them. They make more fuss about the loss of an apple or of a pear than of an inheritance.

They have no memory for past kindness. They clamour and snatch greedily at everything they see. They like the talk and ideas of boys like themselves and shun the company of the old. They do not keep a secret but repeat tactlessly everything they see or hear. They suddenly laugh, they suddenly cry, they make a ceaseless noise and endless chatter. They hardly shut up for sleep. As soon as they have been washed they make themselves filthily dirty. They make violent resistance when their mothers wash or comb them. They only think of their own stomachs . . . and are scarcely out of bed before they demand food.

From *Bartholomew the Englishman,*
translated by John of Trevisa

JEAN FROISSART'S BOYHOOD, c. 1363

In my boyhood I was one who l.ked too well to have a good time; and I still do . . . When I was only twelve years old I was very eager for dances and carols, to hear minstrels and lively talk. And I always liked those who loved dogs and birds. And when they sent me to school . . . there were little girls there of my own age, and I, innocent as I was, gave them pins or an apple or a pear or a little glass ring, and it seemed to me wonderful when they were pleased . . .

And when Lent came I had under a stool a great storehouse of shells for which I would not have accepted any money. And then of an afternoon, with the shell which had holes in it, I played with the children of our street; and when we threw it into the air, I would say to them, 'Toss it high . . . ' And when the moon was bright, we played at 'Pinch Me', and in the spring I was very cross when they interfered with my playing. We played games called 'Follow the Leader', and 'Trot-trot Merlot', and pebbles [marbles?], and 'Heads or Tails'. And I have often made of a stick a horse called Grisel. We used to make helmets of our hats; and often, before the girls, we beat one another with our caps. Sometimes we played at charades (or riddles), at 'Hare and Hounds', at 'Cow's Horn in the Salt', and throwing leaden pennies or pebbles against a fence. And then we rolled nuts . . . I amused myself night and morning with a spinning top; and I've often made soap bubbles in a little pipe, two or three or four or five. I loved to watch them.

When I was a little wiser, I had to control myself, for they made me learn Latin; and if I made mistakes in saying my lessons, I was beaten; and when I was beaten or afraid of being beaten,

I did better. Nevertheless, away from my master I could never rest till I fought with the other boys; I was beaten and I beat, and I was so knocked about that often my clothes were torn. I went home and there I was scolded and beaten again, but to be sure one gets used to all that, for I never had the less fun for it. But when I saw my companions passing before me down the street, I dropped everything and ran after them to play.

Jean Froissart, 'L'Espinette amoureuse', *Œuvres ·de Froissart*:
poésies, edited by Auguste Scheler.

'That [Chaucer] knew Froissart . . .is practically certain, for Froissart was a member of Queen Philippa's household from 1361 to 1366 . . . and Chaucer was also at this time probably attached to some member of the royal family.'

J. M. Manly, Chaucer, *Canterbury Tales*

THE WIFE OF BATH

A worthy woman from beside Bath city
Was with us, somewhat deaf, which was a pity.
In making cloth she showed so great a bent
She bettered those of Ypres and of Ghent.
In all the parish not a dame dared stir
Towards the altar steps in front of her,
And if indeed they did, so wrath was she
As to be quite put out of charity.
Her kerchiefs were of finely woven ground;
I dared have sworn they weighed a good ten pound,
The ones she wore on Sunday, on her head.
Her hose were of the finest scarlet red
And gartered tight; her shoes were soft and new.
Bold was her face, handsome, and red in hue.
A worthy woman all her life, what's more
She'd had five husbands, all at the church door,
Apart from other company in youth;
No need just now to speak of that, forsooth.
And she had thrice been to Jerusalem.
Seen many strange rivers and passed over them;
She'd been to Rome and also to Boulogne,
St James of Compostella and Cologne,
And she was skilled in wandering by the way.
She had gap-teeth, set widely, truth to say.
Easily on an ambling horse she sat
All wimpled up, and on her head a hat

18. Sir Geoffrey Lnttrell at the main meal of the day.

As broad as is a buckler or a shield;
She had a flowing mantle that concealed
Large hips, her heels spurred sharply under that.
In company she liked to laugh and chat
And knew the remedies for love's mischances,
An art in which she knew the oldest dances.

Geoffrey Chaucer, *Canterbury Tales,*
Prologue translated by Nevill Coghill

AN ESQUIRE'S SUMMARY OF THE CONTENTS OF HIS HOUSE AT SALISBURY, 1410

George Meryet, Esquire, of St Thomas's Parish, Salisbury, included in his will 'all my goods and utensils in my inn [private dwelling house].' To wit, covers, blankets, linens, coverlets, mattresses, testers [canopy over a bed], painted cloths, rugs, napkins, towels, washbasins, candelabra of bronze, marble, and silver-gilt, bronze pots and pans, twelve silver spoons, spits, poles, iron pots, vessels of silver-gilt and lead for beer, silver-gilt salt cellars, three iron braziers, and boards for tables, and trestles.

Prerogative Court of Canterbury, 21 March

A HORSE-MILL, 1436

Yet she left not the world altogether, for she now bethought herself of a new housewifery. She had a horse-mill. She got herself two good horses and a man to grind men's corn, and thus she trusted to get her living. This enterprise lasted not long, for in a short time after, on Corpus Christi Eve, befell this marvel.

This man, being in good health of body, and his two horses sturdy and gentle, had pulled well in the mill beforetime, and now he took one of these horses and put him in the mill as he had done before, and this horse would draw no draught in the mill for anything the man might do. The man was sorry and essayed with all his wits how he should make this horse pull. Sometimes he led him by the head, sometimes he beat him, sometimes he cherished him and all availed not, for he would rather go backwards than forward. Then this man set a sharp pair of spurs on his heels and rode on the horse's back to make him pull, and it was never the better. When the man saw it would work in no way, he set up this horse again in the stable, and give him corn, and he ate well and freshly. And later he took the other horse and put him in the mill, and like his fellow did, so did he, for he would not draw for anything the man might do. Then the man forsook his service and would no longer remain with the aforesaid creature. Anon, it was noised about the town of [Lynn] that neither man nor beast would serve the said creature.

Then some said she was accursed; some said God took open vengeance on her; some said one thing and some said another. Some wise men, whose minds were more grounded in the love of Our Lord, said it was the high mercy of Our Lord Jesus Christ that called her from the pride and vanity of the wretched world.

The Book of Margery Kempe, A modern version by
W. Butler-Bowdon

TRAINING A SERVANT, c. 1460

I will that you eschew forever the 'simple conditions' of a person that is not taught.

Do not claw your head or your back as if you were after a flea, or stroke your hair as if you sought a louse.

Be not glum, nor twinkle with your eyes, nor be heavy of cheer; and keep your eyes from winking and watering.

Do not pick your nose or let it drop clear pearls, or sniff, or blow it too hard, lest your lord hear.

Twist not your neck askew like a jackdaw; wring not your hands with picking or trifling or shrugging, as if you would saw wood; nor puff up your chest, nor pick your ears, nor be slow of hearing.

Retch not, nor spit too far, nor laugh or speak too loud. Beware of making faces and scorning; and be no liar with your mouth. Nor yet lick your lips or drivel.

Do not have the habit of squirting or spouting with your mouth,

19. A domestic scene in the fifteenth century.

or gape or yawn or pout. And do not lick a dish with your tongue to get out dust.

Be not rash or reckless—that is not worth a clout.

Do not sigh with your breast, or cough, or breathe hard in the presence of your sovereign, or hiccough, or belch, or groan never the more. Do not trample with your feet, or straddle your legs, or scratch your body—there is no sense in showing off. Good son, do not pick your teeth, or grind, or gnash them, or with puffing and blowing cast foul breath upon your lord.

'The duties of a Panter or Butler' in John Russell's 'Book of Nurture'; *The Babees Medieval Manners for the Young done into modern English from Dr Furnivall's Texts* by Edith Rickert

A BATH, c. 1460

If your lord wishes to bathe and wash his body clean, hang sheets round the roof, every one full of flowers and sweet green herbs, and have five or six sponges to sit or lean upon, and see that you have one big sponge to sit upon, and a sheet over so that he may bathe there for a while, and have a sponge also for under his feet, if there be any to spare, and always be careful that the door is shut. Have a basin full of hot fresh herbs and wash his body with a soft sponge, rinse him with fair rose-water, and throw it over him; then let him go to bed; but see that the bed be sweet and nice; and first put on his socks and slippers that he may go near the fire and stand on his foot-sheet, wipe him dry with a clean cloth, and take him to bed to cure his troubles.

> John Russell, *Book of Nurture,* from Edith Rickert,
> *The Babees' Book: Medieval Manners for the Young:*
> *Done into Modern English from Dr Furnivall's Texts*

A BATH OF BOILED HERBS, c. 1460

Boil together hollyhock, mallow, wall pellitory and brown fennel, danewort, St John's wort, centaury, ribwort and camomile, heyhove, heyriff, herb-benet, bresewort, smallage, water speedwell, scabious, bugloss, and wild flax which is good for aches— boil withy leaves and green oats together with them, and throw them hot into a vessel and put your lord over it and let him endure it for a while as hot as he can, being covered over and closed on every side; and whatever disease, grievance or pain ye be vexed with, this medicine shall surely make you whole, as men say.

> John Russell, *Book of Nurture*

THE DEMAUNDES JOYOUS, Fifteenth Century

Question What thing is it that never was nor never shall be?
Answer Never mouse made her nest in a cat's ear.
Question Why come dogs so often to church?
Answer Because, when they see the altars covered, they think their masters go there to dine.
Question Why doth a dog turn himself about three times before he lies down?
Answer Because he knoweth not his bed's head from the foot.
Question Why do men make an oven in the town?
Answer Because they cannot make the town in the oven.
Question What thing is it that hath no end?
Answer A bowl.

Question What is it that never freezeth?
Answer   That' is hot water.
Question What thing is it, the less it is the more it is dreaded?
Answer   A bridge.
Question How many straws go to a goose's nest?
Answer   None, for lack of feet.
Question Who was he that slew the fourth part of the world?
Answer   Cain, when he slew his brother Abel, in which time
          there were but four persons in the world.

Reliquae Antiquae, where it is described as 'From a unique copy in the Public Library of the University of Cambridge, printed by Wynken de Worde.' It shows medieval amusements round the evening fire. Wynken de Worde came to London *c.* 1477 and became Caxton's assistant, inheriting his press on Caxton's death in 1491.

COURTING IN THE FIFTEENTH CENTURY

The same day that I come to Northleach on a Sunday before mattins from Burford William Midwinter welcomed me and in our communication he asked me if I were in any way of marriage. I told him nay, and he informed me that there was a young gentlewoman whose father's name is Lemryke and her mother is dead and she shall inherit from her mother £40 a year as they say in that country, and her father is the greatest ruler as richest man in that country . . . . When I had packed [the wool] at Camden and William Midwinter departed I came to Northleach again to make an end of packing, and on Sunday next after, the same man that William Midwinter brake first came to me and told me that he had broken to his master according as Midwinter desired him . . . and if I would tarry till May Day I should have a sight of the young gentlewoman, and I said I would tarry with a good will . . . to mattins the same day come the young gentle-woman and her mother-in-law, and I and William Bretten were saying mattins when they come into church, and when mattins were done they went to a kinswoman of the young gentlewoman and I sent to them a pottle of white romnay and they took it thankfully for they had come a mile afoot that morning and when mass was done I come and welcomed them and kissed them and they thanked me for the wine and prayed me to come to dinner with them, and I excused me and they made me promise to drink with them after dinner, and I sent them to dinner a gallon of wine and they sent me a roast heron, and after dinner I come and drank with them and took William Bretten with me and we had right good communication, and the person pleased me well, as by the first communication she is young, little and very well-favoured and witty and the country speaks much good by her. Sir, all this matter abideth the coming of her father to London that we may understand what sum he will depart with and how he likes me. He will be here within three weeks. I pray send me a letter how you think by this manner . . . Writ at London on the 13 day of May per Richard Cely.

The Cely Letters, quoted J. J. Bagley, *Historical Interpretation*

RELATIONS BETWEEN PARENTS AND CHILDREN

The want of affection in the English is strongly manifested towards their children; for after having kept them at home till they arrive at the age of 7 or 9 years at the utmost, they put them out, both males and females, to hard service in the houses of other people . . . and few are born who are exempted from this fate, for every one, however rich he may be, sends his children into the houses of others, whilst he, in return, receives those of strangers into his own. And on enquiring the reason for the severity, they answered that they did it in order that their children might learn better manners.

Italian Relation of England

Food and Drink

KITCHENS, Twelfth Century

In a kitchen there should be a small table on which cabbage may be minced, and also lentils, peas, shelled beans, beans in the pod, millet, onions, and other vegetables of the kind that can be cut up. There should also be pots, tripods, a mortar, a hatchet, a pestle, a stirring stick, a hook, a cauldron, a bronze vessel, a small pan, a baking pan, a meathook, a griddle, small pitchers, a trencher, a bowl, a platter, a pickling vat, and knives for cleaning fish. In a *vivarium* [aquarium] let fish be kept in which they can be caught by net, fork, spear, or light hook, or with a basket. The chief cook should have a cupboard in the kitchen where he may store many aromatic spices, and bread flour sifted through a sieve—and used also for feeding small fish—may be hidden away there. Let there be also a cleaning place where the entrails and feathers of ducks and other domestic fowl can be removed and the birds cleaned. Likewise there should be a large spoon for removing foam and skimming. Also there should be hot water for scalding fowl.

Have a pepper mill and a hand [flour?] mill. Small fish for cooking should be put into a pickling mixture, that is, water mixed with salt. . . . To be sure, pickling is not for all fish, for these are of different kinds. . . There should be also a *garde-robe* pit through which the filth of the kitchen may be evacuated. In the pantry let there be shaggy towels, tablecloth, and an ordinary hand towel which shall hang from a pole to avoid mice. Knives should be kept in the pantry, an engraved saucedish, a saltcellar, a cheese container, a candelabra, a lantern, a candlestick, and baskets. In the cellar or storeroom should be casks, tuns, wineskins, cups, cup cases, spoons, ewers, basins, baskets, pure wine, cider, beer, unfermented wine, mixed wine, claret, nectar, mead, . . . pear wine, red wine, wine from Auvergne, clove-spiced wine for gluttons whose thirst is unquenchable.

U. T. Holmes, Jr., *Daily Living in the Twelfth Century, based on The Observations of Alexander Neckham*

67

20. A royal banquet, Jean de Wavrin's *Chronique d'Angleterre,* late fifteenth century. John I of Portugal entertains John of Gaunt.

PUTRID FOOD AT COURT, 1160

I often wonder how anyone who has been used to the service of scholarship and the camps of learning can endure the annoyances of a court life. Among courtiers there is no order, no plan, no moderation, either in food, in horse exercise, or in watchings. A priest or a soldier attached to the court has bread put before him which is not kneaded, nor leavened, made of the dregs of beer, bread like lead, full of bran and unbaked; wine spoiled either by being sour or mouldy—thick, greasy, rancid, tasting of pitch and vapid. I have sometimes seen wine so full of dregs put before noblemen that they were compelled rather to filter than drink it, with their eyes shut and teeth closed.

The beer at court is horrid to taste and filthy to look at. On account of the great demand, meat is sold whether it be fresh or not. The fish one buys is four days old, yet the fact that it stinks does not lessen its price. The servants care nothing whatever whether the unlucky guests become ill or die provided they load their masters' tables with dishes. Indeed the tables are sometimes filled with putrid food, and were it not for the fact that those who eat it indulge in powerful exercise, many more deaths would result

from it. But if the courtiers cannot have exercise (which is the
case of the court for a time in town) some of them always are left
behind at death's door. . . .

Peter of Blois, Letters

A MULTITUDE OF DISHES, 1179

And as he sat there at the high table with the Prior [of
Canterbury] and the seniors, he noted two things, the multitude
of the dishes and the excessive superfluity of signs which the monks
[forbidden to speak] made to one another. For there was the
Prior giving so many dishes to the serving monks, and they in
their turn bearing these gifts to the lower tables; and there were
those, to whom these gifts were brought, offering their thanks,
and all of them gesticulating with fingers, hands and arms, and
whistling one to another in lieu of speaking, all extravagating in
a manner more free and frivolous than was seemly; so that
Giraldus seemed to be seated at a stage-play or among actors
and jesters. It would therefore be more consonant with good

21. The cook is serving meat from the iron cauldron hanging from an
adjustable ratchet over a wood fire. On the left, a sheep is being slaughtered.
This illustration was made in the thirteenth century.

order and decency to speak modestly in human speech than with signs and whistlings thus jocosely to indulge in dumb garrulity. And as to the dishes and the number thereof, what I shall say, save that I have oft heard Giraldus himself declare that sixteen very costly dishes or even more were placed upon the table in order, not to say contrary to all order. Finally, potherbs were brought to every table but were little tasted. For you might see so many kinds of fish, roast and boiled, stuffed and fried, so many dishes contrived with eggs and pepper by dexterous cooks, so many flavourings and condiments, compounded with like dexterity to tickle gluttony and awaken appetite. Moreover you m'ght see in the midst of such abundance 'wine and strong drink', metheglin [spiced mead], claret, must, mead, and mulberry juice, and all that can intoxicate, beverages so choice that beer, such as is made at its best in England and above all in Kent, found no place among them. There beer among other drinks is as potherbs are among made dishes. Such extreme superfluity and extravagance might you behold both in food and drink, as might not only beget loathing in him that partook thereof, but weariness even in him that beheld it.

> *The Autobiography of Giraldus Cambrensis,* edited and translated by H. E. Butler

A ROYAL MEAL, 1260

. . . At feasts, first meat is prepared and arrayed, guests be called together, forms and stools be set in the hall, and tables, cloths, and towels be ordained, disposed and made ready. Guests be set with the lord in the chief place of the board, and they sit not down at the board before the guests wash their hands. Children be set in their place, and servants at a table by themselves. First knives, spoons and salt be set on the board, and then bread and drink, and many divers messes; household servants busily help each other to do everything diligently, and talk merrily together. The guests be gladded with lutes and harps. Now wine and now messes of meat be brought forth and departed. At the last cometh fruit and spices, and when they have eatèn, board, cloths, and relief are borne away, and guests wash and wipe their hands again. Then grace is said, and guests thank the lord. When all this is done at meat, men take their leave, and some go to bed and sleep, and some go home to their own lodgings.

> Bartholomaeus Anglicus, *De Proprietatibus Rerum*

THE FARE OF A FARMER IN EDWARD III's REIGN
'I have no penny,' quoth Piers, 'Pullets for to buy
Nor neither geese nor piglets, but two green [new] cheeses,
A few curds and cream and an oaten cake
And two loaves of beans and bran to bake for my little ones.
And besides I say by my soul I have no salt bacon,
Nor no little eggs, by Christ, collops for to make.
But I have parsley and leeks and many cabbages,
And besides a cow and a calf and a cart mare
To draw afield my dung the while the drought lasteth.
And by this livelihood we must live till lammas time [August].
And by that I hope to have harvest in my croft.
And then may I prepare the dinner as I dearly like.
All the poor people those peascods fatten.
Beans and baked apples they brought in their laps.
Shalots and chervils and ripe cherries many
And proffered pears these present . . .
Then poor folk for fear fed hunger eagerly
With great leeks and peas . . .
By then it came near harvest. New corn came to market.
Then were folk glad and fed hunger with the best,
With good ale as Glutton taught and got hunger to sleep.
And when wasters wouldn't work but wander about
Nor no beggar eat bread that beans within were
But two sorts of fine white or else of clean wheat
Nor no halfpenny ale in nowise drink,
But of the best and the brownest that in town is to sell,
Labourers that have no land to live on, only their hands,
Deigned not to dine each day on herbs not fresh gathered,
Have no penny ale given them, nor no piece of bacon,
But if it be fresh flesh or fish, fried or baked,
And that warm or hot to avoid chilling their bellies.

William Langland, *Piers Plowman, c.* 1370

GLUTTON GOING TO CHURCH, STEPS INTO A LONDON TAVERN
Then in goes Glutton, and great oaths welcomed him.
Cis the sempstress sat on the bench,
Walt the gamekeeper and his wife—drunk;
Tom the tinker and two of his 'prentices,
Hick the hackneyman, Hogg the needler,
Clarice of Cock Lane and the parish clerk;

Parson Piers of Pray-to-God and Pernel the Flemish woman,
Daw the ditcher and a dozen more of them;
A fiddler, a ratter and a cheapside scavenger,
A ropemaker, a lackey and Rose the retailer,
A watchman and a hermit and the Tyburn hangman;
Godfrey the garlic-seller and Griffin the Welshman,
All early in the morning welcomed Glutton gladly
To try the good ale.
There was laughing and chattering and 'Pass the cup round',
Bargains and toasts and songs, and so they sat till evensong,
And Glutton had gulped down a gallon and a gill.
He could neither step nor stand till he had his staff;
Then he 'gan walk like a blind singer's dog,
Now to this side, now to that, and sometimes backward,
Like a man who lays lines to catch wild birds;
And when he drew to the doorstep, then his eyes grew dim,
He stumbled on the threshold and fell flat on the floor.

William Langland, Piers Plowman, c. 1370

LOVE OF SPICES SHOWN IN A GROCER'S BILL, 1380

Robert Passeleive, knight, was summoned to answer Edmund
Fraunceys, citizen and grocer of London, in a plea that he pay
£6 . . . whereof Edmund says that, whereas Robert, between the
Feast of Pentecost, 2 Richard 11, and the Feast of Easter following,
in the parish of St Stephen in the ward of Walbrook at divers
times purchased of Edmund pepper, saffron, ginger, cloves, dates,
almonds, rice, saunders [horse parsley], powder of ginger, powder
called 'pouderlumbard', powder of cinnamon, figs, raisins, myrrh,
and canvas for the said £6, payable on the Feast of the Ascension
[May 3] nert following the said Easter, though often required,
Robert has not paid, and has hitherto refused to pay.

Common Pleas, Plea Roll 487m. 438d.

MEAL AND GUESTS, 1398

. . . at feasts first meat is prepared and arranged, then guests are
called together, forms and stools set in the hall, and tables, cloths
and towels ordained, dispersed and made ready. Guests are sat
with the lord in the chief place of the board, and they sit not down
at the board before the guests wash their hands. Children are sat
in their place, and servants at a table by themselves. First knives,
spoons and salt are set on the board, and then bread and drink
and many different dishes. Household servants busily help each
other to everything diligently, and talk merrily together. The

guests are gladdened with lutes and harps. Now wine and dishes of meat are brought forth and despatched. At the last cometh fruit and spices, and then they have eaten, board cloths and scraps are borne away, and guests wash and wipe their hands again. Then graces are said and guests thank the lord. Then for gladness and comfort drink is brought yet again. At the end men take their leave, and some go to bed and sleep, and some go home to their own lodgings.

All that is rehearsed before of dinners and feasts accordeth to the supper also. Many things are necessary and proper for supper . . .

The first is convenient time, . . . not too early, not too late. The second is convenient place, large, pleasant and secure . . . The third is the hearty and glad cheer of him that maketh the feast: the supper is not worthy to be praised if the lord of the house be heavy cheered. . . . The fourth is many divers dishes, so that who that will not of one may taste of another. . . . The fifth is divers wines and drinks. . . . The sixth is courtesy and honesty of servants. . . . The seventh is kind friendship and company of them that sit at the supper. . . . The eighth is mirth of song and of instruments of music: noble men use not to make suppers without harp or symphony. . . . The ninth is plenty of light of candles and tapers and of torches, for it is shame to sup in darkness and perilous also for flies and other filth. Therefore candles and tapers are set on candlesticks to burn. The tenth is the deliciousness of all that is set on the board, for it is not used at supper to serve men with great meat and common as it is used at dinner, but with special light meat and delicious. . . . The eleventh is long during of the supper, for men use after full end of work and travail to sit long at the supper. For meat eaten too hastily grieveth against night, therefore at the supper men should eat by leisure and not too hastily. . . . The twelfth is sureness, for without harm and damage every man shall be prayed to the supper, and after supper that is freely offered it is not honest to compel a man to pay his share. The thirteenth is softness and liking of rest and of sleep. After supper men shall rest, for then sleep is sweet and liking . . . for . . . when smoke of meat cometh into the brain, then men sleep easily.

John of Trevisa, translation of Bartholomaeus Anglicus,
De Proprietatibus Rerum

FROM A FIFTEENTH-CENTURY ACCOUNT ROLL, 1425

Expenses of the Kitchen

For 20 fowls bought by the cook at the feast of St Kalixtus, 20d., and for a quarter of beef bought in Burcester [Bicester] market on the feast of St Thomas Apostle for salting, 16d., and for 1 cade [barrel] of red herrings bought of Harmand Banbury, 8d. And for pork bought for the clerks of the Lord Archbishop sitting at an inquiry at Burchester the Wednesday next before the past of the Conversion of St Paul, 19d., and 1 frayle [basket made of rushes] of figs, 3s. 4d., and for 12 lbs. of sparrows' eggs, 13d., and for 3 couple of green fish with a lyng (of the cod family), 3 congers and, a couple of hake, 9s. 7d., and for a great chopper called a flesh axe, 15d., and for a saltstone bought for the dovecot, 2½d.

Further Provisions

For white bread bought at sundry times for the Prior and guests, 3s. 10d,, and for beer, to wit, 132½ gallons bought for John Spinan, Alice Bedale and other brewers, 4s. 10d., and for 32 galls. of red wine bought of Richard Brayser of Burcester at 8d. a gallon, 21s. 4d., and for 3 gallons, 3 quarts of sweet wine bought of the same, at 16d. a gallon, 5s., and for canvas bought at London by Richard Dymby before the feast of St Osith Virgin for making sheets, 3s.

Other Necessary Provisions

And for one great candle bought at the feast of St Kalixtus, Pope this year 2d., and for parchment bought at St Frideswide's fair 6d., and for paper bought at the same time, 4d., and for a box chair bought at London on the feast of St Thomas Apostle, 9s., and in payments to the sub-prior for copperas and galls bought for making ink at the same time 2d., and for 2 lbs. candles bought for the Prior's lantern at Christmas this year, 12d., and for 8 lbs. of wax bought at Oxford the same year to make 2 torches against Christmas for the Prior's Hall, 3s., . . . and for soap bought for washing the Prior's Hall, 1d., and for 8 snodes of pack thread bought for making a net for snaring rabbits, 6d., and 1 lb. of birdlime, 3d., and for two hand baskets, 7d., and for 4 matts, 13d.

Account Roll of the Manors of Miaxter Priory, quoted in
Hone, *Manor and Manorial Records,* R. B. Morgan,
Readings in English Social History.

KITCHEN GOODS OF SIR JOHN FASTOLF, c. 1430

1 great brass pot	3 cupboards
6 coarse brass pots	1 frying pan

4 little brass pots
4 great brass pots
3 brass pike pans
2 ladles and 2 skimmers of brass
1 cauldron
1 'dytyn' pan of brass
1 dropping pan
1 gridiron
4 rakes
3 trivets
1 dressing knife
1 fire shovel
2 trays

1 slice
2 great square spits
2 square spits
1 brass sieve
1 brass mortar and 1 pestle
1 grate
1 wooden sieve or cullender
1 flesh hook
2 pot hooks
1 pair tongs
1 strainer
1 vinegar bottle

Paston Letters, number 336

LARDED MILK, c. 1450

Take milk scalding hot and take eggs, the yolks and the white, and draw them through a strainer and cast to the milk. And then draw the juice of herbs, whichever thou wilt, so that they be good, and draw them through a strainer. And when the milk beginneth to curdle, cast the juice thereto if thou wilt have it green. And if thou wilt have it red take saunders [horse parsley] and cast to the milk when it curdleth, and leave the herbs. And if thou wilt have it yellow, take saffron and cast to the milk when it curdleth, and leave the saunders. And if thou wilt have it of all these colours, take a pot with milk and juice of herbs, and another pot with milk and saffron, and another pot with milk and saunders, and put them all in a linen cloth and press them all together. And if thou wilt have it of one colour, take but one cloth and strain it in a cloth in the same manner, and beat on the cloth with a ladle or a skimmer to make it solid and flat. And slice it fair with a knife, and fry the slices in a pan with a little fresh grease, and take a little and put it in a dish and serve it forth.

Two Fifteenth-Century Cookery-Books, edited by Thomas Austin
from Harl. MS., British Museum

HOW TO COOK A CABBAGE, c. 1430

Take fair cabbages, and cut them, and pick them clean, and clean wash them, and parboil them in fair water, and then press them on a fair board; and then chop them, and cast them in a fair pot with good fresh broth, and with marrowbones, and let it boil; then take fair grated bread, and cast thereto saffron and salt; or else take good gruel made of fresh flesh, draw through a strainer, and cast thereto. And when thou servest it in, knock out the marrow of the bones, and lay the marrow two pieces or three in a dish, as seemeth best, and serve forth.

Two Fifteenth-Century Cookery-Books, edited by Thomas Austin from Harl. MS., British Museum

WAFERS, OR BISCUIT OF PIKE, c. 1430

Take the belly of a full-grown pike and seethe it well, and put it on a mortar, and put cheese thereto; grind them together; then take flour and white of eggs and beat together; and look that thine eggs be hot, and lay thereon of thine paste, and then make thin wafers and serve in.

Two Fifteenth-Century Cookery-Books, edited by Thomas Austin from Harl. MS., British Museum

BRUET OF ALMAYNE, c. 1430

Take almonds and draw a good milk thereof with water. Take capons, coneys, or partridges; cut up the capon, or kid, or chickens, or coneys; the partridge shall be whole. Then blanch the flesh and cast on the milk; take bacon fat and mince it and cast thereto; take and mince onions and cast thereto enough; put cloves and small raisins thereto; cast whole saffron thereto; then put it to the fire and stir it well. When the flesh is [done] enough, set it off the fire, and put thereto sugar enough. Take powdered ginger, galingale, cinnamon and temper it with vinegar and cast thereto. Season it with salt and serve forth.

Two Fifteenth-Century Cookery-Books, edited by Thomas Austin from Harl. MS., British Museum

TO MAKE WHITE WINE INTO RED AT THE TABLE, Fifteenth Century

Take in spring the flowers that grow in wheat, which are called darnel or passerose, and dry them until they can be powdered. Put some of this, without being observed, into the wine glass, and the wine will turn red.

Sloane MS. 1313 fol. 12v., British Museum

TO MAKE WHITE SALT, Fifteenth Century

To make white salt, take of coarse salt one pint and three pints of water, and put them on the fire until the salt is melted; then strain through a cloth, towel, or sieve. Place on the fire again and make it boil hard and skim it. When it has boiled almost dry, so that the little bubbles which the water throws up are all dry, then take the salt out of the pail and spread it out on a cloth in the sun to dry.

Sloane MS. 1313 fol. 126, British Museum

MARGERY KEMPE, CUNNING IN BREWING, 1436

Then for pure covetousness, and to maintain her pride, she began to brew, and was one of the greatest brewers in the town of [Lynn] for three years or four, till she lost much money, for she had never been used thereto. For, though she had ever such good servants, cunning in brewing, yet it would never succeed-with them. For when the ale was as fair standing under barm as any man might see, suddenly the barm would fall down, so that all the ale was lost, one brewing after another, so that her servants were ashamed and would not dwell with her.

Then this creature thought how God had punished her aforetime —and she could not take heed—and now again, by the loss of her goods. Then she left and brewed no more.

Then she asked her husband's mercy because she would not follow his counsel aforetime, and she said that her pride and sin were the cause of her punishing, and that she would amend and that she had trespassed with good will.

The Book of Margery Kempe, A modern version
by W. Butler-Bowden

TAKE GOOD HEED TO THE WINES, c. 1460

Look ye have two wine-augers, a greater and a less, some gutters of boxwood that fit them, also a gimlet to pierce with, a tap and a bung, ready to stop the flow when it is time. So when you broach a pipe, good son, do after my teaching: pierce or bore with an auger or gimlet, slanting upward, four fingers' breadth from the lower rim, so as not to cause the lees to rise—I warn you especially. . . .

Take good heed to the wines, red, white, and sweet; look to them every night with a candle, to see that they neither ferment nor leak. Never forget to wash the heads of the pipes with cold water every night; and always carry a gimlet, adze and linen clouts, large and small. If the wine ferment, ye shall know by its singing, so keep at hand a pipe of *couleur de rose* (a red malmsey wine) that has been spent in drinking and add to the fermentation the dregs of this, and it shall be amended. . . .

'The Duties of a Panter or Butler' in John Russell's
'Book of Nurture'; *The Babees' Book Medieval Manners
for the Young done into modern English from Dr Furnivall's
Texts* by Edith Rickert

THE PANTRY, c. 1460

. . . In the pantry, you must always keep three sharp knives, one
to chop the loaves, another to pare them, and a third sharp and
keen, to smooth and square the trenchers with.

Always cut your lord's bread, and see that it be new; and all
other bread at the table one day old ere you cut it, all household
bread three days old, and trencher bread four days old.

Look that your salt be fine, white, fair, and dry; and have your
salt-plane of ivory, two inches wide and three long; and see to it
that the lid of the salt-cellar touch not the salt.

Good son, look that your napery be sweet and clean, and that
your table-cloth, towel, and napkin be folded neatly, your
table-knives brightly polished and your spoon fair washed—ye wot
well what I mean.

'The Duties of a Panter or Butler' in John Russell's 'Book
of Nurture'; *The Babees' Book Medieval Manners for the
Young done into modern English from Dr. Furnivall's Texts*
by Edith Rickert

GOOD TABLE MANNERS, c. 1475

Cut your bread with your knife and break it not. Lay a clean
trencher before you, and when your pottage is brought, take your
spoon and eat quietly; and do not leave your spoon in the dish,
I pray you.

Look ye be not caught leaning on the table, and keep clear of
soiling the cloth.

Do not hang your head over your dish, or in any wise drink
with full mouth.

Keep from picking your nose, your teeth, your nails at mealtime
—so we are taught.

Advise you against taking so muckle meat into your mouth but
that ye might right well answer when men speak to you.

When ye shall drink, wipe your mouth clean with a cloth, and
your hands also, so that you shall not in any way soil the cup, for
then shall none of your companions be loth to drink with you.

Likewise, do not touch the salt in the salt-cellar with any meat;
but lay salt honestly on your trencher, for that is courtesy.

Do not carry your knife to your mouth with food, or hold the meat with your hands in any wise; and also if divers goodmeats are brought to you, look that with all courtesy ye assay of each; and if your dish be taken away with its meat and another brought, courtesy demands that ye shall let it go and not ask for it back again.

And if strangers be set at table with you, and savoury meat be brought or sent to you, make them good cheer with part of it, for certainly it is not polite when others be present at meat with you, to keep all that is brought you, and like churls vouchsafe nothing to others.

Do not cut your meat like field-men who have such an appetite that they reck not in what wise, where or when or how ungoodly they hack at their meat; but, sweet children, have always your delight in courtesy and in gentleness, and eschew boisterousness with all your might.

When cheese is brought, have a clean trencher, on which with a clean knife ye may cut it; and in your feeding look ye appear goodly, and keep your tongue from jangling, for so indeed shall ye deserve a name for gentleness and good governance, and always advance yourself in virtue.

Edith Rickert, *The Babees' Book Medieval Manners for the Young done into Modern English from Dr Furnivall's Texts*

TO MAKE WATER FOR WASHING THE HANDS
AT TABLE, Fifteenth Century
Boil some sage, and pour off the water, and let it cool until it is a little more than warm. Add to it camomile or marjoram or rosemary, and boil it with orange peel. Laurel leaves are also good.

Sloane MS. 1313 fol. 126v., British Museum

STEWED PARTRIDGE IN THE FIFTEENTH CENTURY
Take a moderately strong broth of beef or of mutton when it is boiled enough, and strain it through a strainer, and put it in an earthenware pot. And take a good quantity of wine, as it were half a pint. And take partridge, cloves, maces and whole pepper, and cast into the pot, and let boil well together. And when the partridge been enough, take the pot from the fire, and then take fair bread cut in thin browes and couch them in a fair charger, and lay the partridge on top. And take powder of ginger, salt, and hard yolks of eggs minced, and cast into the broth, and pour the

22. A roadside tavern with its ale-stake, early fourteenth century.

broth upon the partridge into the charger, and serve it forth, but
let it be coloured with saffron.

J. J. Bagley, Historical Interpretation

A FIFTEENTH-CENTURY SONG IN PRAISE OF GOOD ALE

Bring us in good ale, and bring us in good ale;
For our blesséd Lady's sake, bring us in good ale!
Bring us in no brown bread, for that is made of bran,
Nor bring us in in no white bread, for therein is no gain,
      But bring us in good ale!
Bring us in no beef, for there is many bones,
But bring us in good ale, for that goeth down at once;
      And bring us in good ale!
Bring us in no bacon, for that is passing fat,
And bring us in good ale, and give us enough of that;
      And bring us in good ale!
Bring us in no mutton, for that is often lean,
Nor bring us in no tripes, for they be seldom clean;
      But bring us in good ale!
Bring us in no eggs, for there are many shells,
But bring us in good ale, and give us nothing else.
      And bring us in good ale!
Bring us in no butter, for therein are many hairs;
Nor bring us in no pig's flesh, for that will make us boars:
      But bring us in good ale!
Bring us in no puddings, for therein is all God's good;
Nor bring us in no venison, for that is not for our blood;
      But bring us in good ale!
Bring us in no capon's flesh, for that is ofter dear;
Nor bring us in no duck's flesh, for they slobber in the mere;
      But bring us in good ale!

Reprinted in T. Wright, Songs and Carols, Percy Society

23. Roasting sucking-pig and fowl on a spit.

Dress

LOVE OF DRESS IS A SNARE

In order that ye may compass men's praise ye spend all your labour on your garments—on your veils and your kirtles. Many of you pay as much to the sempstress as the cost of the cloth itself; it must have shields on the shoulders, it must be flounced and tucked all round the hem; it is not enough for you to show your pride in your very buttonholes, but you must also send your feet to hell by special torments, ye trot this way and that way with your fine stitchings. Ye busy yourselves with your veils, ye twitch them hither, ye twitch them thither; ye gild them here and there with gold thread; ye will spend a good six months' work on a single veil . . . when thou shouldest be busy in the house with something needful for the goodman, or for thyself, or thy children, or thy guests, then art thou busy instead with thy hair, thou art careful whether thy sleeves sit well, or thy veil or thy headdress, wherewith thy whole time is filled.

Berthold von Regensburg, *Sermons, c.* 1260

ABOUT WEARING FUR, 1281

. . . No woman of the City shall from henceforth go to market, or in the King's highway, out of her house, with a hood furred with other than lambskin or rabbitskin, on pain of losing her hood to the use of the Sheriffs; save only those ladies who wear furred capes, the hoods of which may have such furs as they may think proper. And this, because that regratresses [retailers], nurses and other servants, and women of loose life, bedizen themselves, and wear hoods furred with gros vair [great vair] and with miniver, in guise of good ladies.

City Letter Book Regulations about wearing fur, 1281
H. T. Riley, *Memorials of London and London Life*

THE SEARCH FOR FALSE HATS, 1311

At the request of the hatters, and of the dealers of the City who bought and sold hats, it was ordered that, immediately after the

24. A twelth-century MS. illustration of women in long tunics
with pendant cuffs. One is wearing a silk sheath over her hair.

25. Man in a cotehardie and a hood with liripipe (a long tail from the pointed cowl). From The Luttrell Psalter, 1340.

26. Man in a garnache (the tabard style but with cape-like sleeves at elbow length). Also large, wide hat over the hood. From the Luttrell Psalter, 1340.

Feast of Easter, diligent scrutiny should be made throughout all the City as to false hats [made of prohibited material], by three or four good men of either calling; and that such good men should at once cause all such false hats as they might find, to be brought here to the Guildhall before the Mayor and Aldermen, to be examined, and to have judgment pronounced as to the same. . . . Afterwards a scrutiny having been made as to such false hats, the examiners aforesaid brought into the Guildhall . . . certain hats, white, black, and grey, which had been found upon divers *haberdasshers* and hatters. And the said hats were examined. . . . And it was found, upon the oath of the said examiners, that 40 grey and white hats, and 15 black hats, belonging to the hatters aforesaid, were of false workmanship, and a mixture of wool and flocks. Therefore it was adjudged that they should be burnt in the street of Chepe.

City Letter-Book, 1311, H. T. Riley, *Memorials of London and London Life*

REGULATION ISSUED IN 1363 ABOUT CLOTHING AND WORKING CONDITIONS

It is ordained . . . first, as to grooms, as well the servants of great men as of traders and craftsmen, that they shall be served once a day with meat or fish, the rest with other food, as milk, cheese, butter, and other such victuals according to their estate. And they shall have cloth for their apparel whereof the whole cloth does not exceed two marks. . . . And that they shall not use any article of gold or silver or embroidered or enamel, or of silk. . . .

And their wives, daughters and children shall be of the same condition in their apparel; they shall wear no veils exceeding 12d. each. . . .

And the carters, ploughmen, drivers, oxherds, cowherds, shepherds, swineherds, dairywomen, and other keepers of beasts, threshers of corn and all manner of men engaged in husbandry, and other people who have no goods and chattels worth 40s., shall wear no cloth save blanket and russet, 12d., the yard. They shall wear no girdles, and shall have linen according to their condition. They shall live upon such food and drink as is suitable, and then not in excess.

Sumptuary Ordinance issued at the request of the Commons

COSTUME, c. 1380

Some [common people] in wide surcoats reaching to the loins,

27. From the Holkham Bible, fourteenth century. The lady wears a long gown and a wimple (linen or silk wrapped round the front of the neck and chin, the ends fastened to the hair above the ears. Usually worn with a fillet or veil).

some in a garment reaching to the heels, close before and strutting out on the sides, so that at the back they make men seem like women, and this they call by a ridiculous name, gowne. Their hoods are little, tied under the chin, and buttoned like the women's, but set with gold, silver, and precious stones. Their liripipes, or tippets, pass round the neck, and hanging down before reach to the heels, all jagged. They have another weed of silk,

which they call a paltock [short coat]. Their hose are of two colours,
or pied with more, which they tie up to their paltocks with white
lachets, called herlots, without any breeches. Their girdles are of
gold and silver, and some of them worth twenty marks. Their
shoes and pattens are snouted and picked more than a finger long,
crooking upwards, what they call crackowes, resembling devil's
claws, and fastened to knees with chains of gold and silver.

Eulogium, quoted by William Caxton

THE ART OF DRESSING WELL, c. 1460

See that your lord has a clean shirt and hose, a short coat, a
doublet, and a long coat, if he wear such, his hose well brushed,
his socks at hand, his shoes or slippers as brown as a water-leech.

In the morning, against your lord shall rise, take care that his
linen be clean, and warm it at a clear fire, not smoky if the weather
be cold or freezing.

When he rises make ready the foot-sheet, and forget not to place
a chair or some other seat with a cushion on it before the fire, with
another cushion for the feet. Over the cushion and chair spread
this sheet so as to cover them; and see that you have a kerchief
and a comb to comb your lord's head before he is fully dressed.

Then pray your lord in humble words to come to a good fire
and array him thereby, and there sit or stand pleasantly; and wait
with due manners to assist him. First hold out to him his tunic,
then his doublet while he puts in his arms, and have his stomacher
well aired to keep off harm, as also his vamps [ankle socks] and so
shall he go warm all day.

Thus draw on his socks and his hose by the fire, and lace or
buckle his shoes, draw his hosen on well and truss them up to the
height that suits him, lace his doublet in every hole, and put round
his neck and on his shoulders a kerchief; and then gently comb
his head with an ivory comb, and give him water wherewith to
wash his hands and face.

Then kneel down on your knee and say thus: 'Sir, what robe or
gown doth it please you to wear today?' Then get him such as he
asks for, and hold it out for him to put on, and do on his girdle,
if he wear one, tight or loose, arrange his robe in the proper
fashion, give him a hood or hat for his head, a cloak or
cappe-de-buse [house cap or cape], according as it be fair or foul,
or all misty with rain; and so shall ye please him. Before he goes,
brush busily about him, and whether he wear satin, sendal [silk],

28. The bridegroom in a low-belted houppelande, the bride in horned head-dress. From John Lydgate's *Sege of Troye*, c. 1420

velvet, scarlet [cloth] or grain [crimson cloth], see that all be clean
and nice.

'The Office of a Chamberlain' in John Russell's 'Book of
Nurture'; *The Babees' Book Medieval Manners for the Young
done into modern English from Dr Furnivall's Texts*
by Edith Rickert

29. The man on the left wears a short jacket over a doublet; the others are
in long gowns. All are wearing piked shoes (having long points stuffed with
tow), *c.* 1470.

Education

OF SCHOOLS, 1173

In London three principal churches have by privilege and ancient dignity famous schools, yet very often by support of some personage, or of some teachers who are considered notable and famous in philosophy; there are also other schools by favour or permission. On feast days the masters have festival meetings in the churches. Their scholars dispute, some by demonstration, others by dialectics, some recite enthymemes [a syllogism with one premise omitted], others do better in using perfect syllogisms. Some are exercised in disputation for display, as wrestling with opponents; others for truth, which is the grace of perfectness. Sophists who feign are judged happy in their heap and flood of words. Others paralogise [mislead by false reasoning]. Some orators, now and then, say in their rhetorical speeches something apt for persuasion, careful to observe rules of their art, and to omit none of the contingents. Boys of different schools strive against one another in verses, and contend about the principles of grammar and rules of the past and future tenses.

William Fitz-Stephen, *Descriptio Nobilissimae Civitatis Londonae*

IN BITTER PROTEST MASTERS AND SCHOLARS LEAVE OXFORD UNIVERSITY

About this time, 1209, a certain clerk who was studying in Arts at Oxford slew by chance a certain woman, and, finding that she was dead, sought safety in flight. But the mayor and many others, coming to the place and finding the dead woman, began to seek the slayer in his hostel which he had hired with three other clerks his fellows. And, not finding the guilty man, they took his three fellow-clerks aforesaid, who knew nothing whatsoever of the homicide, and cast them into prison. And, after a few days, at the King's bidding but in contempt of all ecclesiastical liberties, these clerks were led out of the city and hanged.

Whereupon some three thousand clerks, both masters and scholars, departed from Oxford, so that not one of the whole

University was left; of which scholars some pursued their study of the liberal Arts at Cambridge, and others at Reading, leaving Oxford utterly empty.

Roger of Wendover, *Chronicle*

HENRY III WRITES TO THE MAYOR AND BAILIFFS OF CAMBRIDGE IN 1231

The King to the Mayor and Bailiffs of Cambridge: Greeting. It is well known to you that a multitude of scholars flows together to our city of Cambridge for the sake of study, from various places at home and abroad; which we hold right pleasing and acceptable, for that from thence no small profit comes to our kingdom and honour to ourself; and above all you, amongst whom the students have their daily life, should rejoice and be glad. But we have heard that in letting your lodgings you are so heavy and burdensome to the scholars dwelling amongst you, that unless you behave yourselves more measurably and modestly towards them in this matter of your exactions, they must leave our city, and, having abandoned the University, depart from our land, which we in no respect desire. And therefore we command you . . . that, concerning the letting of the aforesaid lodgings . . according to the custom of the University, you should estimate the aforesaid lodgings by two masters and two good legal men of your town, and according to their estimate should permit them to be hired. . . .

Witness the King at Oxford the third day of May.

Heywood and Wright, King's College and Eton College Statutes

UNIVERSITY EXPENSES, 1374

Also, for the board of the said Thomas, during the said 13 years; 2 shillings per week being paid by the same Robert while he was at the Schools at Oxford, for his board there, and the same throughout the said time, making 104 shillings yearly, and in the whole—67L. 12s.

Also,—for the clothes, linen and woollen, and shoes, of the same Thomas for the said 13 years, at 40 shillings yearly, expended by the said Robert—26L.

Also,—for the teaching of the same Thomas for ten years out of the said thirteen, at 2 marks yearly, by the same Robert paid, making 20 marks.

Also,—for sundry expenses, namely, his riding at Oxford and elsewhere, and for moneys laid out upon a master for the said Thomas, at the rate of 20 shillings yearly, making in the whole 13L.

H. T. Riley, *Memorials of London*

30.   Education in the twelfth century. The verse reads:

'Wisdom that is not willing
                    sought,
With the rod must needs be
                    taught.'

DANGERS OF GRAMMAR AND INKHORNS
Walsingham is speaking of Wat Tyler and his followers
We must judge them by their works; for they slew the father of the whole clergy, the head of the English Church, the Archbishop of Canterbury. See too what they did against the faith; how they compelled masters of grammar schools to swear that they would never again teach grammar to children! And what more? They strove to burn all ancient muniments, and slew all such as could be found capable of commemorating to posterity either ancient records or modern events; it was perilous to be recognized as a clerk, and far more perilous if any were caught bearing an inkhorn at his side.

Thomas de Walsingham, *Historia Brevis*, 1381

STUDENT RIOT, OXFORD, 1388-9

In these days there happened at Oxford a grave misfortune. For, during two whole years was there great strife between the men of the south and the men of Wales on the one side and the northerners on the other. Whence arose broils, quarrels, and oft-times loss of life. In the first year the northerners were driven clean away from the university. And they laid their expulsion chiefly to my charge. But in the second year, in an evil hour, coming back to Oxford, they gathered by night, and denying us passage from our quarters by force of arms, for two days they strove sorely against us, breaking and plundering some of the halls of our side, and slaying certain of our men. Howbeit, on the third day our party, bravely strengthened by the help of Merton Hall, forced our adversaries shamefully to fly from the public streets, which for the two days they had held as a camp, and to take refuge in their own quarters. In short, we could not be quieted before many of our number had been indicted for felonious riot; and amongst them I, who am now writing, was indicted, as the chief leader, and abettor of the Welsh, and perhaps not unrighteously. And so indicted we were hardly acquitted, being tried by jury before the king's judge. From that day forth I feared the king, hitherto unknown to me in his power, and his laws, and I put hooks into my jaws.

Chronicle of Adam of Usk, 1377-1421, translated by
E. Maunde Thompson

'CHAMBERDEACONS'

Seeing that the peace of this kindly University is seen to be frequently broken by divers persons who, under pretence of being scholars, wait and lurk within the University and its precincts, but outside the Halls and under no tutelage of no Principal—men known by the abominable name of 'Chamberdeacons', who sleep all day and by night haunt the taverns and brothels for occasion of robbery and manslaughter—therefore it is decreed by the said University that all and every scholar do dwell in that Hall or College wherein his common contributions are registered, or in Halls thereunto annexed, which share with the aforesaid in commons and battels, under pain of imprisonment for the first offence. If, moreover, having been once admonished by the Chancellor or his Commissary, or by the Proctors, they neglect to transfer themselves to those abodes aforesaid, then let them be banished and cut off from the University, as rotten members thereof, within eight days.

Anstey, *Munimenta Academica*, Oxford Statute of 1432

31. Higher education in early fourteenth century.

A BOY AT ETON WRITES TO HIS BROTHER
To his worshipful brother, John Paston, be this delivered in haste.
    Right reverend and worshipful brother, I recommend me unto
you, desiring to hear of your welfare and prosperity, letting you
weet [know] that I have received of Alweder a letter and a noble
in gold therein; furthermore . . . Master Thomas heartily

recommended him to you, and he prayeth you to send him some money for my commons, for he saith ye be 20s. in his debt, for a month was to pay for, when he had money last; also I beseech you to send me a hose cloth, one for the holydays of some colour, and another for the working days how coarse soever it be it maketh no matter, and a stomacher, and two shirts, and a pair of slippers; and if it like you that I may come with Alweder by water, and sport me with you at London a day or two this term time, then ye may let all this be till the time that I come, and then I will tell you when I shall be ready to come from Eton by the grace of God, who have you in his keeping. Written the Saturday next after Allhallows day with the hand of your brother,

WILLIAM PASTON

Eton, Saturday,
7th November, 1478
18 E. IV.

ST RICHARD OF CHICHESTER, THE POOR SCHOLAR

Richard therefore hastily left both [his father's] lands and the lady [he was to marry], and all his friends, and betook himself to the University of Oxford and then to that of Paris, where he learned logic. Such was his love of learning, that he cared little or nothing for food or raiment, for, as he was wont to relate, he and two companions who lodged in the same chamber had only their tunics, and one gown [statutory for all university students] between them, and each of them a miserable pallet. When one, therefore, went out with the gown to hear a lecture, the others sat in their room, and so they went forth alternately; and bread with a little wine and pottage sufficed for their food. For their poverty never suffered them to eat flesh or fish, save on the Sunday or on some solemn holy day or in the presence of companions or friends; yet he hath oftentimes told me how, in all his days, he had never after led so pleasant and delectable a life.

John Capgrave, *Life of St Richard of Chichester,* fifteenth century

SCHOOL OF A PARISH PRIEST IN THE FIFTEENTH CENTURY

. . . First was he a master of learning to the 'smale petites', such as learn to read, spell and sing. The children that were under his discipline he taught not only their lessons on the book, but besides this, he taught for to play in due time, and here plays taught he that they should be honest and merry withouten clamour or great

32.   A university lecture, *c.* 1400.

noise. For though he had not at that time experience of the good customs which be used among religious men in monasteries, yet had our Lord God at that age put in his breast these holy exercises, for he taught . . . that (*they*) had to keep silence in the church; all at one hour to go to bed and eke to rise to their lessons; all went they together to their play or any other thing.

John Capgrave, *Life of St Gilbert*

FIFTEENTH CENTURY REGULATIONS AT KING'S COLLEGE, CAMBRIDGE

We ordain that our students go not about alone, without a fellow or scholar of the said King's College, or one of the common servants thereof, or some other companion of mature age and good character; and let them walk modestly and without confusion— save only to processions, sermons, churches, or the Schools, for which purposes we permit them to go alone if they cannot well find such a companion. Further, we prohibit all and singular the fellows and scholars aforesaid from wearing red or green hosen, piked shoes, or striped hoods, on any pretext, within or without the University or the town of Cambridge, either publicly or privately, except for some necessary cause to be approved by the Provost, or by the Vice-Provost, Deans, and Bursars. Furthermore we ordain that no scholar or fellow let his hair or beard grow; but that all wear the crown and tonsure, accordant to their order, degree, and condition, honestly and duly and decently.

Since it befitteth not poor men, and specially such as live by charity, to give the children's bread unto dogs . . . therefore we command, ordain and will that no scholar, fellow, chaplain, clerk, or servant whatsoever to the said King's College, do keep or possess dogs, hunting or fishing nets, ferrets, falcons or hawks; nor shall they practise hunting or fishing. Nor shall they in any wise have or hold within our Royal College, singly or in common, any ape, bear, fox, stag, hind, fawn, or badger, or any other such ravening or unaccustomed or strange beast, which are neither profitable nor unprofitable. Furthermore, we forbid and expressly interdict the University. . . . And it is Our will firmly and expressly to prohibit games of dice, hazard, ball and all noxious inordinate unlawful and unhonest sports, and especially all games which afford a cause or occasion for loss of coin, money, goods or chattels of any kind whatsoever, whether within King's College or elsewhere within the all of the aforesaid fellows &c. from shooting arrows, or casting or hurling stones, javelins, wood, clods or anything whatsoever, and

from making or practising, singly or in common, in person or by
deputy, any games or castings whatsoever, within the aforesaid
King's College or its enclosed precincts or gardens, whereby,
directly or indirectly, the Chapel or Hall or other buildings or
edifices of our said College may suffer any sort of harm or loss in
the glass windows, walls, roofs, coverings, or any other part thereof
within or without. Item: whereas through incautious and
inordinate games in the Chapel or Hall of our said King's College,
which might perchance be practised therein by the wantonness of
some students, the said Chapel and Hall might be harmed and
even deformed in its walls, stalls, paintings and glass windows; we
therefore, desiring to provide against such harm, do strictly
command that no casting of stones or balls or of anything else
soever be made in the aforesaid collegiate Chapel, Cloister, Stalls,
or Hall; and we forbid that dancing or wrestling, or other
incautious and inordinate sports whatsoever, be practised at any
time within the Chapel, Cloister or Hall aforesaid.

King's College and Eton College Statutes, translated by
G. G. Coulton

The Arts

MODE OF SINGING, 1188

In their musical concerts they [the Welsh] do not sing in unison like the inhabitants of other countries, but in many different parts; so that in a company of singers, which one very frequently meets with in Wales, you will hear as many different parts and voices as there are performers, who all at length unite, with organic melody, in one consonance and the soft sweetness of B flat. In the northern district of Britain, beyond the Humber, and on the borders of Yorkshire, the inhabitants make use of the same kind of symphonious harmony, but with less variety; singing only in two parts, one murmuring in the' base, the other warbling in the acute or treble. Neither of the two nations has acquired this peculiarity by art, but by long habit, which has rendered it natural and familiar; and the practice is now so firmly rooted in them, that it is unusual to hear a simple and single melody well sung; and, what is still more wonderful, the children, even from their infancy, sing in the same manner. As the English in general do not adopt this mode of singing, but only those of the northern countries, I believe that it was from the Danes and Norwegians, by whom these parts of the island were more frequently invaded, and held longer under their dominion, that the natives contracted their mode of singing as well as speaking.

Gerald the Welshman, Description of Wales, translated by
Sir R. C. Hoare

SCRIBES, Twelfth Century

Let him have a razor or knife for scraping pages of parchment or skin; let him have a 'biting' pumice for cleaning the sheets, and a little scraper for making equal the surface of the skin. He should have a piece of lead and a ruler with which he may rule the margins on both sides—on the back and on the side from which the flesh has been removed.

There should be a fold of four sheets [a quaternion]. . . . Let

99

33. This is the opening of the Latin chronicle, the *Historia Novorum in Anglia,* in the handwriting of the author, Eadmer, (*d.* 1124), a monk of Canterbury, and friend and biographer of Anselm.

these leaves be held together at top and bottom by a strip [of parchment threaded through]. The scribe should have a bookmark cord and a pointed tool. . . . Let him sit in a chair with both arms high, reinforcing the back rest, and with a stool at his feet.

Let the writer have a heating basin [of hot charcoal] covered with a cap; he should have a knife with which he can shape a quill pen; let this be prepared for writing with the inside fuzzy scale scraped out, and let there be a boar's or goat's tooth for polishing the parchment, so that the ink of a letter may not run. . . . He should have something with which letters can be canceled. Let him have an indicator or line marker in order that he may not make costly delay from error. There should be hot coals in the heating container so that the ink may dry more quickly on the parchment in foggy or wet weather. Let there be a small window through which light can enter; if perchance the blowing of the north wind attacks the principal window, let this be supplied with a screen of linen or of parchment, distinct in color; green and black offer more comfort to the eyes. Whiteness, when too intense, disturbs the sight and throws it into disorder. There should be red lead for forming red . . . letters or capitals. Let there be dark powder and blue. . . .

U. T. Holmes, Jr., *Daily Living in the Twelfth Century, based on the Observations of Alexander Neckham*

ROGER BACON'S FORECASTS, c. 1270

I will now proceed, therefore, to relate the works of art and miracles of nature, that I may afterwards expound the cause and manner thereof; wherein there is nothing magical; nay rather, all magical power would seem inferior to such works, and unworthy of them. And first I will discourse through the figure and reason of art alone. For vessels might be made to move without oars or rowers, so that ships of great size might move on sea or on river, at the governance of a single man, more swiftly than if they were strongly manned. Moreover, chariots might be made to move without animal impulse at an incalculable speed; such as we suppose those scythed chariots to have been wherewith men were wont to fight in ancient days. Again, flying instruments might be made, so that a man might sit in the midst thereof, turning a certain machine whereby wings of artful composition should beat the air, after the fashion of a bird in her flight. Another instrument might be made of small size, to raise or lower weights of almost infinite greatness; than which nothing could be more useful in certain cases. For, by means of an instrument of the height and breadth of three fingers, and less bulk than they, a man might free himself and his companions from all peril of prison, lifting them and lowering them again. Moreover, an instrument might easily be

34. A twelfth-century organ and musicians.

made whereby one man could violently draw a thousand men to himself against their will, and so also of the attraction of other things. Again, instruments might be made for walking in the sea, or in rivers, even to the very bottom, without bodily danger: for Alexander the Great used these to see the secrets of the sea, as is related by Ethicus the Astronomer. For these things were done of old, and have certainly also been done in our own times; except possibly the flying machine, which I have never seen, nor have I met any man who hath seen it; but I know a wise man who hath excogitated this artifice. And almost innumerable things of this kind might be made; bridges over rivers without pier or prop whatsoever, and unheard of machines and engines.

Roger Bacon, *Epistola de Secretis,* translated by G. G. Coulton

THREE KINDS OF ACTORS, 1300

There are three kinds of play actors [*histrionum*]. Some transform and transfigure their own bodies by base contortions and base gestures, or by basely denuding themselves, or by wearing horrible masks; and all such are to be damned unless they abandon their calling. Others, again do no work, but commit criminal deeds, having no fixed abode, but haunting the courts of great men and backbiting the absent opprobriously and ignominiously in order to please others. Such men also are to be damned; for the Apostle bids us take no food with such men as this; and such men are called wandering buffoons, for they are good for nothing but gluttony and backbiting. There is also a third kind of actors who have musical instruments for men's delight; and such are of two kinds. Some haunt public drinkings and wanton assemblies, where they sing divers songs to move men to wantonness; and such are to be damned like the rest. But there are others called jongleurs [*joculatores*], who sing the deeds of princes and the lives of the saints, and solace men in their sickness or in their anguish, and do not those innumerable base deeds which are done by dancing-men and dancing-women and others who play in indecent figures, and make men see a certain show of phantasms by enchantment or in any other way. If, then, these do no such thing, but sing to their instruments of the deeds of princes and other such profitable things, for the solace of their fellow-Christians, as is aforesaid, then such may well be borne with, as was said by pope Alexander III. For, when a jongleur asked of him whether he could have his soul in that calling, the Pope asked him whether he knew any other work for his livelihood; and he made answer that he knew none. Then

35. *Sumer is icumen in* is an early thirteenth-century rota or round, 'a spring song for four tenor voices in canon (a tune begun by one voice first and by another later) and two bass voices repeated many times with variations'. It was written at Reading Abbey *c.* 1226.

36. An artist preparing his colours inside an initial from Jacobus's *Omne bonum*, a fourteenth-century manuscript.

the Pope permitted him to live by that calling, so long as he abstained from the aforesaid base and wanton practices. And it must be noted that all commit mortal sin who give any of their goods to buffoons or jesters or the aforesaid play-actors; for to give to play-actors is no other than to throw our money away.

> Thomas de Cabham, sub-dean of Salisbury, *Penitential,* or guide-book for confessors. Translated by G. G. Coulton

THE ENGLISH LANGUAGE, c. 1327

It is plain that there are as many languages as there are races in this island. As the Scottish and Welsh are untainted by other peoples they keep their speech practically in its virgin purity, unless maybe the Scots have assimilated somewhat into their speech by association with the Picts with whom they once mixed as allies. But the Flemings who colonise the Western extremity of Wales have abandoned barbarism and speak in a sufficiently Saxon way. Although the Angles originally inherited a threefold tongue [viz. southern, midland and northern], as originating from three Teutonic tribes, their native language has been corrupted in many particulars by intermixture first with the Danes and then with the Normans and thus they acquire alien accents and rhythms. This corruption of the native tongue now largely proceeds from two factors: contrary to the custom of other peoples, boys in schools since the Conquest have been forced to abandon their own language and to form sentences in French, and furthermore the sons of the nobility have been educated in the French idiom from their very cradles. The rustics have wanted to ape them in order that they may thus seem more respectable and so they have striven with might and main to frenchify themselves. So it really seems amazing how the indigenous native language of the Angles, confined as it is in a single island, varies so widely in its pronunciation, while the Norman speech, imported as it is, maintains the same pronunciation among all of the people. The threefold language of the Saxons hardly survives today among a handful of rustics, and those in the East have a dialect which resembles that of the folk in the West (as under the same latitude) more than the peoples of North and South. . . The whole language of the Northumbrians, especially those of York, rasps in such an uncouth way, that we southerners can hardly understand it. . . .

> From Ralph Higden, *Polychronicon*

ILL-TREATMENT OF BOOKS, 1345

You will see perchance some headstrong youth, sitting slothfully at his studies . . . his finger-nails are filthy, black as jet, and with them he marks the place where the matter takes his fancy. He distributes innumerable straws, laying them conspicuously in divers places of the book, that the wheatstalk may recall whatsoever his memory may let slip. These straws, which are never withdrawn, remain undigested in the book's belly, first distending it to the bursting of its wonted clasps, and then rotting in the neglect and oblivion to which they have been left. He shrinketh not from eating fruit or cheese over his open book, nor from moving his cup carelessly over it; and, having no bag at hand, he leaves in his book the fragments that remain. . . . Then he leans his elbows on the book and takes a long sleep in exchange for his brief study, and bends back the margins of the leaves to smooth out the wrinkles, to the no small detriment of the volume. Now the rain is over and gone, and the flowers appear on our earth; and this scholar whom we describe, this neglector rather than inspector of books, will stuff his volume with violets, primroses, roses and four-leaved clover. Then he will paw it over with hands wet with water or sweat; then with dusty gloves he will fumble over the white parchment, and hunt for his page, line by line, with a forefinger clad in this ancient leather. Then, at the prick of some biting flea, the sacred volume is cast aside, scarce to be closed again for another month, when it is so clogged and swollen with dust that it resists all efforts to close it.

But we must specially keep from all touch of our books those shameless youths who, when they have learned to shape the letters of the alphabet, straightway become incongruous annotators of all the fairest volumes that come in their way, and either deck with their monstrous alphabets all broader margins that they can find around the text, or rashly presume to write with unchastened pen whatsoever frivolous stuff may happen to run at that moment in their heads.

> *Philobiblon* by Richard de Bury, tutor to Edward III, later
> bishop of Durham. Translation by G. G. Coulton, in
> *Social Life in Britain from the Conquest to the Reformation*

THE START OF THE SECULAR STAGE

We have heard, not without grave disquietude, that a certain abominable sect of evil-minded men, named the Order (let us rather say, the Error) of Brothelyngham [a parody on the English monastic Order, Sempringham], hath lately arisen by inspiration of

37. Thomas Occleve presenting a copy of his poetic works to Prince Hal,
c. 1410.

him who soweth all evil deeds. Which men, forming no true convent but rather a plainly unlawful and sinister conventicle, have chosen for their head a certain crazy lunatic, of temper most suitable to their evil purpose. This man they call their Abbot; they dress him in monastic garb, set him up upon a stage, and adore him as their idol. Then, at the sound of a horn, which they have chosen instead of a bell, they led him not many days since through the lanes and streets of the said city of Exeter, with a great throng of horse and foot at their heels; in which procession they laid hold on clergy or laity whom they found in their way—nay, they even drew some from their own houses—and held them so long in durance, with rash, headlong, and sometimes with sacrilegious spirit, until they had extorted from them certain sums of money by way of sacrifice—nay, rather, of sacrilege. And, though they seem to do this under colour and cloak of play, or rather of buffoonery, yet this is beyond doubt no other than theft and rapine, since the money is taken from the unwilling.

Mandate of Bishop John de Grandisson to the Official of the Archdeacon of Exeter and two other Commissioners, 11 July 1348

LIMNERS AND TEXT-WRITERS, 1403

Be it remembered, that on the 12th day of July, in the 4th year etc., the reputable men of the craft of Writers of text-letter, those commonly called 'Limners' [painters and decorators of manuscripts], and other good folks of London, who are wont to bind and to sell books, presented here . . . a certain petition, in these words, that it may please your sagenesses to grant unto them, that they may elect yearly two reputable men, the one a *lymenour* the other a text-writer, to be Wardens of the said trades; and that the names of the Wardens so elected may be presented each year before the Mayor, for the time being, and they be there sworn well and diligently to oversee, that good rule and governance is had and exercised by all folks of the same trades in all works unto the said trades pertaining, to the praise and good fame of the loyal good men of the said trades, and to the shame and blame of the bad and disloyal men of the same. And that the same Wardens may call together all the men of the said trades honourably and peaceably, when need shall be, as well as for the good rule and governance of the said city, as of the trades aforesaid. And that the same Wardens, in performing their due office, may present from time to time all the defaults of the said bad and disloyal men to the

Chamberlain at the Guildhall, for the time being; to the end that the same may there, according to the wise and prudent discretion of the governors of the said city be corrected, punished and duly redressed. And that all who are rebellious against the said Wardens, as to the survey and good rule of the same trades, may be punished, according to the general Ordinance made as to rebellious persons in trades of the said city. . . . And that it may please you to command that this petition, by your sagenesses granted, may be entered of record for time to come; for the love of God, and as a work of charity.

Which petition having been read before the said Mayor and Aldermen, and fully understood, for the reason especially that it concerned the common weal and profit, that transgressors of the Ordinance aforesaid should be severely punished, as before stated; it was unanimously granted by them that the Ordinance should thereafter be faithfully observed, and that transgressors should be punished in manner as above stated.

H. T. Riley, *Memorials of London*

38. William Caxton's printer's mark, *c*. 1476.

PRINTING, 1471

Thus ende I this book whyche I have translated after my auctor as nyghe as God hath gyven me connyng to whom be gyven the laude and preysyng. And for as moche as in the wrytyng of the same my penne is worn, myn hande wery and not stedfast, myn eyen dimmed with overmoche lokyng on the whit paper, and my corage not so prone and redy to laboure as hit hath ben, and that age crepeth on me dayly and febleth all the bodye, and also because I have promysid to dyverce gentilmen and to my frendes to addresse to hem as hastely as I myght this sayd book. Therefore I have practysed and lerned at my grete charge and dispense to ordeyne this said booke in prynte after the maner and forme as ye may here see. And it is not wreton with penne and ynke as other bokes ben to thende that every man may have them attones. For all the bookes of this storye named the recule of the historyes of Troyes thus emprynted as ye here see were begonne in oon day, and also fynysshed in oon day.

William Caxton in *The Recuyell of the Histories of Troye*, 1471

Sports and Pastimes

ROYAL HUNTSMEN, c. 1136

Each of four *Hornblowers* 3d. a day. Twenty *Serjeants*: Each 1d. a day. *Fewterers* [Keepers of Greyhounds]: Each 3d. a day, and 2d. for their men; and for each greyhound a halfpenny a day. The *King's Pack of Hounds*: 8d. a day. *Knight-Huntsman*: Each 8d. a day. *Huntsmen*: Each 5d. *Leader of the Lime-Hound* [a leashed hound only loosed to kill a stag at bay] and the limehound a halfpenny. *Berner* [feeder of hounds]: 3d. a day. *Huntsmen of the Hounds on the Leash*: Each 3d. a day. Of the great leash four hounds 1d. And of the small leashes six should have 1d. For the great leashes two men, each 1d. a day; and for the small, two men, each 1d. a day. *Brach-Keepers* [small hounds hunting by scent]: Each 3d. a day. *Wolf-Hunters*: 20d. a day for horses, men and hounds: and they should have twenty-four running hounds and eight greyhounds, and £6 a year to buy horses; but they say 'eight'. Each of the *Archers* who carried the King's bow 5d. a day; and the other archers as much. Bernard, Ralf the Rober, and their fellows 3d. a day.

Establishment of the Royal Household, *c.* 1136, translated in
*Dialogues de Scaccario The Course of the Exchequer and
Constitutio Domus Regis*

HAWKING, c. 1160

King Henry the Second of England (or his son Richard; I name both, but shun to distinguish clearly since my tale is to his dishonour) in the early days of his reign cast off his best falcon at a heron, for the sake of that cruel pastime. The heron circled higher and higher; but the falcon, being swifter, had already wellnigh overtaken him, when the king felt certain of victory and cried aloud, 'By God's eyes or His gorge . . . that bird shall not now escape, even though God Himself had sworn it!' (for they had learned thus to swear in their youthful insolence; and such habits may scarce be unlearnt; even as Henry II's grandfather, Henry I, was wont to swear *By God's Death*). At these words the heron

111

39. Life of St Cuthbert, twelfth-century MS. In a rough ball game he is hurt.
In 1385, boys were excommunicated for playing destructive games inside and
outside St. Paul's Cathedral.

turned forthwith to bay; and, by a most miraculous change from
victim to tormentor, stuck his beak into the falcon's head, dashed
out his brains, and (himself whole and unhurt) cast the dying
bird to the earth at the king's very feet.

    Giraldus Cambrensis (Gerald of Wales), *Gemma Ecclesiastica*

SPORTS OF LONDON, c. 1180

Furthermore let us consider also the sports of the City; since it is
not meet that a city should only be useful and sober, unless it
also be pleasant and merry. . . .

    London in place of shows in the theatre and stage-plays has
holier plays, wherein are shown forth the miracles wrought by
Holy Confessors or the sufferings which glorified the constancy of
Martyrs.

    Moreover, each year upon the day called Carnival—to begin
with the sports of boys (for we were all boys once)—boys from the

schools bring fighting-cocks to their master, and the whole forenoon is given up to boyish sport; for they have a holiday in the schools that they may watch their cocks do battle. After dinner all the youth of the City goes out into the fields in a much-frequented game of ball. The scholars of each school have their own ball, and almost all the workers of each trade have theirs also in their hands. Elder men and fathers and rich citizens come on horseback to watch the contests of their juniors, and after their fashion are young again with the young; and it seems that the motion of their natural heat is kindled by the contemplation of such violent motion and by their partaking in the joys of untrammelled youth.

Every Sunday in Lent after dinner a 'fresh swarm of young gentles' goes forth on war-horses, 'steeds skilled in the contest', of which each is 'apt and schooled to wheel in circles round'. From the gates burst forth in throngs the lay sons of citizens, armed with lance and shield, the younger with shafts forked at the end, but with steel point removed. 'They wake war's semblance' and in mimic contest exercise their skill at arms. Many courtiers come too, when the King is in residence; and from the households of Earls and Barons come young men not yet invested with the belt of knighthood, that they may there contend together. Each one of them is on fire with hope of victory. The fierce horses neigh, 'their limbs tremble; they champ the bit; impatient of delay they cannot stand still'. When at length 'the hoof of trampling steeds careers along', the youthful riders divide their hosts; some pursue those that fly before, and cannot overtake them; others unhorse their comrades and speed by.

At the feast of Easter they make sport with naval tourneys, as it were. For a shield being strongly bound to a stout pole in mid-stream, a small vessel, swiftly driven on by many an oar and by the river's flow, carries a youth standing at the prow, who is to strike the shield with his lance. If he break the lance by striking the shield and keep his feet unshaken, he has achieved his purpose and fulfilled his desire. If, however, he strike it strongly without splintering his lance, he is thrown into the rushing river, and the boat of its own speed passes him by. But there are on each side of the shield two vessels moored, and in them are many youths to snatch up the striker who has been sucked down by the stream, as soon as he emerges into sight or 'once more bubbles on the topmost wave'. On the bridge and the galleries above the river are spectators of the sport 'ready to laugh their fill'.

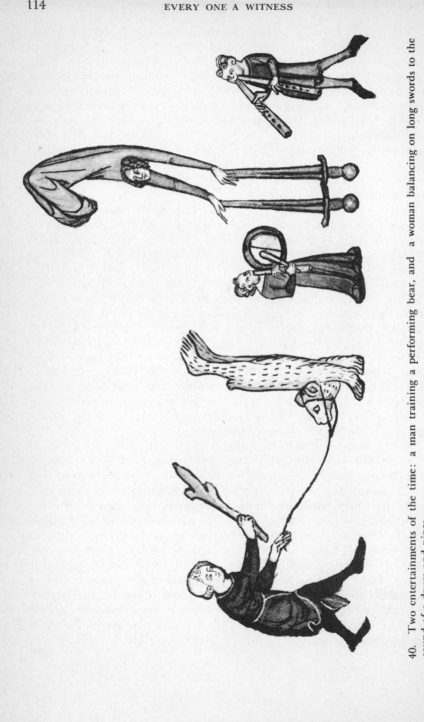

40. Two entertainments of the time: a man training a performing bear, and a woman balancing on long swords to the sound of a drum and pipes.

On feast-days throughout the summer the youths exercise themselves in leaping, archery and wrestling, putting the stone, and throwing the thonged javelin beyond a mark, and fighting with sword and buckler. 'Cytherea leads the dance of maidens and the earth is smitten with free foot at moonrise.'

In winter on almost every feast-day before dinner either foaming boars and hogs, armed with 'tusks lightning-swift', themselves soon to be bacon, fight for their lives, or fat bulls with butting horns, or huge bears, do combat to the death against hounds let loose upon them.

When the great marsh that washes the northern walls of the City is frozen, dense throngs of youths go forth to disport themselves upon the ice. Some gathering speed by a run, glide sidelong, with feet set well apart, over a vast space of ice. Others make themselves seats of ice like millstones and are dragged along by a number who run before them holding hands. Sometimes they slip owing to the greatness of their speed and fall, every one of them, upon their faces. Others there are, more skilled to sport upon the ice, who fit to their feet the shin-bones of beasts, lashing them beneath their ankles, and with ironshod poles in their hands they strike ever and anon against the ice and are borne along swift as a bird in flight or a bolt shot from a mangonel. But sometimes two by agreement run one against the other from a great distance and, raising their poles, strike one another. One or both fall, not without bodily hurt, since on falling they are borne a long way in opposite directions. . . .

Many of the citizens delight in taking their sport with birds of the air, merlins and falcons and the like, and with dogs that wage warfare in the woods. The citizens have the special privilege of hunting in Middlesex, Hertfordshire and all Chiltern, and in Kent as far as the river Cray.

William FitzStephen, *A Description of London,* prefixed to his *Life of Thomas à Becket,* translated by H. E. Butler, Historical Association, 1934

HAWKS AND FALCONS, 1188

I ought not to omit mentioning the falcons of these parts, which are very large, and of a generous kind, and exercise a most severe tyranny over the river and land birds. King Henry II remained here for some time, making preparations for his voyage to Ireland; and being desirous of taking the diversion of hawking, he accidentally saw a noble falcon perched upon a rock. Going sideways round him, he let loose a fine Norway hawk, which he

text·cox non obsti
tuo cuxpe·suis·
in unitas i suntipii

pellitur·s·ille·cui qui muna familiaritate quin
e·ff·oc·y·sig·m·l litry·amicos·xcp·leuos·immi
nò cutungitur·legathi·ff·ccabonnen·le·l·uy·mfi·si·

41. A King hunting the hart; early fourteenth century.

carried on his left hand. The falcon, though at first slower in
its flight, soaring up to a great height, burning with resentment,
and in his turn becoming the aggressor, rushed down upon his
adversary with the greatest impetuosity, and by a violent blow
struck the hawk dead at the feet of the king. From that time the
king sent every year, about the breeding season, for the falcons
of this country, which are produced on the sea cliffs; nor can
better be found in any part of his dominions.

Gerald the Welshman, *Description of Wales*, translated by
Sir R. C. Hoare

BOXING DAY IN THE CEMETERY,
BURY ST. EDMUNDS, Late Twelfth Century

On the day after Christmas there were gatherings in the cemetery,
wrestling bouts and matches between the Abbot's servants and the
burgesses of the town; and from words they came to blows, and
from buffets to wounds and bloodshed. But the Abbot when he
heard of it, after calling to him in private certain persons who had
gathered to watch the show, but had stood afar off, ordered the
names of the evil-doers to be written down, and caused all of them
to be brought before him in the chapel of St. Denys on the day
after the feast of St. Thomas; and in the meantime he abstained
from inviting a single burgess to his table, as he used formerly to
do during the first five days of Christmas. So on the appointed day,
having sworn sixteen law-worthy men and heard their testimony,
the Abbot said, '. . . because they are laymen and do not understand
how great a crime it is to commit such sacrilege, I will, that other
may be the more afraid, excommunicate these by name and in

public, and that there may be no failure of justice in any respect, I will begin with my own household and servants'. And so it was done, when we had put on stoles and lighted candles. Then all of them went out of the church and, after taking counsel, they stripped themselves and, naked save for their drawers, they prostrated themselves before the door of the church. And when the Abbot's assessors, both monks and clerks, came and told him with tears that more than a hundred men were lying thus naked, the Abbot also wept. . . . Therefore after they had all been smartly scourged and then absolved, they all swore that they would stand by the judgment of the Church concerning the commission of sacrilege. And on the morrow they were given penance according to the rule laid down by the canons, and thus the Abbot recalled them all to unity and concord, uttering terrible threats against all those who by word or deed should give cause for dissension. But he publicly forbade all gatherings and shows in the cemetery. So all having been brought back to the blessing of peace, the burgesses feasted with their lord during the days that followed with much rejoicing.

The Chronicle of Jocelin of Brakelond concerning the Acts of Samson, Abbot of the Monastery of St. Edmund, translated by H. E. Butler

A WRESTLING MATCH IN THE CITY OF LONDON, 1222

On St. James's Day, the inhabitants of the City of London met at the hospital of Queen Matilda, outside the city, to engage in wrestling with the inhabitants of the district round the city, to see which of them was possessed of the greatest strength. After they had contended for a length of time amidst the shouts of both parties, the citizens, having put their antagonists into disorder, gained the victory. Amongst others, the seneschal of the Abbot of Westminster was defeated, and went away in deep deliberation as to how he could revenge himself and his companions.

At length he fixed on the following plan of revenge: he offered a prize of a ram on St. Peter's Day, and sent word throughout the district for all to come and wrestle at Westminster, and whoever should prove himself the best wrestler should receive the ram for a prize. He, in the meantime, collected a number of strong and skilful wrestlers, that he might thus gain the victory; but the citizens, being desirous of gaining another victory, came to the sport in great strength.

The contest having been commenced by both parties, they continued to throw each other for some time. The seneschal,

42.   Minstrels; early fourteenth-century.

however, with his suburban companions and fellow-provincials, who sought revenge rather than sport, without any reason flew to arms, and severely beat the citizens, who had come there unarmed, causing bloodshed amongst them.

Roger of Wendover, *Flores Historiarum*

HUNTING THE HARE AND THE HART,
Early Fourteenth Century

When the Hare is taken, and they [the hounds] have chased it, you ought to blow the prize [a blast on the horn], and you ought to give the hounds the halow. What is the halow? The sides, and the shoulders, and the neck, and the head; and the loin shall remain for the kitchen. When the Hart is taken you ought to blow *four moots* [long blasts on the horn], and he shall be undone [cut to pieces] like any other beast. And then if it should happen that his hounds are bold, and if they have taken the Hart by force, the Huntsman shall have the hide, and he that flays the head shall have the shoulder by right [as a perquisite], and the hounds shall be rewarded with the neck, and with the bowels, and with the liver, and it shall be eaten upon the hide. . . . The head shall be carried to the house before the Lord, and the heart, and the tail, and the gullet on a fork. And the menee ought to be blown at the door of the hall, when he is taken to the house. When the buck is taken you ought to blow the prize, and you ought to reward the hounds with the paunch and with the bowels.

> H. Dryden, *The Art of Hunting or Three Hunting MSS., a
> revised edition of the Art of Hunting by William Twici,
> Huntsman of King Edward II*, 1844, revised, Northampton,
> William Mark, 1908

TOURNAMENT, 1347

And a little before the feast of St. Michael at London in Chepe there were very beautiful lists. Here the lady Queen Philippa with a great party of her ladies fell to the ground from the pavilions which had been newly built so that they could watch the knightly deeds; but they were not hurt. That most pious queen would not allow the carpenters to be punished for this, but she assuaged the anger of the king and his courtiers with prayers on bended knee. This merciful act of the queen aroused the love of all towards her when they considered her piety.

> G. Le Baker, *Chronicon*, edited by E. M. Thompson

ARCHERY IN DISREPUTE, 1363

The King [Edward III] to the Lord-lieutenant of Kent, greeting:

Whereas the people of our realm, rich and poor alike, were accustomed formerly in their games to practise archery—whence by God's help, it is well known that high honour and profit came to our realm, and no small advantage to ourselves in our warlike

43. A tournament, *c.* 1475. The Earl of Warwick has the Bear and Ragged Staff on his crest; his page has the emblem of the Ragged Staff on his back. Judges, on the left, examine the tilting lances.

enterprises—and that now skill in the use of the bow having fallen almost wholly into disrepute, our subjects give themselves up to the throwing of stones and of wood and of iron; and some to handball and football and hockey; and others to coursing and cockfights, and even to other unseemly sports less useful and manly; whereby our realm—which God forbid—will soon, it would appear, be void of archers:

We, wishing that a fitting remedy be found in this matter, do hereby ordain, that in all places in your county, liberties or no liberties, wheresoever you shall deem fit, a proclamation be made to this effect: that every man in the same county, if he be able-bodied, shall upon holidays, make use, in his games, of bows and arrows . . . and so learn and practise archery.

Moreover we ordain that you prohibit under penalty of imprisonment all and sundry from such stone, wood and iron throwing; handball, football, or hockey; coursing and cock-fighting; or other such idle games.

Rymer, Foedera III, R. B. Morgan, Readings in English
Social History

A TOURNAMENT AT SMITHFIELD, 1390

The ceremonies were to take place on the Monday, and the sixty knights to be prepared for tilting courteously, with blunted lances, against all comers. The prize for the best knight of the opponents was a rich crown of gold, that for the tenants of the lists, a very rich golden clasp. They were to be given to the most gallant tilter, according to the judgment of the ladies who should be as spectators. On Tuesday the tournaments were to be continued by squires against others of the same rank who wished to oppose them. The prize for the opponents was a courser saddled and bridled, and for the tenants of the lists a falcon.

Accordingly when Sunday came, about three o'clock, there pounded from the Town of London, which is situated in the Square of St. Catherine, on the banks of the Thames, sixty barbed coursers ornamented for the tournament, and on each was mounted a squire of honour. Then came sixty ladies of rank mounted on palfreys most elegantly and richly dressed, following each other, every one leading a knight with a silver chain completely armed for tilting. And in this procession they moved on through the streets of London, attended by numbers of minstrels and trumpets to Smithfield. The Queen of England and her ladies and damsels had already arrived, also the King.

44. May Festivities. The people in the boat are going for a picnic; their wine
bottle is hanging in the river. Men are dancing in the market square. Early
sixteenth-century Book of Hours.

When the ladies who led the knights reached the square, the servants were ready to assist them to dismount from the palfreys, and conduct them to the apartments prepared for them. The knights remained until the squires of honour had dismounted and brought them their coursers, which having mounted, they had their helmets laced on, and prepared themselves in all points for the tilt. When the tournament began every one exerted himself to the utmost, many were unhorsed, and many more lost their helmets. The jousting continued, with great courage and perseverance, until night put an end to it. The company then retired, and when supper-time was come, the lords and ladies attended. The prize for the opponents at the tournament was adjudged, by the ladies, lords and heralds, to the Count d'Ostrevant, who far eclipsed all who had tilted that day; that for the tenants was given to a gallant knight of England, called Sir Hugh Spencer.

On the morrow, Tuesday, the tournament was renewed by the squires, who tilted until night in the presence of the king, queen, and all the nobles. The supper was as before at the bishop's palace, and the dancing lasted until daybreak. On Wednesday the tournament was continued by all knights and squires indiscriminantly. The remainder of the week was spent in feasting, and the king conferred the Order of the Garter on Count d'Ostrevant—a circumstance at which the King of France and many of his people were much annoyed.

Jean Froissart, Chronicles

DEER STALKING

Harts and hinds betake themselves to the hills; and the fox and polecat seek their earths; the hare squats by the hedges, hurries and hastens thither to her forme and prepares to lurk there. As I stood in that place the idea of stalking came to me, so I covered both body and bow with leaves, turned in behind a tree and waited there awhile. And as I gazed in the glade near by me I saw a hart with tall antlers: the main stem was unburnished and in the middle very strong. And he was full grown and adorned with horns of six and five tines, and was large, broad and big of body: whoever might catch him, he was a dish for a king. But there followed him a fourth-year buck that most eagerly attended him, and aroused and warned him when the wind failed, so that no one should be sly enough to harm him in his sleep by stealth. He went in front of him when any danger was to be feared.

I let the leash fall to the ground quietly, and settled down my hound by the bole of a birch tree, and took careful note of the wind from the fluttering of the leaves. I stalked on very quietly so as to break no twigs, and crept to a crab-apple tree and hid underneath it.

Then I wound up my bow and prepared to shoot, drew up the tiller and aimed at the hart, but the buck who attended the hart lifted up his nose, looked cautiously around, and eagerly snuffed about.

Then, perforce, I had to stand without moving, and to stir no foot, although gnats grievously troubled me and bit my eyes, for if I had tried to move, or made any sign, all my sport, that I had so long awaited, would have been lost. The hart paused, went on cautiously, staring here and there, but at last he bent down and began on his feed. Then I hauled to the hook [i.e. the trigger of the cross-bow] and smote the hart. It so happened that I hit him behind the left shoulder and the blood streamed out on both sides. He stopped: brayed and then brushed through the thickets, as if everything in the wood had crashed down at the same moment. Soon the attending buck went off to his mates, but they were terrified by his manner and took to the fells. I went to my hound, and quickly grasped him and untied his leash, and let him cast about. The briars and the bracken were smeared with blood, and the hound picked up the scent and pursued the hart to where he was for he had crept into a cave, and, crouched to the earth, had fallen down—dead as a door-nail.

> *The Parlement of the Three Ages,* modernized by
> H. S. Bennett, *Life on the English Manor*

THE ENGLISH LONGBOW

Justices now be no Justices; there be many good acts made for this matter already. Charge them upon their allegiance, that this singular benefit of God may be practised, and that it be not turned into cheating and whoring within the towns: for they be negligent in executing these laws of Shooting.

In my time, my poor father was as diligent to teach me to Shoot, as to learn me any other thing, and so I think other men did their children. He taught me how to draw, how to lay my body in my bow, and not to draw with strength of arms as other nations do, but with strength of the body. I had my bows bought me, according to my age and strength: as I increased in them, so my bows were made bigger and bigger: for men shall never Shoot well, except they be brought up in it. It is a goodly Art, a wholesome kind of exercise, and much commended in Physic. Marcilius Phicinus in his book *de triplici vita* (it is a great while since I read him now) but I remember he commendeth this kind of exercise, and saith, that it wrestleth against many kinds of diseases. In the reverence of God let it be continued. Let a proclamation go forth, charging the Justices of peace, that they see such Acts and Statutes kept, as were made for this purpose.

Hugh Latimer, *Sixth Sermon before King Edward VI*

Health

THE BLACK DEATH, 1348

The grievous plague penetrated the sea coasts from Southampton and came to Bristol, and there almost the whole strength of the town died, struck as it were by sudden death; for there were few who kept their beds more than three days, or two days, or half a day; and after this the fell death broke forth on every side with the course of the sun. There died at Leicester in the small parish of St. Leonard more than 380; and in the parish of the Holy Cross more than 400; and so in each parish a great number. . . . In the same year there was a great plague of sheep everywhere in the realm, so that in one place there died in one pasturage more than 5,000 sheep, and so rotted that neither beast nor bird would touch them. And there were smaller prices for everything on account of the fear of death. For there were very few who cared about riches or anything else. For a man could have a horse which before was worth 40s. for 6s. 8d., a fat ox for 4s., a cow for 12d., a heifer for 6d., a fat wether for 4d., a sheep for 8d., a lamb for 2d., a big pig for 5d., a stone of wool for 9d. Sheep and cattle went wandering over fields and through crops and there was no one to go and drive or father them, so that the number cannot be reckoned which perished in the ditches in every district for lack of herdsmen; for there was such a lack of servants that no one knew what he ought to do.

In the following autumn no one could get a reaper for less than 8d. with his food, a mower for less than 12d. with his food. Wherefore, many crops perished in the fields for want of someone to gather them; but in the pestilence year, as is above said of other things, there was such abundance of all kinds of corn that no one much troubled about it.

. . . Priests were in such poverty that many churches were widowed and lacking the divine offices, masses, matins, vespers, sacraments, and other rites . . . but within a short time a very great multitude of those whose wives had died in the pestilence flocked

45. Early thirteenth century.
  i At the apothecary's shop: weighing the herbs; pounding them; heating
     them over a fire.
 ii A patient breathing the fumes; another with a skin disease.
iii A surgeon examines with a knife; the operation takes place, the patient
     is held down, an assistant asks for payment.

into orders, of whom many were illiterate and little more than laymen, except so far as they knew how to read, although they could not understand.

Meanwhile the King sent proclamation into all the counties that reapers and other labourers should not take more than they had been accustomed to take under the penalty appointed by statute. But the labourers were so lifted up and obstinate that they would not listen to the King's command, but if any wished to have them he had to give them what they wanted, and either lose his fruit and crops or satisfy the lofty and covetous desires of the workmen . . . after the aforesaid pestilence many buildings, great and small, fell into ruins in every city, borough and village for lack of inhabitants, likewise many villages and hamlets became desolate, all having died who dwelt there.

> Henry Knighton, *Chronicle,* II. Rolls Series. *Readings in English Social History,* edited by R. B. Morgan

THE RAPIDITY OF THE BLACK DEATH, 1348

The plague, which first began in the country of the Saracens, spread to such a degree that, without sparing any country, it visited with the scourge of sudden death every place in all the kingdoms stretching from that country northwards, even as far as Scotland.

Now in England it started in the county of Dorsetshire, about the festival of St. Peter in Chains [1 August], in the year of our Lord, 1348; and immediately spreading with great rapidity from place to place, it attacked between morning and noon a very large number of people in perfect health, and rid them of this mortal life. Not one of these so doomed to death was permitted to live more than three or four days at the most. With the exception perhaps of a few, rich persons of every degree were attacked. On the same day, twenty, forty, sixty, and indeed many more bodies received the rites of burial in the same grave.

And about the festival of All Saints [1 November], the plague came to London, and killed off many people every day; and it spread to such an extent that, from the feast of the Purification till after Easter, more than two hundred bodies were buried daily in the new cemetery that had just been made near Smithfield, to say nothing of those buried in the other cemeteries of the city. But by the grace of the Holy Spirit it departed from London at Whitsuntide, and went on its way northwards; and it departed thence about the festival of St. Michael, in the year of our Lord, 1349.

> Robert of Avesbury, *De Gestis Mirabilibus.* Rolls Series

MEDICAL RECIPES, Fourteenth Century

For him that is in the jaundice: take wormwood and seethe it long in water, and wash the sick man with that water thrice right well, and give him to drink ivory shaven small in wine.

Another: take the root of borage, and if he be hard therein stamp it, and temper it with a little ale, and do thereto saffron, and give him .iij sups three days at morn and even.

Another: drink sorrel, plantain, and chickweed tempered with old ale morn and even. . . .

Another: take ivory and saffron, and stamp together, and temper it up with holy water, and drink it morn and even, when thou goest to bed. . . .

Another: take a tench, and cleave it in two all quick, and do away the bones, and lay it to the heart, and to the ribs; the sick man or woman shall drink no strong ale, mixed with feeble ale, nor eat no geese, no duck, no roast, nor no manner of beef nor pork, nor nought that comes of swine, nor drink no wine, nor no new ale, nor anything that is hot, few clothes night and day. . . .

> *Reliquiae Antiquae* (from a fragment of MS. of fourteenth century, in possession of J. O. Halliwell, No. 335)

ANOTHER MEDICAL RECIPE

For him that has a quinsy: take a fat cat, and flay it well, and clean, and draw out the guts, and take the grease of a hedgehog, and the fat of a bear, and resins and fenugreek, and sage, and gum of honeysuckle, and virgin wax; all this crumble small, and stuff the cat within as you stuff a goose; roast it all, and gather the grease and anoint him with it.

Reliquiae Antiquae, from a fragment of MS., fourteenth century

CONCERNING LEPERS, 1370

It is to be observed that leprous persons were always, for the avoiding the danger of infection, to be separated from the sound; God Himself commanding to put out of the host every leper. Whereupon I read that in a provincial synod, holden at Westminster by Hubert, archbishop of Canterbury, in the year of Christ, 1200, the second of King John, it was decreed according to the institution of the Lateran Council, that when so many leprous persons were assembled that might be able to build a church, with a churchyard for themselves, and to have one especial priest of their own, that they should be permitted to have the same without contradiction, so they be not injurious to the old churches by that which was granted to them for pity's sake. And further, it was

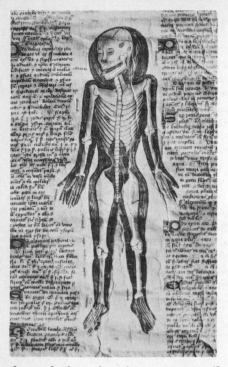

46. A skeleton to teach
anatomy from a manuscript
of the book by John Averne,
the earliest known of great
British surgeons, about 1370.

decreed that they be not compelled to give any tithes of their
gardens or increase of cattle. . . .

And I have read that King Edward the Third, in the twentieth
year of his reign, gave commandment to the mayor and sheriffs of
London . . that they should cause the said lepers to be removed
into some out-places in the fields, from the haunt or company of
sound people; whereupon certain lazar-houses, as may be supposed,
were then builded without the city some good distance—to wit, the
lock without Southwarke, in Kent Street; one other betwixt the
Miles end and Stratford Bow; one other at Kingsland, betwixt
Shoreditch and Stoke Newington; and another at Knightes bridge,
west from Charing crosse. These four I have noted to be erected
for the receipt of leprous people sent out of the city. At that time
also the citizens required of the guardians of Saint Giles Hospital
to take from them, and keep continually, the number of fourteen
persons leprous, according to the foundation of Matilda the queen,
which was for leprous persons in the city of London, and the shire
of Middlesex, which was granted.

John Stow, *Survey of London*

A FAMOUS SURGEON SPEAKS, c. 1370

In clothing and bearing show he the manner of clerks. For why? It is seemly for any discreet man to be dressed in clerk's clothing for to occupy gentlemen's tables. Have the surgeon also clean hands and well-shaped nails and cleansed from all blackness and filth. And he be courteous at lord's table, and displeases he not in words or deeds the guests sitting by; hear he many things but speak he but a few. . . . And when he shall speak, be the words short, and, as much as he may, fair and reasonable and without swearing.

Beware that there be never found double words in his mouth, for if he be found true in his words few or none shall doubt his deeds. . . . A surgeon should tell good tales and of honest that may make the patients laugh, and any other things which are no trouble, while they make or induce a light heart in the patient or the sick man.

John Arderne, from a fifteenth-century translation of his
Treatise on Fistula

AN ANAESTHETIC, c. 1370

An untement slepyng [soporific ointment], with which if any man be anointed he shall be able to suffer cutting in any place of the body without feeling or aching [Recipe, henbane, mandragora, hemlock, black and white poppies, opium etc.]. . . . Also the seed alone [of henbane] given in wine to drink maketh the drinker at once for to sleep, that he shall not feel whatsoever is done to him. And proved I myself for certain. And know then that it speedeth for to draw him that sleepeth so by the nose and by the cheeks and by the beard, that the spirits be quickened, that he sleep not over deeply.

John Arderne, from a fifteenth-century translation of his
Treatise on Fistula

HOW TO PLEASE THE PATIENT

And if the patients or their friends or servants ask by what length of time he hopes to cure the complaint, let the doctor always promise double what he supposes; that is, if the doctor hopes to heal the patient in twenty weeks—that is the common course of curing—let him add so many over. For it is better that the term be lengthened than the cure. For to prolong the cure brings despair to the patient, when trust in the doctor is the strongest hope of cure. And if the patient wonders why he was told the cure would be so long when he was healed in half the time, tell him he was strong-hearted, bore the pain well and had a body to heal quickly. The patient will be proud and delighted to hear such words.

John Arderne, from a fifteenth-century translation of his
Treatise on Fistula, c. 1370

OINTMENT, Fourteenth Century

I bethought myself of collecting a good number of those beetles which in summer are found in the dung of oxen, also of the crickets which sing in the fields. I cut off the heads and the wings of the crickets and put them with the beetles and common oil into a pot; I covered it and left it afterwards for a day and night in a bread oven. I drew out the pot and heated it at a moderate fire, I pounded the whole and rubbed the sick parts; in three days the pain had disappeared.

J. J. Jusserand, *English Wayfaring Life in the Middle Ages,*
translated from the French by Lucy Toulmin Smith

SIGNS THAT THE PATIENT WILL DIE,
Late Fourteenth Century

Again, take the name of the patient, the name of the messenger sent to summon the physician, and the name of the day upon which the messenger first came to you; join all their letters together, and if an even number result, the patient will not escape; if the number be odd, then he will recover.

The following are signs of death: Continuous vomiting, a cold sweat, and cold extremities, excessive eructations, convulsions and delirium, together with bowel obstruction of whatever nature.

Again, if a blister, black in colour, appear upon his belly, the patient will die on the following day; similarly if the face be distorted with a pallid swelling, the eyes become greenish, or the legs swollen. Also the patient will die if the veins around the eyes and in the forehead appear black in colour.

Take the herb Cinquefoil, and, whilst collecting it, say a Paternoster on behalf of the patient, and then boil it in a new jar with some of the water which the patient is destined to drink; and if the water be red in colour after this boiling, then the patient will die. . . .

Johannes de Mirfeld of St. Bartholomew's, Smithfield,
Sir Percival Horton-Smith Hartley and H. R. Aldridge

47.   Scenes in a medieval hospital.

VARIETIES OF EXERCISES, Late Fourteenth Century

There are, however, many different kinds of exercise, according to
the difference of rank and of persons. For some are strong, and
some are weak; some are rich, and some are poor; some are
prelates and men of rank, others are members of religious orders
and are enclosed within their walls; moreover, the season is
sometimes rainy, at other times it is fine. Therefore it is necessary
to have several varieties of exercise. The first and most important
of these is to walk abroad, choosing the uplands where the air
is pure; this is the best of all. Riding is another form of exercise,
but this is only for the wealthy. It behoves prelates, however, to
have some other method of taking exercise. Let such a man,
therefore, have a stout rope, knotted at the end, hanging up in
his chamber; and then, grasping the rope with both hands, let
him raise himself up, and remain in that position for a long time
without touching the ground; then, holding the rope and running
with it as far as possible, let him jump into the air, turning himself
round and round and strutting fiercely about. Or if this pastime

does not please him, let him hold in his hands a stone, weighing thirty pounds, in which a ring has been fixed, and carry it about frequently from one part of his dwelling to another; or let him hold this same stone up in the air for a long time before setting it down, or lift it to his neck, or between his hands: the like also with other methods of exercise, until he begins to tire: or thus: let him hold a staff in his hand, and let another person, pulling straight, try to drag it away from him, if he is able; and let another strive to tear a penny from his closed hand. Another method of taking exercise is to hold the breath and impel it towards the head, or towards the belly, and this is extremely useful. Other forms of exercise are useful for playful youths, such as running, wrestling, jumping, hurling stones, and many other sports in which young men take delight.

Johannes de Mirfeld of St. Bartholomew's, Smithfield,
Sir Percival Horton-Smith Hartley and H. R. Aldridge

MEDICINAL BATHS FOR CONSUMPTIVES,
Late Fourteenth Century
Also here is a bath which has proved to be of value. Take blind puppies, remove the viscera, and cut off the extremities; then boil in water, and in this water let the patient be bathed: let him enter the bath for four hours after his food, and whilst therein keep the head entirely covered, and the chest completely wrapped around with the skin of a small kid, as a preservation against exposure to sudden chill.

Another bath of which the patient may avail himself: Take land-tortoises, and boil them in a cooking pot. Take the tortoises, and boil them in fresh water, and in this water let the patient bathe; and after the bath anoint the chest with either the 'ointment for consumptives', or with one of the others mentioned above.

Sir Percival Horton-Smith Hartley and H. R. Aldridge,
Breviarium Bartholomei, Cambridge

SPECIAL DIET FOR CONSUMPTIVES,
Late Fourteenth Century
. . . Milk is of the greatest possible value, especially if it be that of women; asses' milk is next to be preferred, and then that of goats. The milk ought to be imbibed direct from the udder; but should this be impossible, then take a salver, which has been washed in hot water, and allow it to stand over another full of hot water; then let the animal be milked into the salver and the

48. Doctor treating orthopaedic patients in the fourteenth century. From *On Surgery* by Rogier de Salerne.

milk immediately proferred, for it very quickly turns bad. If it be feared that this has occurred, boil the milk over the fire, add a pinch of salt or honey to it, and let this be absorbed; or drop into the milk either heated stones taken from the river, or a red hot iron. Moreover, wine should not be drunk during the whole period in which the milk remains in the stomach, for the wine causes the milk to coagulate, and this changes it into the nature of a poison. . . .

The patient can also eat the flesh of all the usual kinds of fowl which fly, except of those which live on the water; likewise the flesh of kids, lambs, and unweaned calves, or of the young rabbit; also the extremities of animals (such as the feet and legs of little pigs), hens and their chickens, and the flesh of a year-old lamb: and of all these only a little should be taken, and but rarely, except in the case of flying fowl, and even this should be taken only in such a small quantity as to be digestible. . . .

> Johannes de Mirfeld of St. Bartholomew's, Smithfield, Sir Percival Horton-Smith Hartley and H. R. Aldridge, Breviarium Bartholomei, Cambridge

THE DANGERS OF WATER, 1398

Spring time is the time of gladness and love; for in spring time all things seem glad; for the earth turns green, trees burgeon and spread, meadows bring forth flowers, heaven shines, the sea rests and is quiet, birds sing and make their nests, and all things that seem dead and withered in winter are renewed in spring time. . . . And water in spring time is unwholesome to drink; for it is made great and thick with vapours that must be removed. Also it is infected with frogs and other worms that breed at that time. And therefore, if it be needful to drink water at that time, Constantine counsels to seethe it first, that it may be cleansed and purged by boiling.

> John of Trevisa, Bartholomew

TOOTHACHE, 1398

Worms breed in the cheek teeth . . . and this is known by itching and tickling and continual digging and boring. Worms of the teeth can be slain with myrrh and opium.

> John of Trevisa, Bartholomew

AGAINST TOOTHACHE

Take a candle of mutton-fat, mingled with seed of sea-holly; burn this candle as close as possible to the tooth, holding a basin of cold water beneath it. The worms [which are gnawing the tooth] will fall into the water to escape the heat of the candle.

From *Meddygon Myddveu,* a fourteenth century MS.

Work and Wages

GOLD

The goldsmith should have a furnace with a hole at the top so that smoke can get out by all exits. One hand should operate the bellows with a light pressure and the greatest diligence, so that the air inside the bellows, being pressed through the tubes, may blow up the coals and that the constant spread of it may feed the fire. Let there be an anvil of extreme hardness on which iron and gold may be softened and may take the required form. They can be stretched and pulled with the tongs and the hammer. There should be a hammer also for making gold leaf, as well as sheets of silver, tin, brass, iron, or copper. The goldsmith must have a very sharp chisel by which he can engrave in amber, diamond . . . or marble, or jacinth, emerald, sapphire, or pearl, and form many figures. He should have a hardness stone for testing metals, and one for comparing steel with iron. He must also have a rabbit's-foot for smoothing, polishing, and wiping the surface of gold and silver, and the small particles of metal should be collected in a leather apron. He must have small boxes, flasks, and containers, of pottery, and a toothed saw and a gold file, as well as gold and silver wire, by which broken objects can be mended or properly constructed. The goldsmith should be skilled in feathery work as well as in bas-relief, in fusing as well as in hammering. His apprentice must have a waxed or painted table, or one covered with clay, for portraying little flowers and drawing in various ways. That he may do this conveniently let him have litharge and chalk. He must know how to distinguish solid gold from brass and copper, that he may not purchase brass for gold. . . .

U. T. Holmes, Jr., *Daily Living in the Twelfth Century,*
based on the Observations of Alexander Neckham

RIVALRY BETWEEN MARKETS, 1201

. . . the monks of Ely set up a market at Lakenheath, having the King's assent and a charter to that effect. At first we dealt peaceably with our friends and neighbours, and after sending letters to the

49. Blacksmiths working in the twelfth century.

Lord Bishop of Ely, we sent messengers to the Chapter of Ely, asking them to desist from their enterprise, and adding that, for the sake of peace and for the preservation of our mutual love, we would, in all friendship, pay them fifteen marks, which was the sum given by them to secure the King's charter. I will say no more than this; they refused to desist, and threatening words were bandied to and fro *and Roman spears menaced the spears of Rome* (Horace, *Epistles* I, i, 100). But we secured a writ of recognition to decide whether that market had been set up to our prejudice and to the detriment of the market of St. Edmund. And oath being taken, it was declared that it was done to our detriment. [The King decided against Ely]. . . . The Provost of the Hundred therefore, coming thither on the market day with freemen to bear him witness, publicly on the King's behalf forbade the market, showing the letters both of the King and the Sheriff; but being received with insult and injury, he retired, having accomplished nothing. The Abbot postponed the matter for a time, being then in London; but after consulting wise men on the matter, he ordered his bailiffs to take men of St. Edmund with horses and arms and to remove the market and carry off in chains such buyers and sellers as they could find. Now about midnight some six hundred well-armed men set out for Lakenheath. But since scouts gave warning of their approach, all those who were at the market ran this way and that, so that not one of them was to be found . . . they overthrew the forked poles of the meat-market and the planks of the stalls in the market, and carried them off, and leading with them all the cattle, 'all sheep and oxen, yea, and the beasts of the field', they proceeded towards Icklingham . . . the Bishop of Ely, an eloquent and fluent speaker, complained in person concerning this affair to the Justiciar and magnates of England, saying that an act of unprecedented arrogance had been committed on the land of St. Ethelreda in time of peace; and many others were stirred to indignation against the Abbot by his words.

The Chronicle of Jocelin of Brakelond concerning the Acts
of Samson, Abbot of the Monastery of St. Edmund,
translated by H. E. Butler

THE MANOR FARM, c. 1289

THE PLOUGHMAN

The art of the ploughmen consists in knowing how to draw a straight furrow with yoked oxen without striking, pricking or ill-treating them.

Ploughmen ought not to be melancholy, or irritable, but gay,

50. A vertical loom in the twelfth century. The warp threads were strung vertically on the wooden loom. The shuttle carried the weft through these threads by hand. The women standing on either side of the woman weaving hold sheep shears. On the left, one is winding skeins of wool.

full of song and joyous, so that they may in a sort of way encourage
the oxen at their toil with melody and song; they must take them
their forage and fodder, and they ought to be attached to them,
and sleep in their stable at night, and make much of them, curry
and rub them down, look after them well in every way taking
care that their forage and fodder is not stolen; the allowance of
hay or litter should not be given out for two or three nights at
once, but as much as is required for a day's feed should be given
to them every day, nor should they be permitted to have a candle
unless, as the saying is, it is 'held' [i.e. a lantern].

Other people's beasts found in the ploughmen's pasture ought
to be impounded. It is the duty of the ploughmen and husbandmen
when the tillage season is over, to ditch, thresh, dig, fence, repair
the watercourses in the fields, and to do other such small and
useful tasks.

SHEPHERDS

Shepherds should be intelligent, watchful, and kind men who will
not harry the sheep by their bad temper, but let them graze
peacefully and without disturbing them.

Let each provide himself with a good barking dog and sleep out
every night with his flock. Let him prepare his folds and sheepcotes
and provide good hurdles covered with pelts and thick rushes for
warmth; and he must be careful that the 'sheep in his charge are
not stolen or changed, nor allowed to graze in wet or marshy
places, in thickets, or on low-lying bottoms, or on unhealthy
pastures, lest, for want of good care, they go sick and die, otherwise
he will be held liable for the penalty of the account.

But let there be three folds for the sheep and their lambs, viz.
one for the muttons and wethers, another for the two-tooth ewes,
and a third for hogs of one year and under, if the flock is large
enough, three shepherds must then be put in charge.

All the sheep must be marked with the same mark. The ewes
should not be allowed to be suckled or milked beyond the feast
of the Nativity of the Blessed Mary [8 Sept.]; those which it is not
expedient to keep should be drafted out between Easter and
Whitsuntide, sheared earlier, marked differently from the others,
and be sent at once into the wood pastures where they should be
kept, or in some other pasture in which they will fatten and
improve more rapidly; they may be sold at the feast of the Nativity
of St. John the Baptist [24 June].

Those that are sickly can be recognized by the teeth dropping
out and by the sign of old age; the wool of these may be sold

with the pelts of those dying of murrain; and hence much may
be saved on these by shrewdness, for some careful people have
the flesh of those dying of murrain put into water for the period
between the hour of nine and vespers, and afterwards hung up
so that the water drains off; the flesh is afterwards salted and
dried and they are made worth something and can be distributed
among the workpeople and the household; and to prevent loss
in the account an allowance in the daily expenses according to a
fixed price can be made for the flesh so used. . . .

Fleta, a tract in Latin *c.* 1289. Parts translated in
F. H. Cripps-Day, *The Manor Farm*

A MINSTREL'S LIFE, Thirteenth Century

It is a common story everywhere (as all men and women know) that,
when a man makes a marriage or a feast, whereunto well-nurtured
folk come, the minstrels soon get wind of this; for they ask for
nothing better. Then they flock to this house, up hill and down
dale, some on foot and others on horseback. Cousin William
[pantler to the Count of Poitiers, brother of St. Louis] made
some such marriage feast for the common behoof, whereat many
were fair folk, which seemed both fair and noble. Well they ate
and well they drank; how many we were, I myself cannot tell,
though I was among them. Right joyous was the cheer they made;
it is long since I saw such noble fare or such delights; so help me
God! all the fair folk are departing; good gentility is gone, and
all men think only of their own. So to this spousal came the
minstrels in full riding-boots; none was slow of speech: 'give us'
(quoth they) 'either patronage or money, as is right and reason,
that each may go content to his home'.

Rutebeuf, *Lay of Charlot the Jew, c.* 1260

HAY CARTING ON A HOLY DAY, c. 1297

To the reverend and prudent man, etc. It is my duty to tell your
discretion that last Sunday, the morrow of S. Margaret's day,
H... C..., the Bishop of Winchester's harvester in Harwell,
summoned or caused to be summoned all the tenants of the said
Bishop in the said vill, ordering them to come to the park of the
said Bishop immediately after nine o'clock to cart hay. For this
purpose, while we were at breakfast he called them up to work by
blowing a certain great horn through the whole village, as he is
wont to do on working days. And this seemed to me unbearable,
so I immediately sent Sir Thomas my colleague, chaplain of the

51. A man ploughing with yoked oxen in the thirteenth century.

parish, to prevent such work upon that day, but they would not listen to him or desist from their work. So I warned them three or four times to stop and afterwards threatened them with excommunication if they went on, but I laboured in vain, for the said H... answered me mockingly that he was going to cart the hay whether I liked it or not, nor would he cease work, or permit others to cease, for my threats or warnings. I therefore, being somewhat disturbed, summoned them generally and afterwards had them summoned separately to appear before you in your chapter held on Wednesday the vigil of S. James's day, to hear and receive the sentence which your discretion should declare according to justice. Wherefore I beg your discretion to give them a suitable sentence, punishing them so that others may not be tempted by the lightness of their sentence to follow their example, and let the harvester receive punishment for habitually working on holy days and encouraging others to do the same. He is a powerful man. Farewell and good wishes.

Roger de Marlowe, rector of Harwell complains possibly to the Archdeacon of Berkshire. Rosalind M. T. Hill, 'A Berkshire Letter-Book', *Berkshire Archaeological Journal*

WAGES OF FARM LABOURERS, Late Thirteenth Century

You can well have three acres weeded for a penny, and an acre of meadow mown for fourpence, and an acre of waste meadow for threepence-halfpenny, and an acre of meadow turned and raised for a penny-halfpenny, and an acre of waste for a penny farthing. And know that five men can well reap and bind two

52. Milking in the thirteenth century.

acres a day of each kind of corn, more or less. And where each takes twopence a day then you must give fivepence an acre, and when four take a penny-halfpenny a day and the fifth twopence, because he is binder, then you must give fourpence for the acre. And, because in many places they do not reap by the acre, one can know by the reapers and by the work done what they do, but keep the reapers by the band, that is to say, that five men or women, whichever you will, who are called half men, make a band, and twenty-five men make five bands, and twenty-five men can reap and bind ten acres a day working all day, and in ten days a hundred acres, and in twenty days two hundred acres by five score. And see then how many acres there are to reap throughout, and see if they agree with the days and pay them then, and if they account for more days than is right according to this reckoning, do not let them be paid, for it is their fault that they have not reaped the amount and have not worked so well as they ought.

Printed with *Walter of Henley's Husbandry*, edited by
Elizabeth Lamond

THE GOOD DAIRYMAID, Late Thirteenth Century
The dairymaid ought to be faithful and of good repute, and keep

herself clean, and ought to know her business and all that belongs to it. She ought not to allow any underdairymaid or another to take or carry away milk, or butter, or cream, by which the cheese shall be less and the dairy impoverished. And she ought to know well how to make cheese and salt cheese, and she ought to save and keep the vessels of the dairy, that it need not be necessary to buy new ones every year. And she ought to know the day when she begins to make cheese and of what weight, and when she begins to make two cheeses a day, of how much and of what weight, and then the bailiff and the provost [reeve] ought to inspect the dairy often and the cheeses, when they increase and decrease in weight, and no harm be done in the dairy, nor any robbery by which the weight shall be lessened. And they ought to know and prove and see when the cows make a stone of cheese and butter, and when the ewes make a stone of the same, that they may be

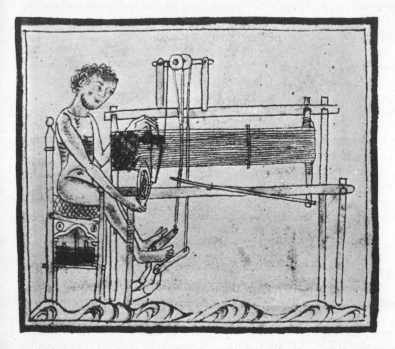

53. Thirteenth-century illustration of a horizontal loom, an improvement on the ancient vertical loom. Now the weaver by use of foot-operated treadles can raise and lower the alternate threads of the warp. Both hands are then free to pass the shuttle through the 'shed'.

able the more surely to answer in the account. No cow shall be milked or suckled after Michaelmas, and no ewe after the feast of our Lady. . . .

The dairymaid ought to help to winnow the corn when she can be present, and she ought to take care of the geese and hens and answer for the returns and keep and cover the fire, that no harm arise from lack of guard.

> Tract on the Office of Seneschal, printed with *Walter of Henley's Husbandry*, edited by Elizabeth Lamond

THE SWINEHERD, Late Thirteenth Century

The swineherd ought to be on those manors where swine can be sustained and kept in the forest, or in woods, or waste, or in marshes, without sustenance from the grange; and if the swine can be kept with little sustenance from the grange during hard frost, then must a pigsty be made in a marsh or wood, where the swine may be night and day. And then when the sows have farrowed, let them be driven with the feeble swine to the manors and kept with leavings as long as the hard frost and the bad weather last, and then driven back to the others. And if there is no wood or marsh or waste where the swine may be sustained without being altogether kept on the grange, no swineherd or swine shall be on the manor, except only such as can be kept in August on the stubble and leavings of the grange, and when the corn is threshed for sale, and as soon as they are in good condition and well, let them be sold. For whoever will keep swine for a year from the cost of the grange alone, and count the cost and the allowance for the swine and swineherd, together with the damage they do yearly to the corn, he shall lose twice as much as he shall gain, and this will soon be seen by whoever keeps account.

> Tract on the Office of Seneschal, printed with *Walter of Henley's Husbandry*

CORN, Late Thirteenth Century

You know surely that an acre sown with wheat takes three ploughings, except lands which are sown yearly; and that, one with the other, each ploughing is worth sixpence, and harrowing a penny, and on the acre it is necessary to sow at least two bushels. Now two bushels at Michaelmas are worth at least twelvepence, and weeding a halfpenny, and reaping fivepence, and carrying in August a penny; the straw will pay for the threshing. At three times your sowing you ought to have six bushels, worth three shillings, and the cost amounts to three shillings and three halfpence, and the ground is yours and not reckoned.

Change your seed every year at Michaelmas, for seed grown on other ground will bring more profit than that which is grown on your own. Will you see this? Plough two selions [arable strips or 'lands'] at the same time, and sow the one with seed which is bought and the other with corn which you have grown: in August you will see that I speak truly.

Walter of Henley's Husbandry, edited by Elizabeth Lamond

FRATERNITY OF GROCERS FOUNDED, 1345

Mem. That all the brethren of the fraternity dined the first time together at the house of the Abbot of Bury on the 12th June, 1345, at which dinner each paid 12 pence, and the whole was expended and 23 pence beside by the Warden. At which dinner we had a surcoat to be made of one livery, for which each paid his proportion. The same day after dinner ended, it was decreed by common consent to take and hire a priest at the Nativity of St. John next, to come to chant and pray for the members of the said company and for all Christians, and to maintain the said priest each one of the fraternity consented to give a penny a week, which amounts to 4s. 4d. to pay now for the year.

Mem. The priest commenced to sing July 3rd, and to receive each week 15d. It was agreed that none should be of the fraternity if he were not of good condition and of their mistery, that is to say a pepperer of Soper Lane, or a canvasser of the Ropery, or a spicer of Cheap, or other man of their mistery wherever he might dwell.

Facsimile, Transcript and Translation of Grocers' Records, 1345-1463. Company of Grocers, J. A. Kingdom; retranslated in G. Unwin, Gilds and Companies of London

'EVERY MAN SHALL SERVE THE MASTER REQUIRING HIM', 1349

Because a great part of the people, and especially of workmen and servants, lately died of the Pestilence, many seeing the necessity of the masters of great scarcity of servants, will not serve unless they receive excessive wages, and some rather willing to beg in idleness than by labour to get their living. We considering the grievous incommodities, which of the lack, especially of ploughman and such labourers may hereafter come, have upon deliberation and treaty with the prelates and nobles, and the learned men assisting us,

54. Two groups of armourers at work in the thirteenth century. The smith in the centre is shaping with a hammer a helmet held on the anvil with a pair of tongs. On the right a man tests by eye so see if a sword blade is straight. On the left two men inspect completed work.

ordained that every man and woman in England of whatever condition they may be, bond or free, able in body and under sixty years of age, not living by merchandise, or being an artificer, and not having property whereby they may live, shall serve the master requiring him or her.

The Statute of Labourers. *Statutes of the Realm,* I, quoted in Henderson's *Historical Documents of the Middle Ages*

THE GUILD SYSTEM SHOWN IN THE REGULATIONS OF THE WHITE TAWYERS [TANNERS] OF LONDON, 1346

In honour of God, of Our Lady, and of all Saints, and for the nuture of tranquillity and peace among the good folks . . . called 'Whittawyers', the folks of the same trade have, by assent of Richard Lacer, Mayor, and of the Alderman, ordained the points under-written.

In the first place they have ordained that they will find a wax candle, to burn before Our Lady in the Church for All Hallows near London Wall. Also that each person of the said trade shall put in the box each sum as he shall think fit, in aid of maintaining the said candle.

Also, if by chance any one of the said trade shall fall into poverty, whether through old age, or because he cannot . . . work . . . he shall have every week from the said box 7d. for his support if he be a man of good repute. . . .

And that no stranger shall work in the said trade . . . if he be not an apprentice, or a man admitted to the franchise of the said city.

And that no one shall take the serving man of another to work with him, during his term, unless it be with the permission of his master.

And if any one of the said trade shall have work in his house that he cannot complete, or if for want of assistance such work shall be in danger of being lost, those of the said trade shall aid him so that the said work be not lost.

. . . And if any of the said trade shall do to the contrary of any point of the Ordinances aforesaid, and be convicted thereof by goodmen of the said trade, he shall pay to the Chamber of the Guildhall of London, the first time 2s., the second time 40d., the third time half a mark, and the fourth time 10s., and shall foreswear the trade.

Also, that the good folks of the same trade shall once a year be assembled in a certain place, convenient thereto, there to choose two men of the most loyal and befitting of the said trade, to be overseers of work and all other things touching the trade, for that year. . . . And if any one of the said trade be found rebellious against the said overseers, so as not to let them properly make their search and assay as they ought to do, . . . he shall pay to the Chamber, upon the first default, 40d., etc.

. . . Also, that all skins falsely and deceitfully wrought in their trade which the said overseers shall find on sale . . . shall be forfeited . . . and the worker thereof amerced in manner aforesaid.

Also, that no one who has not been an apprentice, and has not finished his term of apprenticeship in the said trade shall be made free of the same trade. . . .

Guildhall Letter-Book F; f. Bland, Brown and Tawney

BLACKSMITHS, c. 1350
Swart smoky smiths smutted with smoke

55. Sawyers in the early fourteenth century, using a large two-handled saw and a trestle, still in common use today.

Drive me to death with the din of their dints;
Such noise at night heard no man ever,
Such crying of knaves and clattering of knocks;
The pug-nosed bumpkins cry for 'Coal! coal!'
And blow with their bellow till their brains are all bursting.
'Huff! puff!' says the one; 'Haff! paff!' the other.
They spit and they sprawl and they tell many stories;
They gnash and they gnash, and they groan all together,
And hold them hot with their hard hammers.
Of a bull's hide are their big aprons;
Their shanks are sheathed against sparks of the fire.
Heavy hammers they have that are hard to handle;
Strong strokes they strike on a stock of steel:
'Lus! bus! las! das!' they roar in a row.
Like a dreadful dream—may it go to the devil!
The master stands apart; his stroke is the lighter;
Between the two of them he twines out a treble:
'Tick! tack! hic! hac! ticket! tacket! tick! tack!
Lus! bus! las! das! such a life as they lead us!
All our clothes they smut—Christ give them sorrow!
No man for such water-burners can get a night's rest.

                    Reliquiae Antiquae, edited by Thomas Wright and
                                        J. O. Halliwell

QUARRYMEN, Fourteenth Century

The king to all and singular sheriffs, mayors, bailiffs, ministers and his other faithfuls to whom etc. health. Know that we have appointed our beloved William Cok of Whatelee to have transported both by land and water stone which we have had castle of Wyndsore to the said castle and to take sufficient carriage for the same stone both within the liberties and without excepting the fee of the church at our costs to be paid by the hand of our beloved William de Mulsho, clerk of our said works, and to take and arrest all those whom he finds refractory in this part or rebellious and to arrest and lead them to our said castle to be delivered to our prison there to remain in the same until we decide otherwise about ordaining their punishment. And therefore we order you strictly commanding that ye be attentive helpers and allies in the aforesaid to the same William Cok as often as and provided in quarries at Teynton and Whatele for our works in our according as you are required by him about this on our part. . . . Witness the king at Westminster 28 April. By the king himself.

Commission to get stone for Windsor Castle, 1362, from
P.R.O., Patent Roll

56. Spinning wool by distaff and spindle, early fourteenth century. The spinner held the distaff under one arm, often supporting it in a leather belt, and with that hand picked out strands from the wool tied on the top. The strands were attached to the spindle, which was made to spin by the other hand, so twisting the yarn. The spindle was kept upright by a round ring or 'whorl' attached at the bottom.

152 EVERY ONE A WITNESS

WAGES, 1366

For wage of one man mending collars and gear of a cart for 2 days 10 d. . . .

For 1 carpenter hired to mend carts for 7½ days at 5 d. a day 3 s. 1½ d. . . .

For wage for 1 man making collars and mending harness of cart after 1 August for 2½ days 7½ d. . . .

Paid to 1 roofer for roofing the Peyntidechaumber, chapel, hall and le Chaffons at 4 d. per day for 7 days 2 s. 4 d. . . .

For wage of 1 carpenter mending the door, mending the cart and helping make the kiln for 3 days 15 d.

For wage of 1 carpenter mending the house at the staithe at 5 d. a day for 18 days 7 s. 6 d. . . ,

For wage of 1 roofer roofing the grange, kitchen and the house at the staithe at 4 d. a day for 9 days 3 s. . . .

In costs of washing and shearing the lord's sheep as seen by the auditor by the details examined 2 s. 11 d.

For 1 man hired at 3 d. a day for 4½ days to wash and hang herrings 13½ d.

For 3 men hired for 1 day for same 12 d. . . .

For thrashing at 3 d. a quarter 60 quarters and 2 bushels of wheat, 4 bushels of rye and 5 quarters of peas.

For 275 quarters 4 bushels of barley and 27 quarters of oats thrashed at 2½ d. a quarter 63 s. ¼ d.

For winnowing said corn nothing, as it was done by the manor house maid. . . .

For weeding the lord's corn this year 18 d. . . .

For mowing and binding ½ acre of wheat 7d.

For mowing and binding 5½ acres of rye at 15 d. each plus 1½ d. in all 7s.

For reaping and binding 2 acres of rye 2 s.

For reaping 14 acres 3 rods of barley at 12 d. an acre 14 s. 9 d.

For reaping 2 acres 3 rods of barley 24 d. . . .

Wage for 1 hired reaper as above at the lord's board for 7 weeks 11 s.

Wage for 2 men reaping, binding and sometimes carting for 5½ weeks at the lord's board 18 s.

Wage of 1 other reaper and binder for all autumn 9 s.

Extracts from the bailiff's account for the Abbot of Dereham

57. This early fourteenth-century illustration shows an overshot water-wheel. It was contrived that the water flowed down a sluice into the buckets of the wheel driving it, probably for the grinding of corn in the mill. In the flowing water are two eels-traps.

PRICES, 1366

Issues of the manor.
3000 sheaves of barley straw sold at 6 d. a hundred 15 s.
7000 do. at same price a hundred 35 s.
A quantity of pea straw sold 10 s.
100 sheaves of wheat straw 13 d.
100 sheaves of rye straw 13 d.
Garden produce 12 s.
6 acres ploughed for the chief lord for seed corn 8 s.
Profit of 1 pig killed for fat 6 d.
9 quarters 6 bushels wheat sold at 6 s. 8 d. a quarter 65 s.
2 quarters 2½ bushels peas at 4 s. a quarter 9 s. 3 d.
Barley sold in February at 4 s. 3 d. a quarter £8.10.
83 quarters 7 bushels barley as above £17. 16 s. 5½ d.
18 quarters oats at 3 s. 4 d. a quarter 60 s.
40 quarters of barley at 4 s. 4 d. £8 13 s. 4 d.
4 quarters of malt at 5 s. 4 d. a quarter 21 s. 4 d.
2 store cows sold 30 s.
2 store pigs sold 16 s.
[Expenses include:]
1 new plough bought 13 d. [Various parts were extra].
200 bindings for roofing houses 4 d.
2 stots [horses or steers] for the lord's house at the staithe [wharf] 6 d.
50 keys 3 d.
50 sheaves of thatch for roofing 12 d.

200 bindings 4 d.
150 gross of rods for binding the rof 6 d.
18 hurdles for the lord's fold at 1½ d. each 2 s. 3 d.
18 do. at 1¾ d. each plus ½ d. extra 2 s. 8 d.
12 hurdles do. plus 1 d. extra 22 d.
1 iron stake 14 d.
4 bushels beans 2 s.
1 cow 10 s. 6 d.

     Extracts from the bailiff's account for the Abbot of Dereham

FOR BAD TO WORSE, c. 1375

The world goeth fast from bad to worse, when shepherd and cowherd for their part demand more for their labour than the master bailiff was wont to take in days gone by. Labour is now at so high a price that he who will order his business aright must pay five or six shillings now for what cost two in former times. Labourers of old were not wont to eat of wheaten bread; their meat was of beans or coarser corn, and their drink of water alone. Cheese and milk were a feast to them, and rarely ate they of other dainties; their dress was of hodden grey [coarse woollen cloth made without dyeing]; then was the world ordered aright for folk of this sort. . . .

     Three things, all of the same sort, are merciless when they get the upper hand; a water-flood, a wasting fire, and the common multitude of small folk. For these will never be checked by reason or discipline; and therefore, to speak in brief, the present world is so troubled by them that it is well to set a remedy thereunto. Ha! age of ours, whither turnest thou? for the poor and small folk, who should cleave to their labour, demand to be better fed than their masters. Moreover, they bedeck themselves in fine colours and fine attire, whereas (were it not for their pride and their privy conspiracies) they would be clad in sackcloth as of old. . . . Ha! age of ours, I know not what to say; but of all the estates that I see, from the highest to the lowest, each decayeth in its own degree. Poor man or lord, all alike are full of vanity; I see the poor folk more haughty than their lords; each draweth whither he pleaseth.

               John Gower, *Mirour de l'Omme*

A TRICKY SALESMAN, c. 1376-1379

Fraud also of its trickery
Oftentimes in mercery
Cheats people diversely,

58. Early fourteenth-century illustration showing masons engraving stone slabs with chisel and mallet. The lady in the centre, probably a widow, gives instructions for a gravestone to the master mason.

Being full of artifice,
Of joking and of nonsense,
To make fools of silly people
So as to get their money,

And smooth and soft he talks to them
And is the best of company
With his mouth, but in his thinking
He is slyly after his lucre
Under pretence of courtesy.
He who is born of such a nest
Is never dumb for lack of words,
But cries out like the sparrowhawk,
When he sees people he doesn't know,
Pulls them and drags them with hue and cry,
Saying: 'Come on! Come in!
Beds and kerchiefs, ostrich feathers,
Silks and satins, and cloths imported—
Come, I will give you a look at them,
For if you are thinking of buying,
You have no need to go farther;
Here is the best in the street!'
But about one thing be careful

In entering his premises:
Have a mind to your buying;
For Fraud does not show his true colours,
But by subtle flattery
Chalk for cheese he can sell you.
You would think by his language
That the wild nettle he offers
Was a precious rose,
So much courtesy he will show you;
But if you wish to go uncheated,
Have no faith in his pretences.

John Gower, *Mirour de l'Omme*

59. An illustration from the fifteenth-century MS. 'The Ordinall of Alchemy',
by Thomas Norton of Bristol. These alchemists are preparing colours. The
chief one, above, is weighing the ingredients using a balance in a glass case.
His assistants are distilling materials; using small furnaces, retorts and flasks.

HOW TO SUCCEED AS A LAWYER, c. 1376-1379

It is the custom at Westminster
That whose would learn the trade
Of the law, for this purpose needs
Some money, in order to mount up high.
It is a situation to prize:
According to this practice
On money he will grow wise;
If he makes a start with money,
Later on he will know how to use it
To his own advantage and the harm of others:
By means of money his heart
Is turned to the love of money.
The apprentices in their degree
Taste blood from the beginning,
In pleading at the assizes;
Like dogs they seize as their prey
The silver that is given them,
So that always for the penny
They can run well without check;
I do not say without fault,
For wrong that gives a rich fee
Takes from them the scent of the straight course,
So that they often lose track
And run far from charity.
And then after the apprentice
A certain time has fulfilled
What is sufficient for pleading,
He wishes to have the coif placed
Upon his head, and to his own honour
Wishes to bear the name of sergeant.
But if before this time
In one thing he was greedy,
Now is he a thousand times inflamed;
For he becomes so ravenous
That part is not enough for him:
He must devour the whole country.
But they have also a custom
That the apprentice who is so advanced
To the estate of sergeantry
Must make a donation
Of gold, which is not without meaning;

For the gold that he gives means .
That all the rest of his life after
He must be getting it back.
But this will be a great return,
That for giving a single time,
He takes all the bread, by no means holding
The scales in equal balance.

John Gower, *Mirour de l'Omme*

THE VISION CONCERNING ENGLAND, c. 1377

One summer season, when the sun was warm, I rigged myself out in shaggy woollen clothes, as if I were a shepherd, and in the garb of an easy-living hermit I set out to roam far and wide through the world, hoping to hear of marvels. But on a morning in May, among the. Malvern Hills, a strange thing happened to me, as though by magic. For I was tired out by my wanderings, and as I lay down to rest under a broad bank by the side of a stream and leaned over gazing into the water, it sounded so pleasant that I fell asleep.

And I dreamt a marvellous dream. I was in a wilderness, I could not tell where, and looking Eastwards I saw a tower high up against the. sun, and splendidly built on top of a hill; and far beneath it was a great gulf, with a dungeon in it, surrounded by deep, dark pits, dreadful to see. But between the tower and the gulf I saw a smooth plain, thronged with all kinds of people, high and low together, moving busily about their worldly affairs.

Some laboured at plowing and sowing, with no time for pleasure, sweating to produce food for the gluttons to waste. Others spent their lives in vanity, parading themselves in a show of fine clothes. But many, out of love for our Lord and in the hope of Heaven, led strict lives devoted to prayer and penance—for such are the hermits and anchorites who stay in their cells, and are not forever hankering to roam about, and pamper their bodies with sensual pleasures.

Others chose to live by trade, and were much better off—for in our worldly eyes such men seem to thrive. Then there were the professional entertainers, some of whom, I think, are harmless minstrels, making an honest living by their music; but others, babblers and vulgar jesters, are true Judas' children! They invent fantastic tales about themselves, and pose as half-wits, yet they show wit enough whenever it suits them, and could easily work for a living if they had to! I will not say all that St. Paul says about them; it is enough to quote, 'He who talks filth is a servant of the Devil.'

And there were tramps and beggars hastening on their rounds, with their bellies and their packs crammed full of bread. They lived by their wits, and fought over their ale—for God knows, they go to bed glutted with food and drink, these brigands, and get up with foul language and filthy talk; and all day long, Sleep and shabby Sloth are at their heels.

And I saw pilgrims and palmers banding together to visit the shrines at Rome and Compostella. They went on their way full of clever talk, and took leave to tell fibs about it for the rest of their lives. And some I heard spinning such yarns of the shrines they had visited, you could tell by the way they talked that their tongues were more tuned to lying than telling the truth, no matter what tale they told.

Troops of hermits with their hooked staves were on their way to Walsingham, with their wenches following after. These great long lubbers, who hated work, were got up in clerical gowns to distinguish them from laymen, and paraded as hermits for the sake of an easy life.

I saw the Friars there too—all four Orders of them—preaching to the people for what they could get. In their greed for fine clothes, they interpreted the Scriptures to suit themselves and their patrons. Many of these Doctors of Divinity can dress as handsomely as they please, for as their advances, so their profits increase. And now that Charity has gone into business, and become confessor-in-chief to wealthy lords, many strange things have happened in the last few years; unless the Friars and Holy Church mend their quarrel, the worst evil in the world will soon be upon us.

There was also a Pardoner, preaching like a priest. He produced a document covered with Bishops' seals, and claimed to have power to absolve all the people from broken fasts and vows of every kind. The ignorant folk believed him and were delighted. They came up and knelt to kiss his documents, while he, blinding them with letters of indulgence thrust in their faces, raked in their rings and jewellery with his rolled parchment!—So the people give their gold to support these gluttons, and put their trust in dirty-minded scoundrels. If the Bishop were worthy of the name, if he kept his ears open to what went on around him, his seal would not be sent out like this to deceive the people. But it is not by the Bishop's leave that this rogue preaches; for the parish priest is in league with the Pardoner, and they divide the proceeds between them—

money which, but for them, would go to the poor of the parish.

Then I heard parish priests complaining to the Bishop that since the Plague their parishes were too poor to live in; so they asked permission to live in London, where they could traffic in Masses, and chime their voices to the sweet jingling of silver. Bishops and novices, Doctors of Divinity and other great divines—to whom Christ has given the charge of men's souls, and whose heads are tonsured to show that they must absolve, teach, and pray for their parishioners, and feed the poor—I saw them all living in London, even in Lent. Some took posts at Court counting the king's money, or in the Courts of Exchequer and Chancery, where they claimed his dues from the wards of the City and his right to unclaimed property. Others went into the service of lords and ladies, sitting like stewards managing household affairs—and gabbled their daily Mass and Office without devotion. Indeed, I fear that there are many whom Christ, in His great Consistory Court, will curse for ever.

William Langland, *Piers Plowman, c.* 1370

A YEOMAN, 1387

There was a Yeoman with him at his side,
No other servant, so he chose to ride.
This Yeoman wore a coat and hood of green,
And peacock-feathered arrows, bright and keen
And neatly sheathed, hung at his belt the while,
—For he could dress his gear in yeoman style,
His arrows never drooped their feathers low—
And in his hand he bore a mighty bow.
His head was like a nut, his face was brown.
He knew the whole of woodcraft up and down.
A saucy brace was on his arm to ward
It from the bow-string, and a shield and sword
Hung at one side, and at the other slipped
A jaunty dirk, spear-sharp and well-equipped.
A medal of St. Christopher he wore
Of shining silver on his breast, and bore
A hunting-horn, well slung and burnished clean
That dangled from a baldrick of bright green.
He was a proper forester I guess.

Geoffrey Chaucer, *Canterbury Tales,*
prologue translated by Nevill Coghill

THE LIBRARIAN, 1412

. . . the Librarian, who was to be in holy orders, should once a year hand over to the Chancellor and Proctors the keys of the library: if after visitation he was found to be fit in morals, fidelity, and ability he received them back. Should he desire to resign his office a month's notice was required. His salary was fixed at £5 6s. 8d. a year, for which modest sum he not only took charge of the library, but said masses for the souls of benefactors. He was, however, permitted to claim a robe for every beneficed scholar at graduation. There is a special clause stating that the Proctors should be bound to pay the Librarian's salary half-yearly, for the curious, but very excellent, reason that if his pay were in arrears his care and efficiency might slacken. Lest by too great a number of students the books mighty receive damage, or study be hindered, admission was restricted to those who had studied in the schools for eight years, an exception being made in the case of the sons of lords who had seats in Parliament. Moreover, every reader had to subscribe to the following oath: 'You shall swear when you enter the Library of the University, to treat in a reasonable and quiet manner all the books contained therein, and to injure no book maliciously, by erasing, or by detaching sections and leaves. The library was to be open from 9 till 11 and from 2 till 4, except on Sundays and the greater Saints' days; and lest too close attention to his duties might affect his health, the Librarian was to be allowed a month's holiday in the Long Vacation. . . . Lastly, a board was to be suspended in the library on which were to be recorded in a fair and elegant hand the titles of the books, with their donors' names; and all books were to be closed at night and the windows fastened.

Summary of Library Statutes of 1412, Strickland Gibson,
Some Oxford Libraries, 1914

CORN DEALERS, 1419

And whereas some buyers and brokers of corn do buy corn in the City of country folks who bring it to the City to sell, and give, on the bargain being made, a penny or halfpenny by way of earnest; and tell the peasants to take the corn to their house, and that there they shall receive their pay. And when they come there and think to have their payment directly, the buyer says that his wife at his house has gone out, and has taken the key of the room, so that he cannot get at his money; but that the other must go away, and come again soon and receive his pay. And when he comes back a second

60.   A woman's shop offering mirrors, combs, curlers and cosmetics; fifteenth
century.

time, then the buyer is not to be found; or else, if he is found, he
feigns something else, by reason whereof the poor men cannot have
their pay. And sometimes, while the poor men are waiting for their
pay, which was agreed upon, they are told to wait until such a
day as the buyer shall choose to name, or else to take off a part of
the price; which if they will not do, they may take their corn and
carry it away; a thing which they cannot do, because it is wetted,
and in another state than it was in when they sold it. And by such
evil delays on part of the buyer, the poor men lose half of their
pay in expenses before they are fully settled with. It is provided,
that the person towards whom such knavishness shall be committed,
shall make complaint unto the Mayor; and if he shall be able to
make proof, and convict the buyer before the Mayor of the wrong
so done to him, the buyer shall pay the vendor double the value,
and full damages as well, in case the Mayor shall see that the value
aforesaid does not suffice for the damage which he has received;
and nevertheless, let him also be heavily amerced [fined] unto the
King, if he have the means. And if he have not the means of
paying the penalty aforesaid, or of finding the amercement, then
he shall be put in the pillory, and remain there one hour in the
day at least, a Serjeant of the City standing by the side of the
pillory with good hue and cry as to the reason why he is so
punished.

Liber Albus, the White Book of the City of London compiled
in A.D. 1419 by John Carpenter and Richard Whittington,
translated by H. T. Riley

FROM A FIFTEENTH-CENTURY ACCOUNT ROLL, 1425

Building Expenses

To William Hykkedon, working for 4 days making an entrance from the parlour to the Prior's hall, 16d., and for keys bought of John Bette for the same door, 12d., and for hinges, 8d., and to John Coventry with two servants tiling the room called Clykchamber towards the court for 4 days, 3s. 4d., and for 2 iron workers working for 10 days covering with iron the slabs of elm for making the doors and windows, 6s. 8d. And for wainscote bought at Steresbrugge (Stourbridge), 2s. 3d.

To William Skerne and his fellows hired to dig stones for walls at the quarry beyond Crokkewell, 23s. 4d., and to divers men hired to break stones in the Priory for making mortar, 14d., and to John Chepyn for making and cutting 18 corbelstones to place on the aforesaid wall, 5s. 4d. And to John Coventry of Banbury, tiler, for roofing the aforesaid house, 41s. 1d., and for iron standards

61. Fifteenth-century craftsmen; a free-mason and a carpenter proving their skill with a 'masterpiece' before a Gild Warden.

weighing 28lbs. with two ventilators, to wit, vanes of tin bought of the smith at Cherlton to place upon either end of the aforesaid dormitory, 5s. 2d., and to divers men hired to take down and carry away the old timber material and stones, 10d.

Account Roll of the Manors of Miaxter Priory, quoted in Hone, *Manor and Manorial Records*

FROM A FIFTEENTH-CENTURY ACCOUNT ROLL, 1425

Fees with Wages of Servants

For fee of John Langston, steward, holding the court per annum, 26s. 8d. For fee of William Suleman, the Prior's attorney in London, per annum, 6s. 8d.

And for wages of John Baldwyn, the Prior's groom of the chamber, this year 13s. 4d. And for wages of William Puffe, baker, hour (half-day). This was probably the dinner hour, and the strict per annum 15s. And for wages of William Skynner, his assistant, 10s., and for wages of his wife drying malt this year, 10s., And for wages of William Gulde, barber this year, 6s., and for wages of Catherine Colyers making towels for the kitchen this year, 20d., and for wages of the laundress per annum, 6s.

Wages of Labourers

For John Leseby, making fences at the sheepfolds of Wrechwyk and Crockwell, 13d., and to John Soler, cutting 21 cartloads of late coming'; 'for telling of tales'; 'for chiding'; 'for fighting' (half-day); 'for breaking a shovel'; 'for playing'; 'for letting of (obstructing) his fellows' (whole day); 'for keeping of the whole underwood at Bernwood, 3s. 2d., and to a certain stranger hired to drive the plough and harrow for 12 days, 12d.

Account Roll of the Manors of Miaxter Priory, quoted in Hone,, *Manor and Manorial Records*

ARCHITECTURE: WAGES AND DISCIPLINE

The number of men employed varied according to the work, and the season of the year. The wage-books show that the 'masons called freemasons' and the 'masons called hardhewers', were retained all the year round. They received sixpence a day; and the former were allowed their wages on Saints' days, when no work was done; the latter not, except sometimes by special command of the king. Sixpence a day was the rate of wages for all men, except the labourers, who received fourpence or fivepence.

Discipline was very strict, and a system of fines was enforced, by which men who misbehaved themselves lost a whole day, or half a day, for each misdemeanour. A few of these may be cited (from the accounts of Roger Keys, 1448-1449): 'for he lost a shovel'; 'for observance of it by the men seems to have been a grievance with the clerk of the works, for Robert Goodgrome is fined 'for he would keep his hour and never go to work till the clock smight'. His example apparently caused something like a mutiny, for twenty-one men are fined a whole day because 'they would not go to their work till ij of clock, and all maketh Goodgrome'. Another lost three days 'for spoiling of a load of straw'; and another a whole week 'for he will not labour but as he list himself'.

Willis and Clark, *Architectural History of the University of Cambridge*

62. A harvest scene, *c*. 1500. The scene below shows boys throwing sticks at a cock tied to a large stick.

THE BAKERS' STRIKE, 1484

That in the month of December the year aforesaid the Bakers of the said city in great number riotously disposed assembled them and unlawfully conferred, intending the reproach of the said Mayor, suddenly departed out of the said City unto Bakynton, leaving the said City destitute of bread; whereupon not only strangers resorting to the said City and the inhabitants of the same were unvictualled, but also harming the said City and the said Mayor and all the officers thereof. Of which riot divers of the said Bakers were indicted, as· appeareth of record in the said City etc. Which said Bakers coming to a right mind, resorted and came unto the said Mayor and humbly submitted themselves unto his correction. Whereupon they were committed to ward, and their fine assessed by the said Mayor and other Justices of the Peace within the said City at xxli., of which sum xli was given to them again etc., the other xli was received . . . [and to give surety to obey the Mayor's orders and keep the assize for the future, or pay 20s. fine].

The Coventry Leet Book, Early English Text Society

BORROWING MONEY TO MAINTAIN THE HONOUR OF HIS HOUSE 1172-1180

. . . Abbot Hugh was grown old and his eyes waxed somewhat dim. Pious he was and kindly, a strict monk and good, but in the business of this world neither good nor wise. For he trusted those about him overmuch and gave them too much credence, relying always on the wisdom of others rather than his own. Discipline and religion and all things pertaining to the Rule were zealously observed within the cloister; but outside all things were badly handled, and every man did, not what he ought, but what he would, since his lord was simple and growing old. The townships of the Abbot and all the hundreds were given out to farm; the woods were destroyed, the houses of the manors threatened to fall in ruin, and day by day all things went from bad to worse. The Abbot found but one remedy and one consolation—to borrow money, that thus at least he might be able to maintain the honour of his house. No Easter nor Michaelmas came round during the eight years before his death but that one or two hundred pounds were added to his debt; the bonds were continually renewed, and the interest as it grew was turned into capital. This infirmity from the head to the members—from the superior to the subjects. And so it came about that each obedientiary [departmental bursar] had

his own seal and bound himself in debt to Jews and Christians as
he pleased. Often silken copes and flasks of gold and other
ornaments of the church were placed in pawn without the
knowledge of the Convent. I saw a bond given to William Fitz
Isabel for one thousand and forty pounds, and have never known
the why or the wherefore. I saw another bond given Isaac the son
of Rabbi Joce for four hundred pounds, but I know not why; and
yet a third to Benedict the Jew of Norwich for eight hundred and
fourscore; and the cause of this last debt was as follows: our
chamber was fallen in ruin, and the Sacrist, willy-nilly, undertook
to restore it, and secretly borrowed forty marks at interest from
Benedict the Jew and gave him a bond sealed with the seal that
used to hang from the feretory [box of relics] of St. Edmund, and
with which the instruments of the guilds and fraternities used to
be sealed: it was broken up afterwards, at the bidding of the
Convent, but all too late. Now when this debt had increased to one
hundred pounds, the Jew came with letters from our Lord the King
concerning the Sacrist's debt, and at last that which had been
hidden from the Abbot and the Convent was revealed. . . . The
same Jew also held a number of bonds for smaller debts and one
that was of fourteen years' standing, so that the total debt due to
him amounted to twelve hundred pounds not counting the
accumulated interest. . . .
*The Chronicle of Jocelin of Brakelond concerning the Acts of
Samson, Abbot of the Monastery of St Edmund,* translated by
H E. Butler

USURERS IN ENGLAND, 1235

In these days the abominable plague of Caursins [usurers were
called Caursini, or Lombards, because Cahors and other towns
in the South of France competed with those of North Italy in this
practice] raged so fiercely that there was scarce any man in all
England, especially among the prelates, who was not entangled in
their nets. The King himself [Henry III] also was in debt to them
for an incalculable amount. They circumvented the indigent in
their necessities, cloaking their usury under the pretence of trade,
and feigning not to know that whatsoever payment is added to the
principal is usury, under whatsoever name it be called . . .

That same year Roger, Bishop of London, a learned and
religious man, when he saw how these Caursins practised their
usury publicly and unabashed, and led a most unclean life, and
harried Religious folk with divers injustices, cunningly amassing
money and compelling many folk under their yoke, he was moved

to wrath. Then, kindled with righteous zeal, he admonished them all, as schismatics, to cease from these enormities as they loved the salvation of their own souls, and to do penance for the past.

They for their part scorned his words with mockery and derision and threats. Wherefore the Bishop girded on his weapons of spiritual justice and involved them all under a general anathema. Moreover, he strictly and expressly ordered that all such should be removed from the city of London, which had hitherto been free from this plague, lest his diocese should be infected therewith. But the usurers were proud and puffed-up, as men who trusted in the Pope's protection; and indeed, without difficulty or delay, they obtained their own will at the Court of Rome.

The Bishop—an old man, weak and failing in health—was peremptorily cited to cross the sea and appear at Rome before certain judges, friends of the Caursins, whom they themselves had chosen at their will, and to answer for the injury done to the Pope's merchants. The Bishop, willing rather to follow Shem in covering his father's shame than to discover it with Ham, appeased the tumult by peaceful methods, dissembling and passing on. For he commended this arduous cause to his patron St Paul, who had himself written in defence of the strict faith and righteousness 'Though an angel from heaven preach the contrary of these things, let him be accursed'.

Matthew Paris, Chronica Majora, 1235

LIES AND FRAUD IN TRADE

Ye that work in clothing, silks or wool or fur, shoes or gloves or girdles; men can in no wise dispense with you; men must needs have clothing, therefore should ye so serve them as to do your work truly; not to steal half the cloth, or to use other guile, mixing hair with your wool or stretching it out longer, whereby a man thinketh to have gotten good cloth, yet thou hast stretched it to be longer than it should be, and makest a good cloth into useless stuff. Nowadays no man can find a good hat for thy falsehood; the rain will pour down through the brim into his bosom. Even such deceit is there in shoes, in furs, in skins; a man sells an old skin for new; and how manifold are your deceits no man knoweth so well as thou and thy master the devil. . . . Thou, trader, shouldst trust God that He will find thee a livelihood with true winnings, for so much hath He promised thee with His divine mouth. Yet now thou swearest so loudly how good thy wares are, and what profit thou givest the buyer thereby; more than ten or thirty times takest thou the names of all the saints in vain—God and all His saints—

for wares scarce worth five shillings! That which is worth five shillings thou sellest, maybe, sixpence higher than if thou hadst not been a blasphemer of our Lord. Ye yourselves know best what lies and frauds are busy in your trade!

Berthold von Regensburg, *Sermons, c.* 1260

MENDIP SILVER

Know, my lord, that your workmen have found a splendid mine of lead on the Mendips to the east of Priddy, and one that can be opened up with no trouble, being only five or six feet below the ground. And since these workmen are so often thieves, craftily separating the silver from the lead, stealthily taking it away, and when they have collected a quantity fleeing like thieves and deserting their work, as has frequently happened in times past, therefore your bailiffs are causing the ore to be carried to your court at Wookey where there is a furnace built at which the workmen smelt the ore under supervision of certain persons appointed by your steward. And as the steward, bailiffs, and workmen consider that there is a great deal of silver in the lead, on account of its whiteness and sonority [ringing sound], they beg that you will send them as soon as possible a good and faithful workman upon whom they can rely. I have seen the first pieces of lead smelted there, of great size and weight, which when it is struck rings almost like silver, wherefore I agree with the others that if it is faithfully worked the business should prove of immense value to yourself and to the neighbourhood, and if a reliable workman is obtained I think that it would be expedient to smelt the ore where it is dug, on account of the labour of carrying so heavy a material such a distance. The ore is like grains of sand.

A letter from a landreeve to the Bishop of Bath and Wells, in Ancient Correspondence in the Public Record Office, translated by L. F. Salzman, *English Industries in the Middle Ages*

COINAGE, Late Thirteenth Century

. . . there are in the London Mint two persons concerned with keeping the king's dies; one on behalf of the king, whose duty it is to buy the iron and steel, and to have the finished plates conveyed from the smith to the hands of the engraver of the dies, and to deliver the dies engraved duly prepared for use as often as money has to be struck and coined, and to see that the moneyers strike the blanks in view of the public; and another on behalf of John de Botetourt, who is married to the daughter and heir of Thomas FitzOtho, who has the hereditary duty of cutting the king's dies

used throughout England, and receives for the engraving and
fashioning of every dozen dies, seven shillings. It is also his duty to
deface the worn-out dies so that they may not be used again, and
to keep in his hands all the old dies to the use of his master, and
for his fee. But because an indenture is made between these two
keepers, both of the new dies and of the old and worn out ones, and
both of their deliveries and their restitutions, and because it is their
affair to answer to the Barons of the King's Exchequer and to their
Warden how many pounds have been coined with each worn-out
die at London, Canterbury, St. Edmund's, Durham and elsewhere,
when coining has been going on all over Englad by the aforesaid
indenture and by a tally made between the smith, the engraver
and themselves; it is expedient and well worth while that the
Warden of any mint, as often as he sends to London for dies and
receives new dies from the keepers and restores the old ones,
should enrol the day of the receipt of the new dies and the
restitution of the old and the sum of money struck with them, to
the best of his recollection. . . . When the Master of the Mint has
brought the pence, coined, blanched and made ready, to the
place of trial, e.g. the Mint, he must put them all at once on the
counter which is covered with canvas. Then, when the pence have
been well turned over and thoroughly mixed by the hands of the
Master of the Mint and the Changer, let the Changer take a
handful in the middle of the heap, moving round nine or ten
times in one direction or another, until he has taken six pounds.
He must then distribute these two or three times into four heaps,
so that they are well mixed. Then he must weigh out, from these
well mixed pence, three pounds . . . correct to a grain . . . one
pound to the Warden to count, another to the Master of the
Mint, the third to any company or to himself, and they shall
count diligently.

Treatise on the New Money, late thirteenth century, translated in
C. Johnson, *The De Moneta of Nicholas Oresme and English Mint
Documents*, Nelson

PLEADING FOR THE NUMEROUS POOR
The neediest are our neighbours if we give heed to them,
Prisoners in the dungeon, the poor in the cottage,
Charged with a crew of children and with a landlord's rent.
What they win by their spinning to make their porridge with,
Milk and meal, to satisfy the babes,
The babes that continually cry for food—
This they must spend on the rent of their houses;

Aye, and themselves suffer with hunger,
With woe in winter, rising a-nights
In the narrow room to rock the cradle.
Pitiful is it to read the cottage women's woe,
Aye and many another that puts a good face on it,
Ashamed to beg, ashamed to let the neighbours know
All that they need, noontide and evening.
Many the children, and nought but a man's hands
To clothe and feed them; and few pennies come in,
And many mouths to eat the pennies up.
Bread and thin ale are for them a· banquet.
Cold flesh and cold fish are like roast venison;
A farthing's worth of mussels, a farthing's worth of cockles,
Were a feast for them on Friday or fast-days;
It were charity to help these that be at heavy charges,
To comfort the cottager, the crooked and the blind.

> William Langland, *Piers Plowman*, c. 1370

PUNISH THOSE WHO HARM THE POOR

Women that bake and brew, butchers and cooks,
They are the people that harm the poor,
They harm the poor who can but buy in pennyworths,
And privily and oft they poison them.
They grow rich by retailing what the poor should eat;
They buy houses, they become landlords.
If they sold honestly they would not build so high
Nor buy their tenements.
Mayors and their officers, the king's go-betweens
Between the king and the commons to keep the laws,
They should punish these in pillories and stocks.

> William Langland, *Piers Plowman*, c. 1370

Religion

AT CANTERBURY A MONASTIC BATH, c. 1080

On the vigil of Thomas the apostle, if it be not a Sunday, the brethren shall be shaved and let those who will take a bath, in such wise that all shall have taken it two days before Christmas Day. If need be, they may take their bath even on the feast of the apostle. Let the bathing be ordered as follows. On the previous day the abbot or superior should appoint a devout and prudent senior and order him to take charge of the matter, to warn the brethren when to bathe, and to see that they conduct themselves there in an orderly way. This senior shall see that all is ready, and that the right attendants are provided—mature men, neither children nor youths. If he see anything unfitting, let him tell the chamberlain, who shall at once remedy it. Then the senior shall return to the cloister and give notice to as many of the brethren as can be accommodated. Let him take care that the youths and novices go not all together, but with their elders. The brethren whom he has notified shall, when shaved, take their change of clothes and go to the place where the baths are prepared and there, taking off their clothes in due order as they are wont to do in the dormitory, they shall enter the bathing place as directed, and letting down the curtain that hangs before them they shall sit in silence in the bath. If anyone needs anything let him signal for it quietly, and a servant lifting the veil shall quickly take him what he wants and return at once. When he has finished washing himself, he shall not stay longer for pleasure but shall rise and dress and put on his shoes as he does in the dormitory, and having washed his hands shall return to the cloister. The young monks in ward shall go and return with their masters. The brethren may go to the baths at any hour from Prime to Compline, but none shall presume to go without the permission of the brother in charge.

The Monastic Constitutions of Lanfranc, translated by D. Knowles, *Medieval Classics,* Nelson

63. Church of the Holy Sepulchre, Cambridge, early twelfth century. The circular nave is following the fashion of imitating the Church of the Holy Sepulchre in Jerusalem.

THE ORDEAL OF FIRE, Early Twelfth Century

The antiquity [of Glastonbury Abbey], and multitude of its saints, have endued the place with so much sanctity, that, at night, scarcely any one presumes to keep vigil there, or, during the day, to spit upon its floor; he who is conscious of pollution shudders throughout his whole frame: no one ever brought hawk or horses within the confines of the neighbouring cemetery, who did not depart injured either in them or in himself. Within the memory of man, all persons who, before undergoing the ordeal of fire [handling hot iron] or water, there put up their petitions, exulted in their escape, one only excepted: if any person erected a building in the vicinity, which by its shade obstructed the light of the church, it forthwith became a ruin. And it is sufficiently evident, that, the men of that province had no oath more frequent, or more sacred, than to swear by the Old Church, fearing the swiftest vengeance on their perjury in this respect.

William of Malmesbury, *Chronicle of the Kings of England*, translated by J. A. Giles

TITHES

One tenth of the harvest went by right to the Church.

Now about the same time [late twelfth century] there came to pass a thing, which I have also thought worthy of note, namely that a certain man of these parts, one Roger, surnamed Bechet, owed ten stone of wool to his creditor at the time of shearing. Having no more than this amount, he sent the tenth stone, despite the protest of his wife, to his baptismal church of Caereu, and the remaining nine to his creditor at Pembroke, begging him to have patience for he would soon make good the deficiency. Now his creditor, on receiving the wool, weighed it and found the weight to be ten stone; and though he weighed it again and again, he always found the full tale of ten stone; and, so he made answer to his debtor that he had received satisfaction in full. Wherefore by his example, the wool having been miraculously multiplied like the oil of Elisha, many persons on those parts are either converted to the payment of those tithes or confirmed in their readiness to pay.

The Autobiography of Giraldus Cambrensis, edited and translated by H. E. Williams

DORMITORY AT CANTERBURY, Late Twelfth Century

. . . he [a brother] goes to the dormitory and there rests in absolute silence and quiet, so that neither by sound or voice nor by movement of any object does anyone make a noise nor do anything

64. The South Doorway of Kilpeck Church, Herefordshire, 1150-1175.

that may be heard by his neighbour or may in any way be a
nuisance to his brethren. Let him place his habit tidily before his
bed so that he may find it to hand in the morning, and similarly
let him put his footwear at the foot of his bed. If anything is
done or shifted or placed untidily or awkwardly, the watchman,
that is, the monk who remains awake in the dormitory and goes
round often in the night to see if there be anything needing
correction, shall tell of it in the morning at chapter in the presence
of all, and satisfaction shall be made. Therefore we must take care
that nothing be done at night that will be shameful to hear in the
morning. . . .

When day has dawned he should rise straightway when the signal
is heard and take his night shoes and go to the church, and there
say the *Miserere* at the desks until *Deus in adjutorium* is said.
After Prime the seven penitential psalms are straightway said with
the litany and prostration—that is, we prostrate ourselves after the
seven psalms. After the litany and the collects that follow he goes
forthwith to the dormitory and then taking his book, descends into
the cloister, and there sits and studies in his book, each in his
appointed place, until the signal know as the 'shoe-signal' is
heard. Then, shod and carrying knife and comb, he descends again
to the cloister, and putting the books on the seat goes to the
washing-place, and having washed his hands stands again by
his book and combs his hair. Then, book in hand, he goes in order
to church for Terce. . . .

The Monastic Constitutions of Lanfranc

HOLY MEN QUARREL OVER A WINDMILL, 1191

Herbert the Dean set up a windmill on Haberdun; and when the
Abbot heard this, he grew so hot with anger that he would
scarcely eat or speak a single word. On the morrow, after hearing
mass, he ordered the sacrist to send carpenters thither without
delay, pull everything down, and place the timber under safe
custody. Hearing this, the Dean came and said that he had the
right to do this on his free fief, and free benefit of the wind ought
not to be denied to any man; he said also that he wished to grind
his own corn there and not the corn of others, lest perchance he
might be thought to do this to the detriment of neighbouring mills.
To this the Abbot, still angry, made answer, 'I thank you as I
should thank you if you had cut off both my feet. By God's face,
I will never eat bread till that building be thrown down. You are
an old man, and you ought to know that neither the King nor his
Justiciar can change or set up anything within the liberties of this

town without the assent of the Abbot and the Convent. Why have you then presumed to do such a thing? Nor is this thing done without detriment to my mills, as you assert. For the burgesses will throng to your mill and grind their corn there to their heart's content, nor should I have the lawful right to punish them, since they are free men. I would not even allow the Cellarer's mill, which was built of late, to stand, had it not been built before I was Abbot. Go away,' he said, 'go away; before you reach your house, you shall hear what will be done with your mill.' But the Dean, shrinking in fear from the face of the Abbot, by the advice of his son Master Stephen, anticipated the servants of the Abbot and caused the mill which he had built to be pulled down by his own servants without delay, so that, when the servants of the Sacrist came, they found nothing left to demolish.

The Chronicle of Jocelin of Brakelond concerning the Acts of Samson, Abbot of the Monastery of St Edmund,
translated by H. E. Butler

THE CLOCK STRUCK BEFORE MATINS, 1198

There was a wooden platform between the feretory [box for relics] and the High Altar, on which there were two candles, which the guardians of the shrine used to stick and join together in a most unseemly manner by placing one candle on the top of another. And under this platform many things were stored without regard to seemliness, such as flax, thread, wax, and divers utensils; in fact, anything that came into the hands of the guardians was placed there, since the platform had a door and iron walls. So, while the guardians were asleep on the night of the Feast of St. Ethelreda, part of a candle [as is believed] which had been stuck together and had burned down, fell on the aforesaid platform which was covered with cloth, and began to set fire to everything near it both above and below, so that the iron walls were white with the heat. . . . In the same hour the clock struck before Matins, and the master of the vestry, when he arose, perceived and saw the fire, and running with all speed beat upon the board as though to announce a death, and cried with a loud voice that the feretory was burned. And we all of us ran together, and found the flames raging beyond belief and embracing the whole feretory and reaching up nearly to the beams of the Church. So the young men among us ran to get water, some to the well, and others to the clock, while yet others with the utmost difficulty succeeded in extinguishing the fire with their cowls and carried off certain small pyxes [containing the Holy Sacrament], before harm could happen to them. And when cold water was poured upon the front of the feretory, the stones fell and were reduced almost to powder. But the nails, by which the plates of silver were fastened to the feretory fell from the wood, which was burnt beneath them to the thickness of my finger, and the plates hung one from another without any nails to support them. But the golden Majesty on the front of the feretory, together with certain stones, remained firm and intact, and seemed fairer after the fire than it was before, because it was all of gold.

The Chronicle of Jocelin of Brakelond concerning the Acts of Samson, Abbot of the Monastery of St Edmund, translated by H. E. Butler

SIMON, THE ILLITERATE CURATE, 1222

Acts of the Chapter held by William, dean of Salisbury, at Sonning, in the year of our Lord 1222, on the Friday next before the Feast of St Martin. . . . Vitalis, a priest, perpetual vicar of Sonning, presented the chaplain [i.e. curate] named Simon whom he has with him, and whom he lately engaged until Michaelmas. This Simon, examined as to his Orders, said that he was ordained

65. A fresco of souls falling from a ladder into the arms of demons, painted on the west wall of the church of St Peter and St. Paul, Chaldon, Surrey, *c.* 1200.

archdeacon at Oxford by a certain Irish bishop named Albin, then
suffragan to the Bishop of Lincoln, from whom also he received
deacon's orders; and those of priest from Hugh [of Wells] now
Bishop of Lincoln, four years past. He was examined in the Gospel
of the first Sunday in Advent, and was found insufficient, and
unable to understand what he read. Again he was tried in the
Canon of the Mass, at the words *Te igitur, clementissime Pater,*
etc. He knew not the case of *Te,* nor by what word it was governed;
and when we bade him look closely which could most fittingly
govern it he replied: '*Pater,* for He governeth all things.' We asked
him what *clementissime* was, and what case, and how declined, he
knew not. We asked him what *clemens* was; he knew not.
Moreover, the said Simon knew no difference between one antiphon
and another, nor the chant of the hymns, nor even of the hymn
nocte surgentes, nor did he know by heart aught of the service
or psalter. Moreover, he said that it seemed indecent that he
should be examined before the Dean, since he was already in Holy
Orders. We asked him where he was when he received his priest's
Orders: he answered that he had forgotten. He is amply illiterate.

Register of St Osmund, edited by W. H. R. Jones

THE ARRIVAL OF THE FRANCISCANS IN ENGLAND, 1224

In the year 1224 the Friars Minor first landed in England at
Dover; four clerics and five lay-brethren. . . . These nine were
charitably conveyed over to England by the monks of Fécamp, and
hospitably provided with all necessaries. At Canterbury, they abode
two days at the Cathedral Priory; then four went forth to London,
and the other five repaired to the Priests' Spital, where they abode
until they had found an habitation. Soon afterwards, a little room
was granted unto them within the school-house. Here, from day to
day, they sat almost continually enclosed; but at eventide, when
the scholars were gone home, the friars came into their chamber
and lit their fire and sat by the hearth. Here, when the time of
Collation came, they sometimes set on the fire a pot full of beer-
dregs, wherein they dipped a bowl and drank all round, each
saying some word of edification. And (as one hath borne witness
who was of the same pure simplicity, and who was found worthy
to share and partake in holy poverty) their drink was at times so
thick that, when the bowl had to be warmed, they poured water in,
and thus drank cheerfully. The like frequently befell them at
Sarum, where the brethren so jocundly and joyfully drank their
dregs round the kitchen fire at Collation, that each thought

himself happy to snatch them in friendly fashion from the other. It befell also that two brethren came in great distress to one friary, when there was no beer in the house. Then the Warden, taking counsel with the elder brethren, let them borrow a gallon of beer; yet on such terms that the friars of the house, who were entertaining the guests, should make but a false show of drinking thereof, for charity's sake. Even in the London friary, I myself have seen the brethren drink beer so sour, that some preferred water; and I have seen them eat the bread called *tourte* in vulgar parlance. Moreover, when there was no bread I have for some time eaten porridge of spelt [grain] there, in the presence of the Provincial Minister and the guests.

But the four brethren aforesaid, proceeding to London, abode with the Friars Preachers, who received them kindly, and with whom they dwelt fifteen days, eating and drinking of what was set before them as most familiar guests. Then they hired for themselves a house in Cornhill, wherein they built cells, stuffing the partitions with grass. Here they dwelt in their first simplicity until the next summer, without any chapel, for as yet they had no privilege of setting up an altar and celebrating divine service. Here did the sweet Lord Jesus sow that grain of mustard-seed which afterwards became greater than all herbs. It is worthy of note that, in the thirty-second year from the advent of the Friars Minor to England, the brethren living in the English province were numbered at 1,242, in forty-nine friaries.

The first to be received was a youth of great promise, pre-eminent in bodily beauty, brother Solomon. He was wont to tell me that, while he was yet a novice, the care of the temporal things was committed unto him, and he went to beg alms at his sister's house. She, bringing him a loaf, turned away her face, and said 'Cursed be the hour that I ever set eyes on thee!' but he took the bread cheerfully and went his way. He kept so strictly to the prescribed form of extreme poverty, that he sometimes suffered so from cold as to seem on the point of death; and the brethren, having no other means of warming him, were inspired by holy charity to excogitate a pious subtlety; for they all gathered together and warmed him by pressing him to their bosom, as her litter lieth about a sow. [One day] the brethren ate at the table of the Archbishop and came home barefoot to the Canterbury friary, through snow so deep that all who saw it shuddered to see them go. After this [brother Solomon] was taken with an infirmity of one foot, whereof he lay sick in London for two years, so that he could scarcely move from place to place but if another would bear him. In his infirmity he was honoured with a visit from brother Jordan of holy memory, Master of the whole Order of Friars Preachers, who said unto him: 'Brother, be not ashamed if the Father of our Lord Jesus Christ draw thee to Himself by one foot.' When therefore he had thus lain a long while in the cellar, where he had not been able to hear mass (for the brethren sang no mass in the friary, but went to hear divine service and to sing their masses in the parish church), then his infirmity became so desperate that, as the surgeons judged, his foot must needs be cut off. But, when the axe was brought, and the foot had been bared, a little blood and matter came forth, which promised some hope; wherefore that hard judgment was deferred for a while. Meanwhile he conceived a certain hope that, if he were led to some saint, he might recover his foot and his health. Wherefore, when brother Agnello [the Provincial minister] came, he bade that brother Solomon should be taken to some shrine beyond the sea without delay, and as conveniently as might be. It came to pass, then, that his faith belied him not; nay rather, he waxed so strong as to walk without crutch, and to celebrate mass. At Cambridge, the Brethren were received first by the burghers of the town, who granted unto them the Old Synagogue, hard by the Castle. But, seeing that the neighbourhood of the prison was intolerable to them (for the gaolers and the brethren had but one door of entrance) the king gave them ten marks wherewith to buy a rent which should satisfy his exchequer for the rent of their site; and thus the brethren built a chapel so miserably poor that a single carpenter in one day made and set up 14 pairs of rafters.

Thomas of Eccleston, *Chronicle,* translated and abridged by
G. G. Coulton, *Social Life in Britain from the Conquest
to the Reformation*

FRANCISCANS AND DOMINICANS, c. 1240

And that the world might not appear to be devoid of increasing troubles on every side, a controversy arose between the Minorite brothers [Franciscans] and Preachers [Dominicans], to the astonishment of many, because they seemed to have chosen perfection's path, viz. that of poverty and patience. On one side the Preachers declared that they were instituted first, and on that account more worthy; that they were also more decent in their apparel, and had deservedly obtained their name and office from their preaching, and that they were more truly distinguished by the

66. A nunnery in the thirteenth century.

apostolic dignity: on the other side, the Minorites gave answer, that they had embraced, for God, a way of living more rigorous and humble, and so the more worthy, because more holy; and that the brothers could and certainly ought to pass over from the order of Preachers to their order, as from an inferior community to one more rigorous and superior. The Preachers contradicted them to their face, saying, that though the Minorites went barefooted, coarsely clad, and girded with a rope, the privilege of eating flesh or a more delicate article of diet was not denied them even in public, a thing which is forbidden to the community of Preachers, wherefore it could not be allowed that the Preachers could enter the order of Minorites, as one more rigorous and more worthy, but quite the contrary. Therefore, between these, even as between the Templars and Hospitallers, in the Holy Land, through the enemy to the human race sowing the seeds of dissension, a great and scandalous strife arose; and inasmuch as it was between learned men and scholars, it was more dangerous to the Catholic Church, and a sign of great judgment impending at its threshold. And what is terrible, and a sad presage, for three or four hundred years, or more, the monastic order did not hasten to destruction so quickly as their order, of whom now, the brothers, twenty-four years having scarcely elapsed, had first built in England dwellings which rivalled regal palaces in height. These are they who daily expose to view their inestimable treasures, in enlarging their sumptuous edifices, and erecting lofty walls, thereby impudently transgressing the limits of their original poverty, and violating the basis of their religion, according to the prophecy of the German Hildegarde. When noblemen and rich men are at the point of death, whom they know to be possessed of great riches, they, in their love of gain, diligently urge them, to the injury and loss of the ordinary pastors, and extort confessions and hidden wills, lauding themselves and their own order only, and placing themselves before all others. So no faithful man now believes he can be saved, except he is directed by the counsels of the Preachers and Minorites. Desirous of obtaining privileges in the courts of kings and potentates, they act the parts of councillors, chamberlains, treasurers, bridegrooms, and mediators for marriages; they are the executors of the papal extortions; in their sermons they either are flatterers, or most cutting reprovers, revealers of confessions, or impudent accusers. Despising, also, the authentic orders which were instituted by the holy fathers, namely, by St. Benedict and St. Augustine, and also the followers of them (as the thing clearly appears in the case of the church of

Scarborough, when the Minorites shamefully retreated), they set their own community before the rest. They look upon the Cistercian monks as clownish, harmless, half-bred, or rather ill-bred, priests; and the monks of the Black order as proud epicures.

Matthew Paris, *Historia Anglorum,* edited by J. A. Giles

RESPECT FOR GRAVEYARDS, 1240

We believe that graveyards, containing those who are to be saved of whom many are purged and await the robe of glory, are befouled by brute beasts. We therefore enjoin that they be decently enclosed with a hedge or wall. Those responsible are to be compelled thereto by the law of the church.

Also we forbid rectors and priests of churches to feed beasts at the church gates or to let them enter under pain of heavy punishment.

For the respect of both graveyard and church we forbid the holding of markets, the hearing of lawcases concerning blood, and the performance of dishonourable games in graveyards or other holy places, or indeed anyway else on Sundays. This especially applies to the eves of saints days and church feasts, for it rebounds rather to the dishonour than the honour of saints. . . . Nor are any buildings to be raised in churchyards save perhaps in time of war; and if such are made they are to be demolished.

Constitutions of Walter de Cantilupe, Bishop of Worcester, 1240. D. Wilkins, *Concilia Magnae Britanniae et Hiberniae,* 1737

A SERMON TO OXFORD UNDERGRADUATES, 1293

For the serpent said: 'Why are you forbidden to eat of every tree of paradise?' And Eve answered: 'Lest by chance we die.' But the serpent said: 'By no means, but you shall be like gods.' Is not that just the way some go on nowadays, seducing others? 'Why are you forbidden to go into taverns, to play after curfew, to go into the houses of lay folk?' One will reply: 'Lest by chance I am excommunicated or imprisoned or some such evil befall me.' 'By no means,' says another, 'let us go and play; don't let us give it up for such reasons.' And so they draw many after them and deceive them. I have heard this year about some who have in this way persuaded others to play and led them into thieving, have gone to the tavern and then drawn them to the brothel, have persuaded them to a trial of strength and have ended up with manslaughter. I have even found this to be true, that some have

67. The nave of Canterbury Cathedral by Henry Yevele, thirteenth century.

led their friends to the tavern, and when they have got there, others have tried to cut their throats. . . . For who are more obstinate nowadays than clerks? Who is there among the laity that is not kept from evil by the fear of punishment or loss? Who that does not fear the sentence of excommunication? But clerks fear neither the temporal nor spiritual penalty nor excommunication. . . . Remember, O clerk, chosen to God's lot. Your friends perhaps have worked hard to maintain you in the schools, that you may profit yourself and others. Now you are neither profiting yourself nor others, nay you are only hurting them and wasting your parents' money in evil uses. Those who used to have hope of your promotion have now given you up in despair.

> Simon of Ghent, Chancellor of Oxford, Sermon on Ash Wednesday, 1293, *Oxford Theology and Theologians*

ELECTION OF THE ARCHBISHOP OF CANTERBURY IN 1313

Because I made mention above of the death of the Archbishop of Canterbury, I turn now to his successor and the manner of his succession. On the death of the primate, the prior and convent of Christ Church, Canterbury, proceeded to an election, and by a unanimous vote chose Mr. Thomas de Cobham, a nobleman, and a doctor of canon and civil law who at once set out and crossed the sea to prosecute his cause. He was hindered by two circumstances. While the primate was still on his sick-bed the pope had sent his bull reserving for himself the disposition of the archbishopric and the choice of the next pontiff. Also the King of England sent to the pope, praying him that he should see fit to promote his clerk the Bishop of Worcester to the archiepiscopal see. For these reasons the archbishop-elect was frustrated, nor could the assent of the electors profit him, for at the king's instance, and, it is believed, after a large sum had passed, the lord pope granted the archbishopric and set the said bishop over the English church.

O what a difference there was between the elect and the 'preferred'! For the elect was the very flower of Kent, of noble stock; he had lectured in arts and on canon law, and was a master of theology; a man eminently fitted for the see of Canterbury. The bishop, on the other hand, had recently been a mere clerk and was scarcely literate, but he excelled in theatrical presentations, and through this obtained the king's favour. Thus he was taken into the king's household, and soon became the king's treasurer, and from the treasury became Bishop of

Worcester, later Chancellor, and lo! now he is made Archbishop.
Some are surprised at the man's good luck, but I rather am
surprised at the lord pope, why he should reject so excellent a
person, and deliberately adopt an unsuitable one, when the
merits of each were clearly known to him. But My Lady Money
transacts all business in the Curia. If perchance you are ignorant
of the habit and customs of the Roman Curia, pay heed to this.
It loves causes, law suits, quarrels, because they cannot be
expedited without money; and a case once entered upon at Rome
becomes almost immortal .. . .

Life of Edward II, edited by N. Denholm-Young

THE FLAGELLANTS

In the same year [of the Plague] 1349, about Michaelmas, more
than six score men came through Flanders to London, mostly
from Zealand and Holland. These scourged themselves twice a
day in the sight of the people, some in St. Paul's cathedral and
others in other parts of the city; and this was the manner of
their penance. From the waist to the heels they were wrapped in
linen cloth, leaving all the rest of their body naked; each wore
on his head a cap marked before and behind with a red cross;
each in his right hand bare a scourge with three lashes, and in each
lash a knot, from the midst whereof stood out hither and
thither sharp points like needles. Thus then, in the midst of the
procession, these penitents followed one after the other, barefooted,
lashing their bare and bleeding bodies with these scourges
aforesaid, while four of them sang a chant in their own tongue, to
which four others answered at the end, after the fashion of a
Christian Litany. Then, in this procession, all together fell thrice
to the ground, where they lay with hands outstretched in the form
of a cross, chanting all the while as before; and at last each of
these prostrate penitents, stepping over his fellow, smote him with
the scourge there as he lay; and thus from one to the other, from
the first even unto the last; after which each clad himself in his
daily garb, and, with their caps still on their heads, they returned
to their lodgings. And this same penance, it is said, they repeated
every night also.

Robert of Avesbury, *Historia Edwardi Tertii*,
edited by T. Hearne, 1720

LOLLARDS

William Smith, so called from his trade, had an insignificant and
ugly person. Being crossed in love, he renounced all pleasures, and

68.   A brass of Sir John and Lady Harsick, 1384.

became a vegetarian and a total abstainer . . . he taught the
alphabet and did clerking. Various knights used to go round
protecting him from any harm for his profane teaching, for they
had zeal for God but were uninstructed, for they believed what
they heard from the false prophets . . . and when one of them
would come to the neighbourhood of any of them to preach, they
would promptly assemble the local folk with a great ado at some
fixed place or church even if people did not want to but did not
dare to object. . . . They would attend the sermon with sword
and buckler to stop any objections to the blasphemy.

One Richard Waytestathe, priest, and this William Smith, used
to have spells at St. John Baptist's chapel outside Leicester near
the leper hospital. Here other sectaries met for their
conventicles . . . for there was a hostelry and lodging for that
kind of visitor and there they had a school of malignant
doctrines and opinions and a clearing-house of heresy. The chapel
had been dedicated to God but it was now an asylum for
blasphemers who hated Christ's church. Once these two, Richard
the priest, and William Smith, wanted a meal of herbs. They had
the herbs but no fire. One peered into a corner of the chapel and
saw an old image made in honour of St. Catherine, painted
standing up. 'Look, dearly beloved brother,' said he, 'God has
given us kindling to cook our meal. This will make a saintly
fire.' So axe and flame wrought a new martyrdom, if in the
heavenly kingdom the cruelty of modern torturers can make
itself felt. This Lollard sect hated images and worked against
them calling them idols. . . . If anyone mentioned St. Mary of
Lincoln or St. Mary of Walsingham they would call them names
like 'wiche of Lincolle', and 'wiche of Walsyngham'. So one took
the axe and the other took the image, saying, 'Let's test if it's
really a saint, for if it bleeds when we knock the head off we'll
have to adore it, but if not it can feed our fire and cook our
vegetables.' When they came out they could not hide their shame,
but gave themselves away to their cost by boasting about it as
funny. They were soon after turned out of the inn. . . .

The number of people with such beliefs multiplied fast and
filled the kingdom and they became very bold. . . . They were
called followers of Wycliffe, Wychiffes or Lollards. . . . At the
beginning the leaders of this dreadful sect used to wear russet
clothes mostly, to show outwardly an inward simplicity of heart
and thus exercise a subtle attraction, like wolves in sheep's
clothing, in undyed wool. . . . They gained to their sect half or
more than half the people, some genuinely, others intimidated or

shamed into it, for they magnified their adherents as praiseworthy.
. . . They always claimed to act under 'Goddislawe'.

Even the very recently converted strangely acquired a standard
way of speaking in accordance with their tenets, and this change of
language acted on Doctors and women alike. . . . It divided families
and neighbour from neighbour. . . . They were very argumentative
with plenty to say. . . .

There was at Leicester a priest call William de Swynderby
whom the people called a hermit because he once lived as such.
His antecedents are unknown, but it is remarkable how unstable
were his life and manners, ever chopping and changing. . . .
First he preached against female vanity and dress. Although they
behaved well he did not know how to stop, and at last he made
the women of the town, good and bad, so cross that they decided
to stone him out of town. Seeing his theme unprofitable he turned
his sermons against the merchants saying a rich man could not
enter the kingdom of God. He doled out this stuff so often that but
for God's mercy he would have reduced some worthy man to the
sin of desperation. Then he turned hermit, as preaching had not
helped him. He lived for a while at a hermitage in the duke's
wood, sometimes trotting into the town or the country. The
pious of Leicester took the trouble to bring him food as usual,
he must needs refuse it saying that what little he had with the
duke's help would suffice. He began to run short and to be bored,
but shame kept him from moving back to town. He managed to
get taken into the abbey there for a time, for the canons put
him in a room in the church because they had hopes of his
holiness and they supplied him like the other priests. At that
time he visited the country churches. . . . He joined up with
William Smith at St. John Baptist's by the leper hospital and
associated there with other Wycliffes. At that time the sect was
growing so much in repute and number that you could hardly see
two people in the street but one was a Wycliffe. He saw that his
usual kinds of sermons were unpopular and did not attract
converts; so he levelled them against the clergy saying they were
bad, and, as the rest of the sect, said parishioners need not pay
tithes to the impure, to non-residents, or those prevented from
teaching and preaching by ignorance or inaudibility, for the other
Wycliffes said tithes were a voluntary gift and payment to
evil-livers was connivance. He also preached that men might ask
for payment of debt but not sue or imprison for it, that
excommunication for non-payment of tithes was extortion and
that one who lived contrary to God's law was no priest though

69.   People setting off on a pilgrimage in the fourteenth century.

ordained.

Such and other teachings and heresies pleased the people and won their affection. They said they had never seen or heard such an exponent of truth and they loved him like another God.

John Bukkyngham, Bishop of Lincoln, had wind of this and promptly suspended him from all preaching in chapel, church or graveyard. excommunicating any who should listen to him and sending notices of this to various churches. William set himself up a pulpit between two millstones which stood for sale outside the chapel in the High Street, to preach 'in the High Street in the bishop's teeth so long as he have the people's love'. You would have seen crowds from all over the town and country flocking to hear him more than even before the excommunication. The bishop summoned him to appear in Lincoln Cathedral. . . . There he was publicly convicted of heresies and errors and richly deserved to be food for fire. Then his followers cast their hands and heads in wailing to the walls, for many Leicester people would have gone to succour him, though in vain. That day the pious Duke of Lancaster happened to be at Lincoln and he often

protected the Lollards, for their smooth tongues and faces
tricked him and others into thinking them saints of God. He
persuaded the bishop to give William a different sentence. . . .

Henry Knighton, Chronicle, c. 1363

PARSON SLOTH

I have been priest and parson for thirty winters past,
But I cannot solfa or sing, or read a Latin life of saints;
But I can find a hare, in a field or in a furrow,
Better than construe the first Psalm or explain it to the parish.
I can hold a friendly meeting, I can cast a shire's accounts,
But in mass-book or Pope's edict I cannot read a line.

William Langland, Piers Plowman, c. 1370

A TYPICAL PILGRIM

In pilgrim's dress apparelled, he had a staff in his hand,
Bound with broad list like bindweed twisted round it,
A bowl and bag he bare at his side,
And on his hat a hundred flasks of lead,
Many a cross from Sinai, scallop-shells of Spain,
Cross-keys from Rome, and the portraiture of Christ,
Signs of his pilgrimage, that men might know his saints.
The folk required of him whence he had come.
'From Sinai', says he, 'and from our Lord's Sepulchre,
Bethlehem, Babylon, Alexandria, Armenia, and Damascus;
Ye may see by my signs that be upon my hat
Good saints have I sought for my soul's health,
Walking full wide in wet and dry.'

William Langland, Piers Plowman, c. 1370

THE SERF AT THE CONFESSIONAL, c. 1380

Let peasants and serfs be questioned [in the confessional] whether
they have defrauded by withholding or diminishing their tithes,
either of produce or of personal labour: whether they have failed
in reverence to their lords, or have not provided for them in their
necessity: whether they have withheld their bounden service to
their lords; whether they have held markets, or done any
servile work, on holy days, against the precept of the Church . . .
whether they have encroached on their neighbours' ground with
plough or with cattle. Moreover both peasants and serfs and
artisans commonly sin in this: that they will labour fervently
before a man's face, but feebly and remissly behind his back;
and then, if they be rebuked, they will murmur or withdraw from

the work or labour all the worse.

John de Burgo, *Pupilla Oculi,* handbook for medieval clergy

70. Leaden pilgrim's badge of St. Thomas à Becket from the River Thames at Dowgate. The badge is mid-fourteenth century.

THE 'ABSURD' PREACHING OF JOHN BALL, 1381

There happened great commotions among the lower orders in England by which that country was nearly ruined. In order that this disastrous rebellion may serve as an example to mankind, I will speak of all that was done from the information I had at the time. It is customary in England, as well as in several other countries, for the nobility to have great privileges over the commonalty; that is to say, the lower orders are bound by law to plough the lands of the gentry, to harvest their grain, to carry it home to the barn, to thrash and winnow it; they are also bound to harvest and carry home the hay. All these services the prelates and gentlemen exact of their inferiors; and in the counties of Kent, Essex, and Bedford, these services are more oppressive than in other parts of the kingdom. In consequence of this the evil disposed in these districts began to murmur, saying, that in the beginning of the world there were no slaves, and that no one ought to be treated as such, unless he had committed treason against his lord, as Lucifer had done against God; but they had done no such thing, for they were neither angels nor spirits, but men formed after the same likeness as these lords who treated them as beasts. This they would bear no longer; they were determined to be free, and if they laboured or did any work, they would be paid for it. A crazy priest in the county of Kent, called John Ball, who for his absurd preaching had thrice been confined in prison by the Archbishop of Canterbury, was greatly instrumental in exciting these rebellious ideas. Every Sunday after mass, as the people were coming out of church, this John Ball was accustomed to assemble a crowd around him in the market-place and preach to them. On such occasions he would say, 'My good friends, matters cannot go on well in England until all things shall be in common; when there shall be neither vassals nor lords; when the lords shall be no more masters than ourselves. How ill they behave to us! for what reason do they hold us thus in bondage? Are we not all descended from the same parents, Adam and Eve? And what can they show, or what reason can they give, why they should be more masters than ourselves? They are clothed in velvet and rich stuffs, ornamented with ermine and other furs, while we are forced to wear poor clothing. They have wines, spices and fine bread, while we have only rye and the refuse of the straw; and when we drink it must be water. They have handsome seats and manors, while we must brave the wind and rain in our labours in the field; and it is by our labour they have wherewith to support their

71. Corpus Christi procession, *c.* 1400.

pomp. We are called slaves, and if we do not perform our
service we are beaten, and we have no sovereign to whom we can
complain or who would be willing to hear us. Let us go to the
king and remonstrate with him; he is young, and from him we
may obtain a favourable answer, and if not we must ourselves
seek to amend our condition.' With such language as this did
John Ball harangue the people in his village every Sunday after
mass. The archbishop, on being informed of it, had him arrested
and imprisoned for two or three months by way of punishment;
but the moment he was out of prison, he returned to his former
course. Many in the city of London, envious of the rich and
noble, having heard John Ball's preaching, said among themselves
that the country was badly governed, and that the nobility had
seized upon all the gold and silver. These wicked Londoners,
therefore, began to assemble in parties, and to show signs of
rebellion; they also invited all those who held like opinions in

the adjoining counties to come to London; telling them that they would find the town open to them and the commonalty of the same way of thinking as themselves, and that they would so press the king, that there would no longer be a slave in England.

By this means the men of Kent, Essex, Sussex, Bedford, and the adjoining counties, in number about 60,000, were brought to London, under command of Wat Tyler, Jack Straw, and John Ball. This Wat Tyler, who was chief of the three, had been a tiler of houses—a bad man and a great enemy to the nobility.

Jean Froissart, *Chronicles*

SORCERY, 1382

On the 26th day of March, in the 5th year etc., Henry Pot, a *Duchysman,* was attached to make answer, as well to the Mayor and Commonalty of the City of London, as to Nicholas Freman, and Cristina, his wife, in a plea of deceit and falsehood etc.: as to which, the same Nicholas and Cristina made plaint, that whereas one Simon Gardiner had lately lost a mazer cup, the said Henry came to him, and promised that he would let him know who had stolen the cup, and so cause him to regain it. And hereupon, the same Henry made 32 balls of white clay, and over them did sorcery, or his magic art: which done, he said that the same Cristina had stolen the cup; falsely and maliciously lying therein, and unjustly defaming the said Nicholas and Cristina to their manifest scandal and disgrace, and to their grievance.

And the same Henry, being questioned how he would acquit himself thereof, of his own accord acknowledged that he could not deny the same, but expressly admitted that he had done in manner aforesaid. And because that he thus acknowledged the same, and confessed that he had many times before practised divers like sorceries, both within the city aforesaid and without, through which various persons had undeservedly suffered injury in their character and good name; and because that sorcery, or the art magic, manifestly redounds against the doctrine of Sacred Writ; it was awarded that the same Henry should be put upon the pillory, there to remain for one hour of the day. And the Sheriffs were ordered to have proclamation made as to the reason for the same.

Letter Books, in H. T. Riley, *Memorials of London*

SCRUTINY FOR HERESY AT CAMBRIDGE

In the year of Our Lord 1384, this compilation was examined at

Cambridge in this manner. While it was left there by a certain priest, in order to be bound, it was carefully looked at by certain scholars, and read through and presented to the Chancellor of the University and his Council, in order to be examined for defects and heresies, lest the unlearned should carelessly deceive the people through its means, and fallaciously lead them into various errors. Then by command of the Chancellor, before him and the whole Council of the University, it was examined for four days with all care and diligence, and tested in every college on every side, and on the fifth day all the doctors of both laws and the masters of theology, together with the Chancellor, declared and affirmed that it was well and subtly drawn out of the sacred laws and divine books, and that it was alleged, affirmed and founded on the Wherwell, and St. Mary's, Winchester, after his visitation in 1387 authority of all the Doctors of the Sacred Page. Therefore whoever you are, O reader, do not despise this work, because without a doubt, if any defects had been found in it, it would have been burnt before the University of Cambridge.

'*Speculum Vitae*', MS. Bodley 446 folio 1, quoted and translated by W. A. Pantin, *The English Church in the Fourteenth Century*

FRIVOLOUS THINGS IN CHURCH

Item—whereas we have convinced ourselves by clear proofs that some of the nuns of your house bring with them to church birds, rabbits, hounds, and such like frivolous things, whereunto they give more heed than to the offices of the church, with frequent hindrance to their psalmody and that of their fellow-nuns, and to the grievous peril of their souls—therefore we strictly forbid you all and several, in virtue of the obedience due unto Us, that ye presume henceforward to bring to church no birds, hounds, rabbits or other frivolous things that promote indiscipline. . . .

Item—whereas, though hunting-dogs and other hounds abiding within your monastic precincts, the alms that should be given to the poor are devoured, and the church and cloister and other places set apart for divine and secular services are foully defiled, contrary to all honesty—and whereas, through their inordinate noise, divine service is frequently troubled—there we strictly command and enjoin you, Lady Abbess, that you remove these dogs altogether, and that you suffer them never henceforth nor any other such hounds, to abide within the precincts of your nunnery.

Injunctions of Bishop Wykeham to the nunneries of Romsey, Wherwell, and St. Mary's, Winchester, after his visitation in 1387

72. A bishop in the fifteenth century baptizing a child.

FOURTEENTH-CENTURY PILGRIMAGE

Then people long to go on pilgrimages
And palmers long to seek the stranger strands
Of far-off saints, hallowed in sundry lands,
And specially, from every shire's end
In England, down to Canterbury they wend
To seek the holy blissful martyr, quick
In giving help to them when they were sick.
  It happened in that season that one day
In Southwark, at The Tabard, as I lay
Ready to go on pilgrimage and start
For Canterbury, most devout at heart,
At night there came into that hostelry
Some nine and twenty in a company
Of sundry folk happening then to fall
In fellowship, and they were pilgrims all
That towards Canterbury meant to ride.

Geoffrey Chaucer, *Canterbury Tales, Prologue*,
translated by Nevill Coghill

THE PARSON

A holy-minded man of good renown
There was, and poor, the Parson to a town,
Yet he was rich in holy thought and work.
He also was a learned man, a clerk,
Who truly knew Christ's gospel and would preach it
Devoutly to parishioners, and teach it.
Benign and wonderfully diligent,
And patient when adversity was sent
(For so he proved in great adversity)
He much disliked extorting tithe or fee,
Nay rather he preferred beyond a doubt
Giving to poor parishioners round about
From his own goods and Easter offerings.
He found sufficiency in little things.
Wide was his parish, with houses far asunder,
Yet he neglected not in rain or thunder,
In sickness or in grief to pay a call
On the remotest whether great or small
Upon his feet, and in his hand a stave.
This noble example to his sheep he gave,
First following the word before he taught it,
And it was from the gospel he had caught it.

73. Peasants paying their tithes in 1479. One offers a goose, another a lamb.

This little proverb he would add thereto
That if gold rust, what then will iron do?
For if a priest be foul in whom we trust
No wonder that a common man should rust;
And shame it is to see—let priests take stock—
A shitten shepherd and a snowy flock.
The true example that a priest should give
Is one of cleanness, how the sheep should live.
He did not set his benefice to hire
And leave his sheep encumbered in the mire
Or run to London to earn easy bread
By singing masses for the wealthy dead,
Or find some Brotherhood and get enrolled.
He stayed at home and watched over his fold
So that no wolf should make the sheep miscarry.
He was a shepherd and no mercenary.
Holy and virtuous he was, but then
Never contemptuous of sinful men,
Never disdainful, never too proud or fine,
But was discreet in teaching and benign.
His business was to show a fair behaviour
And draw men thus to Heaven and their Saviour,
Unless indeed a man were obstinate;
And such, whether of high or low estate,
He put to sharp rebuke to say the least.
I think there never was a better priest.
He sought no pomp or glory in his dealings,
No scrupulosity had spiced his feelings.
Christ and His Twelve Apostles and their lore
He taught, but followed it himself before.

Geoffrey Chaucer, *Canterbury Tales, Prologue,*
translated by Nevill Coghill

A PRIORESS

There also was a Nun, a Prioress;
Simple her way of smiling was and coy.
Her greatest oath was only 'By St. Loy!'
And she was known as Madame Eglantyne.
And well she sang a service, with a fine
Intoning through her nose, as was most seemly,
And she spoke daintily in French, extremely,
After the school at Stratford-atte-Bowe;
French in the Paris style she did not know.

At meat her manners were well taught withal;
No morsel from her lips did she let fall,
Nor dipped her fingers in the sauce too deep;
But she could carry a morsel up and keep
The smallest drop from falling on her breast.
For courtliness she had a special zest.
And she would wipe her upperlip so clean
That not a trace of grease was to be seen
Upon the cup when she had drunk; to eat,
She reached a hand sedately for the meat.
She certainly was very entertaining,
Pleasant and friendly in her ways, and straining
To counterfeit a courtly kind of grace,
A stately bearing fitting to her place,
And to seem dignified in all her dealings.
As for her sympathies and tender feelings,
She was so charitably solicitous
She used to weep if she but saw a mouse
Caught in a trap, if it were dead or bleeding.
And she had little dogs she would be feeding
With roasted flesh, or milk, or fine white bread.
Sorely she wept if one of them were dead
Or someone took a stick and made it smart;
She was all sentiment and tender heart.
Her veil was gathered in a seemly way,
Her nose was elegant, her eyes glass-grey;
Her mouth was very small, but soft and red,
And certainly she had a well-shaped head.
Almost a span across the brows, I own;
She was indeed by no means undergrown.
Her cloak I noticed, had a graceful charm.
She wore a coral trinket on her arm,
A set of beads, the gaudies tricked in green,
Whence hung a golden brooch of brightest sheen
On which there first was graven a crowned A,
And lower, *Amor vincit omnia*.

> Geoffrey Chaucer, *Canterbury Tales, Prologue*,
> translated by Nevill Coghill

THE LANGUAGE OF CARVING, 1508

The termes of a Kerver be as here followeth:
Breke that dere—lesche that braune—rere that goose—lyste that
swanne—sauce that capon—spoyle that hen—frusche that checkyn [1]

—unbrace that mallarde [duck]—unlace that conye—dismembre that heron—display that crayn—disfigure that pecocke—unjoynt that bytture [bittern]—untache that curlewe—alaye that fesande [pheasant]—wynge that partyche [partridge]—wyng that quayle—myne that plover—thye that pygion—border that pastry—thye that woodcock—thye all smale byrdes—tymbre that fyere—tyere that egge—chynne that samon—strynge that lamprye—splat that pyke—sauce that plaice—sauce that tenche—splaye that breme—syde that haddok—tuske that barbell—culpon that troute—syne that cheven [chub]—trassene that ele—trance that sturgion—under trance that porpose—tayme that crabbe—barbe that lobster. Here endethe the goodly termes of Kervinge.

A PARDONER

There was no pardoner of equal grace,
For in his trunk he had a pillow-case
Which he asserted was Our Lady's veil.
He said he had a gobbet of the sail
Saint Peter had the time when he made bold
To walk the waves, till Jesu Christ took hold.
He had a cross of metal set with stones
And, in a glass, a rubble of pigs' bones.
And with these relics, any time he found
Some poor up-country parson to astound,

74. A friar preaching outside a church, c. 1480.

On one short day, in money down, he drew
More than the parson in a month or two,
And by his flatteries and prevarication
Made monkeys of the priest and congregation.
But still to do him justice first and last
In church he was a noble ecclesiast.
How well he read a lesson or told a story!
But best of all he sang an Offertory,
For well he knew that when that song was sung
He'd have to preach and tune his honey-tongue
And (well he could) win silver from the crowd.
That's why he sang so merrily and loud.

> Geoffrey Chaucer, *Canterbury Tales, Prologue,*
> translated by Nevill Coghill

BURNING OF HERETICS, 1401

With regard to which innovations and excesses [of the Lollards] set forth above, the prelates and clergy aforesaid, and also the commons of the said realm assembled in the same parliament, prayed the said lord king that his royal highness would in the said parliament deign to make provision for a suitable remedy. The same lord king then . . . by the assent of the magnates and other nobles of the said realm assembled in parliament, has granted, ordained, and established . . . that no one within the said kingdom or the other dominions subject to his royal majesty shall presume to preach in public or in secret without having first sought and obtained the licence of the local diocesan, always excepting curates in their own churches, persons who have hitherto enjoyed the privilege, and others to whom it has been granted by canon law; and that henceforth no one either openly or secretly shall preach, hold, teach, or impart anything, or compose or write any book, contrary to the catholic faith or the decisions of Holy Church, or anywhere hold conventicles or in any way have or maintain schools for such a sect and its nefarious doctrines and opinions; and also that in the future no one shall favour anybody who thus preaches, holds such or similar conventicles, has or maintains such schools, composes or writes such a book, or in any such fashion teaches, instructs, or excites the people. . . . And if any person within the said kingdom and dominions is formally convicted before the local diocesan or commissioners of the said nefarious preachings, doctrines, opinions, [holding of] schools, and heretical and erroneous instruction, or any of them, and if he refuses properly to abjure

75.   The Elevation of the Host, from a fifteenth century manuscript.

the same . . . or, after abjuration has been made by the same person, he is declared by the local diocesan or his commissioners to have relapsed, so that according to the sacred canons he ought to be relinquished to the secular court . . ., then the sheriff of the local county and the mayor and sheriffs or sheriff, or the mayor and bailiffs of the city, town, or borough of the same county nearest the said diocesan or his said commissioners . . . shall, after the pronouncement of such sentences, receive those persons and every one of them and shall have them burned before the people in some prominent place, so that such punishment shall inspire fear in the minds of others and prevent such nefarious doctrines and heretical and erroneous opinions, or their authors and protagonists in the said kingdom and dominions, from being supported or in any way tolerated against the catholic faith, the Christian religion, and the decisions of Holy Church—which God forbid! And in all and singular of the aforesaid matters regarding the said ordinance and statute, the sheriffs, mayors, and bailiffs of the counties, cities, towns, and boroughs aforesaid are to be attentive, helpful, and favourable to the said diocesans and their commissioners.

Sources of the Realm, Volume II,
translated by C. Stephenson and F. G. Marcham

BENEVOLENCES, 1483

. . . our lord the king, remembering how the commons of this his realm, through new and unlawful inventions and inordinate avarice, against the law of the realm have been subjected to great servitude and unbearable charges and exactions, and especially so through a new imposition called benevolence, whereby in divers years the subjects and commons of this land have, against their will and freedom, paid great sums of money to their almost complete ruin—for many and divers honourable men of this realm were on that account compelled of necessity to break up their households and to live in great penury and wretchedness, with their debts unpaid and their children unpreferred, and such memorials as they had ordered for their souls' health were set at naught, to the great displeasure of God and the destruction of this realm—therefore wills and ordains by the advice and consent of his said lords and commons in the said parliament assembled, and by the authority of the same, that henceforth his subjects and the commonalty of this his realm shall in no way be burdened with any such charge or imposition called benevolence, or anything like it; and that such exactions called benevolences as before this time have been taken shall not be held as a precedent for placing such or similar charges upon any of his said subjects of this realm in the future, but that they are to be condemned and annulled forever.

Statutes of the Realm (1810-28),
translated by C. Stevenson and F. G. Marcham

A MINSTREL'S TRICK, Fifteenth Century

Jacobus de Vetriaco tells how there was once an abbot of the Cistercian order; and when he was a monk he was a passing hard man, and miserly also. So it happened that he was made a hostler to look after guests in their guest-house, before he was made an abbot.

So one day there came to this abbey a minstrel, and he was seated at dinner in the guest-house. And this said monk served him with passing grey bread, and thin pottage, and a little salt, and no drink but water. And in the evening he was lying in a vile, hard bed.

And next morning this minstrel was very ill-pleased, and bethought how he might avenge himself upon this monk that had served him so badly. So, as he went out of the chamber where he had spent the night, he happened to meet the abbot. This minstrel came up to him, saluted him and said, 'My lord, I thank you and your worthy abbey for the great hospitality I have received here, and for the great cost which I have caused you; also for your good, generous monk, your hostler, who had served me yesterday evening at my supper, worthily, with many different messes of fish, and I drank passing good wine. And now, when I am going, he gave me a pair of new boots, and a good pair of new knives, and a girdle to hold them.'

And when the abbot had heard this, anon he went into the cloister. He called this monk before all the others of his convent, and then he rebuked him grievously, and dismissed him from the office he held.

An Alphabet of Tales (Early English Text Society, 1904).
A fifteenth-century translation, through the French, of Latin
tales for preachers

BECKET'S SHRINE

I saw, one day (being with your Magnificence at Westminster, a place out of London) the tomb of the Saint King Edward the Confessor, in the church of the aforesaid place Westminster; and indeed, neither St. Martin of Tours, a church in France, which I

76. Fountains Abbey, 1170-1500.

have heard is one of the richest in existence, nor anything else that
I have ever seen, can be put into any sort of comparison with it.
But the magnificence of the tomb of St. Thomas the Martyr,
Archbishop of Canterbury, is that which surpasses all belief.
This, notwithstanding its great size, is entirely covered over with
plates of pure gold; but the gold is scarcely visible from the
variety of precious stones with which it is studded, such as
sapphires, diamonds, rubies, balas-rubies [rose-red rubies], and
emeralds; and on every side that the eye turns, something more
beautiful than the other appears. And these beauties of nature are
enhanced by human skill, for the gold is carved and engraved in
beautiful designs, both large and small, and agates, jaspers and
cornelians set *in relievo,* some of the cameos being of such a size,
that I do not dare to mention it: but everything is left far behind
by a ruby, not larger than á man's thumb-nail, which is set to
the right of the altar. The church is rather dark, and particularly
so where the shrine is placed, and when we went to see it the sun
was nearly gone down, and the weather was cloudy; yet I saw that
ruby as well as if I had it in my hand; they say that it was the
gift of a king of France.

The Italian Relation of England, translation by
the Camden Society Editor

Travel

QUICKSANDS, 1188

Continuing our journey, not far from Margam, where the
alternate vicissitudes of a sandy shore and the tide commence,
we forded over the river Avon, having been considerably delayed
by the ebbing of the sea; and under the guidance of Morgan,
eldest son of Caradoc, proceeded along the sea-shore towards the
river Neth [Neath], which, on account of its quicksands, is the
most dangerous and inaccessible river in South Wales. A packhorse
belonging to the author, which had proceeded by the lower way
near the sea, although in the midst of many others, was the only
one which sunk down into the abyss, but he was at last, with
great difficulty, extricated, and not without some damage done
to the baggage and books. Yet, although we had Morgan, the
prince of that country, as our conductor, we did not reach the
river without great peril, and some severe falls; for the alarm
occasioned by this unusual kind of road, made us hasten our
steps over the quicksands, in opposition to the advice of our
guide, and fear quickened our pace; whereas, through these
difficult passages, as we then learned, the mode of proceeding
should be with moderate speed. But as the fords of the river
experience a change by every monthly tide, and cannot be found
after violent rains and floods, we did not attempt the former, but
passed the river in a boat, leaving the monastery of Neth [Neath]
on our right hand, approaching again to the district of St. David's,
and leaving the diocese of Landaf [which we had entered at
Abergavenny] behind us.

Gerald the Welshman, Description of Wales,
translated by Sir R. C. Hoare

THE GREATEST CITY IN EUROPE

On St. John's Eve [23 June 1203] the Crusaders came by ship to
St. Stephen's Abbey, three leagues from Constantinople. There
they had the city in full view, and drew to land, and anchored
their ships. And you may be assured that those who had never

208

77. A fourteenth-century dog cart.

seen Constantinople opened wide eyes now; for they could not believe that so rich a city could be in the whole world, when they saw her lofty walls and her stately towers wherewith she was encompassed, and these stately palaces and lofty churches, so many in number as no man might believe who had not seen them, and the length and breadth of this town which was sovereign over all others. And know that there was no man among us so bold but that his flesh crept at the sight; and therein was no marvel; for never did any men undertake so great a business as this assault of ours, since the beginning of the world.

[When the Greek Emperor had surrendered the city], you may be assured that many of our army went to see this city of Constantinople, and the rich palaces and churches that were so many. Of relics I speak not; for at that time [before the sack of the city] there were as many here as in all the rest of the world.

[When we had sacked the city], the chattels and the spoils were brought together. . . . Rest assured that much riches were there; for, without counting all that was stolen, or the equal share given to the Venetians, four hundred thousand silver marks were brought together, and a good ten thousand horses and mules.

Geoffroy de Villehardouin's *Chronicle, c.* 1205

CARTS

Can you send your long cart to Aldingburn? so that on it I can send your venison up to London, with other garnison, and cloth for the poor, as much as you like, for I bought 300 yards at Winchester fair; I can't send your small carts because the time of sowing is at hand.

Letter to the Bishop of Chichester from his agent, second quarter of the thirteenth century. Translated by Mary Bateson

78. This fourteenth-century coach reminds us of the portable stage
or 'pageant', on which Miracle and Mystery plays were performed.

HORSES AND THEIR EQUIPMENT

Let the horse's back be covered with a canvas, afterwards with a
sweat pad or cloth; next let a saddle be properly placed with the
fringes of the sweat cloth hanging over the crupper. The stirrups
should hang well. The saddle has a front bow or pommel and a
cantle . . . folded clothing may be well placed in a saddlebag
behind the cantle. A breast strap and the trappings for the use
of someone riding should not be forgotten: halter and headstall,
bit covered with bloody foam, reins, girths, buckles, cushion,
padding. . . . An attendant should carry a currycomb.

Let one who is about to ride have a *chape* with sleeves, of
which the hood will not mind the weather, and let him have
boots, and spurs that he may prevent the horse from stumbling,
jolting, turning, rearing, resisting, and make him *bien amblant*,
'possessed of a good gait', and easily manageable. Shoes should be
well fastened with iron nails.

> *Daily Living in the Twelfth Century, based on the*
> *Observations of Alexander Neckam,* U. T. Holmes Jr.

DANGERS IN FOREST WAYS

In woods is the place of deceit and of hunting. For therein wild
beasts are hunted. There is the place of hiding and of lurking:
for often in woods thieves be hid and often in their waiting and
deceit passing men come and are spoiled and robbed, and often
slain.

79. A map of the world drawn in the late fourteenth century in England. Jerusalem is in the centre with Noah's Ark to the left. England is on the bottom. left-hand side. The Pillars of Hercules, the Straits of Gibraltar, seem to support the world.

80. A horse litter, c. 1400

And so, for many and divers ways and uncertain, strange men often err and go out of the way; and take uncertain ways and the way that is unknown rather than the way that is known, and come oft to the place where thieves be in wait, and not without peril. Therefore often knots are made on trees and in bushes, in boughs and in branches of trees, in token and mark of the high way, to show the certain and sure way to wayfaring men. But oft the thieves, in turning and meeting of ways change such knots and signs, and beguile many men and bring them out of the right way by false tokens and signs.

John of Trevisa's translation of Bartholomew the Englishman,
fl. 1250 to 1260

AT THE ENDS OF THE VERY END

Purposing to survey the possessions and buildings appertaining to my see, I travelled to the border parts of Cornwall. That land adjoined England only with its eastern boundary; the rest is everywhere surrounded by the ocean, far beyond which, to the North, be Wales and Ireland. Southwards, it looks straight over to Gascony and Brittany; and the men of Cornwall speak the Breton tongue. To the West of St. Michael's Mount, the

immensity of ocean stretches without bound or limit. My see
possesseth also certain sea-girt islands [Scilly], whereunto no bishop
ever goeth, but they have been wont to send a few friars, as I
have not [yet] done.

Here I am not only at the end of the world but even (if I may
so say) at the ends of the very end. For this diocese, which includes
Devon and Cornwall, is divided from the rest of England, and
girt on all sides but one by an ocean which is rarely navigable,
and frequented only by the natives of the land. It aboundeth
sufficiently in home-fed flesh of beasts and at times in Gascony
wine; but it is less fertile in corn and other things necessary to
man. My episcopal manors I found terribly destroyed and
despoiled, in hatred of my predecessor [John de Berkeley] who
was so inhumanly murdered, my lands waste and untilled, and an
utter default of cattle and seed corn.

Register of John de Grandisson. He was Bishop of Exeter
1327-1369. The description above is translated from two letters
written (*i*) to his patron Pope John XXII., and (*ii*) to cardinals
at the Court of Avignon. Edited by G. G. Coulton, *Social Life in
Britain from the Conquest to the Reformation*

HOW TO ROB TRAVELLERS c. 1370

[Powder] for to make a man sleep against his will, after manner
of Ribaldez and trowans [tramps] in France, that felawshypeth
them [associate themselves] by the way to pilgrimages that they
may rob them of their silver when they are asleep. *Recipe*
[Henbane, darnel, black poppy and bryony root]; break all
together in a brazen mortar into full small powder, of which
powder give him in his pottage or in a cake of wheat or in drink;
and he shall sleep at once, after the quantity that he hath taken.

John Arderne, earliest known English surgeon, from his treatise
on the Fistula, *c̃*. 1370

THE TWO WANDERING 'MUTES', 1380

John Warde, of the County of York, and Richard Lynham, of
the County of Somerset, two imposters, were brought to the Hall
of the Guildhall of London, before John Hadlee, Mayor, the
Aldermen, and the Sheriffs, and questioned for that, whereas they
were stout enough to work for their food and raiment, and had
their tongues to talk with, they the same John Warde and
Richard Lynham, did there pretend that they were mutes, and
had been deprived of their tongues. And went about in divers
places of the city aforesaid, carrying in their hands two ell

81 A fifteenth-century cart

measures [45 inches], an iron hook and pincers, and a piece of
leather, in shape like part of a tongue, edged with silver, and
with writing around it, to this effect, 'This is the tongue of
John Warde'.

With which instruments, and by means of divers signs, they
gave many persons to understand that they were traders, in
token of which they carried the said ell measures; and that they
had been plundered by robbers of their goods; and that their
tongues had also been drawn out with the said hook, and then
cut off with the pincers; they making a horrible noise like unto a
roaring, and opening their mouths; where it seemed to all who
examined the same, that their tongues had been cut off: to the
defrauding of other poor and infirm persons, and in manifest
deceit of the whole of the people.

Wherefore, they were asked how they would acquit themselves
thereof; upon which, they acknowledged that they had done all
the things above imputed to them. It was awarded that they
should be put upon the pillory on three different days, each time
for one hour in the day; the said instruments being hung about
their necks each day.

H. T. Riley, *Memorials of London*

TRAVELLER'S GEAR

A lesson made in English verses, to teach a gentleman's servant, to say at every time when he taketh his horse, for his remembrance, that he shall not forget his gear in his inn behind him.

Purse, dagger, cloak, night-cap, kerchief, shoeing horn, boget [budget] and shoes.

Spear, mail, hood, halter, saddlecloth, spurs, hat, with thy horse-comb.

Bow, arrows, sword, buckler, horn, leisshe [leash], gloves, string, and thy bracer [arm-guard for shooting the bow].

Pen, paper, ink, parchment, reedwax, pommes [pumice], books thou remember.

Penknife, comb, thimble, needle, thread, point, lest that thy girth break.

Bodkin, knife, lyngel [shoemaker's thread], give thy horse meat, see he be shoed well.

Make merry, sing if thou can; take heed of thy gear, that thou lose none.

Sir Anthony Fitzherbert, *Book of Husbandry,*
edited by W. W. Skeat

Law and Crime

THE LAWLESS CRUELTY OF WILLIAM CUMIN, 1143
A monk describes his anarchy.

His soldiers were incessantly making forages; they ranged through every spot in the whole district; whatever they could lay their hands on they plundered; their inroads ceased neither day nor night; all that came in their way was destroyed—some of it they burnt, some they destroyed; all the produce of the fields they ruined either by treading it down or by depasturing cattle upon it; and thus the land which had been cultivated became barren and devastated by being trodden under foot. Just as effectually as locusts give proof of presence by nipping off the leaves and flowers from a tree, so wherever these men passed it became a wilderness. They associated with themselves such as were the most depraved and the most notorious for their excesses; one struggled against the other for mastery in evil; the greater the cruelty the greater the admiration. Even to hear of their doings was terrible; but to see them was something yet worse. Their insolence was not confined to ravages and plunderings only, but was extended to the cruel bodily torments, inflicted not in secret, and in the darkness of the night, and upon only a few individuals, but perpetrated openly; and in the sight of day, and upon men of the nobler rank. Their torments were of many and various kinds, difficult to describe and incredible to believe. Men were hung from the walls of their own houses; cords being tightly twisted round their middle, and heavy armour or large stones tied to the neck and feet, so that the extremities of the body were bent towards the ground, which, however, they did not touch. Upon one occasion more than twelve persons were discovered together suspended in this manner; others of them they plunged into the bed of the river in the depth of winter, after having broken the ice with which it was covered; and having tied ropes round them, they alternately dragged them out of it and thrust them back again, feeding their cruelty with such a spectacle of misery. The feet of some they thrust through holes made in the wall, and thus exposed their naked bodies to the extremity of the cold, leaving them in this misery all the night long. In addition to all these, they employed a most refined piece of cruelty, by which the limbs were wedged together and thrust within a very narrow chest, a novel device in the mystery of tormenting which eclipsed all former efforts. It was in direct antagonism to the older punishment of the rack, which stretched the limbs to an undue length; whereas, by this present device, they were crushed and cramped up into a narrow space, by which process they were sometimes fractured. Who is able to give an account of the immensity of the chains, or the stench of the prison-house, or the sharpness of the hunger to which they were exposed? But let me not be tedious; everywhere throughout the town there were groans and various kinds of deaths. In consequence of such horrible proceedings the place, which had hitherto been so highly honoured, now became a terror to all, and was surnamed the place of the tortures of hell.

Simeon of Durham, translated by Rev. J. Stevenson in
The Church Historians of England

THE LAW OF ENGLISHRY, Twelfth Century

THE MASTER. *Murdrum* is, properly, the secret death of a man whose slayer is unknown; for the word *murdrum* signifieth *secret* or *hidden*. Now, in the earlier state of this realm after the Conquest, those English who were left were wont to lie in wait for the dreaded and hated Normans, and secretly to slay them here and there in woods or secluded places, as opportunity might offer. The kings and their ministers, therefore, did for some years inflict the most exquisite forms of torture upon the English, yet without full effect; until at length they imagined this following device. Wheresoever a Norman was found thus slain, if the slayer did not show himself or even betray himself by flight, then the whole of that district called the Hundred was fined on behalf of the royal treasury, some in thirty-six pounds sterling and some in forty-four, according to the diversity of districts and the frequency of murders; which (as we hear) was decreed in order that this general penalty might secure the safety of wayfarers, and that all men might be spurred on either to punish the crime or to hand over to justice that man who had brought so enormous a loss upon the whole neighbourhood. Thou must know, as aforesaid, that they who sit at the Exchequer are free from the payment of the fines.

THE DISCIPLE. Should not the secret death of an Englishman, as of a Norman, be imputed as *murdrum*?

THE MASTER. Not at the first institution of this law as thou hast heard; and now that English and Normans have lived so long together, and have intermarried, the nations have become so intermingled (I speak of freemen only) that we can scarce distinguish in these days betwixt Englishman and Norman; excepting of course those serfs bound to the land whom we call villeins, and who cannot leave their condition without leave of their masters. Wherefore, in these days, almost every secret manslaughter is punished as *murdrum*, except those of whom (as I have said) it is certain that they are of servile condition.

Richard, Bishop of London and Treasurer, *Dialogue of the Exchequer*. The law above was not repealed till 1339. Translation by W. Stubbs, *Selected Charters*

LONDON CITIZENS RIOT AGAINST THE ABBOT OF WESTMINSTER'S HOUSEHOLD, 1223

In the year of Our Lord 1223 there was strife at London between the Abbot of Westminster's household and some young London citizens; but their laughter was turned to tears. The abbot's household might triumph by night and many were hurt on both sides, but next morning the London people chose a new mayor, publicly hired men-at-arms by proclamation, appointed a captain for themselves and burst into the church of Westminster. They spoiled the abbot's goods, livestock and chattels. After a few days Philip Daubeni, of the royal household, was staying in London and the Abbot of Westminster went to him to complain about the violence which he had suffered. The Londoners learnt this and swarmed round his house like bees, beating his servants and maltreating the soldiers that came with him, and tried to capture the abbot himself. Philip tried in vain to calm the mob while the abbot escaped secretly from the back. He embarked in a small boat on the Thames and thus escaped with difficulty. The justiciar heard of this frenzied outbreak of the citizens and summoned the mayor and chief citizens to inquire who were the ringleaders. Upon concluding this inquiry he arrested Constantine Aloph and his two nephews. They gave a rude reply to his charges and were hung. The citizens murmured at this so the king took sixty hostages from them and sent them in custody to various castles. He deposed the mayor and appointed his own warden in the city. He ordered a great gallows to be prepared and at last after royal threats and many discussions between them and the barons

peace was made between them and the king on payment of many
thousands of marks.

Annals of Dunstable. Translated and appears in R. F. Glover and
R. W. Harris, *Latin for Historians*

THE MANORIAL COURT, 1246-1249

John Sperling complains that Richard of Newmere on the Sunday
next before S. Bartholomew's day last past with his cattle, horses,
and pigs wrongfully destroyed the corn of his [John's] land to his
damage to the extent of one thrave [stook of corn], and to his
dishonour to the extent of two shillings; and of this he produces
suit. And Richard comes and defends all of it. Therefore let him
go to the law six handed [five neighbours who will support his
oath of innocence]. His pledges, Simon Combe and Hugh Frith.

The twelve jurors say that Hugh Cross has right in the bank
and hedge about which there was a dispute between him and
William White. Therefore let him hold in peace and let William
be distrained for his many trespasses. (Afterwards he made fine
for 12*d*.)

The parson of the Church is in mercy for his cow caught in
the lord's meadow. Pledges, Thomas Ymer and William Coke.

From Martin Shepherd 6*d*. for the wound he gave Perkin.

Ragenhilda of Bec gives 2*s*. for being married without licence.
Pledge, William of Primer.

It was presented that Robert Carter's son by night invaded the
house of Peter Burgess and in felony threw stones at his door so
that the said Peter raised the hue. Therefore let the said Robert
be committed to prison. Afterwards he made fine with 2*s*.

All the ploughmen of Great Ogbourne are convicted by the
oath of twelve men . . . because by reason of their default [the
land] of the lord was ill-ploughed whereby the lord is damaged
to the amount of 9*s*. . . . And Walter Reaper is in mercy for
concealing [not giving information as to] the said bad ploughing.
Afterwards he made fine with the lord with 1 mark.

F. W. Maitland, *Select Pleas in Manorial Courts*

ROYAL WRIT OF 1253 FOR WATCH AND WARD

(1) That watches be held in the several townships as hath been
wont, and by honest and able men.

(2) That the hue and cry be followed according to the ancient
use, so that all who neglect and refuse to follow it up shall
be taken into custody as abettors of the wrongdoers, and

shall be delivered up to the Sheriff. Moreover, in every township, let four or six men be chosen according to its size, to follow the hue and cry hastily and swiftly, and to pursue the wrongdoers, if need be, with bows and arrows and other light arms, which should be provided at the common cost of the township and remain ever for the use thereof. And to this end let two free and lawful men be chosen from the most powerful in each hundred, who shall oversee the work and see that the aforesaid watches and pursuits be rightly carried out.

(3) That no stranger abide in the township except by day, and that he depart while it is yet daylight.

(4) That no stranger be harboured in county townships beyond one day, or two at most, save only in time of harvest, unless his host be willing to answer for him. . . .

(5) That the mayor and bailiffs of all cities and boroughs be bidden that, if any merchant or stranger bearing money do show them the said money and beg for safe conduct, then they must so conduct him through the evil passes and doubtful ways; and if he lose aught for default of such conduct or under their conduct, then let him be indemnified by the inhabitants of the said borough or city.

EXTRACTS FROM THE CORONER'S ROLL OF 1266-7

It happened about bedtime on Sunday next before the feast of St. Bartholomew in the fiftieth year of Henry III that Henry Colburn of Barford went out of his house in Barford to drink a tankard of beer and did not return that night; but early the next morning Agnes Colburn, his mother, looked for him and found the said Henry dead. And he was wounded in the body about the heart and in the belly with seven knife-wounds, and in the head with four wounds apparently made with a pickaxe, and also in the throat and the chin and the head as far as the brain. The aforesaid Agnes at once raised the hue and cry and pursuit was made. And she finds pledges: Humphrey Quarrel and Thomas Quarrel of the same Barford.

It happened in the vill of Wilden on Wednesday next before the feast of Simon and Jude in the fiftieth year that unknown malefactors came to the house of Jordan Hull of Wilden and broke into the said house while the said Jordan was absent. And the said malefactors wounded the said Agnes, wife of the said

Jordan, and killed Emma, his eight-year-old daughter. Afterwards they carried off all the goods from the house. . . . Inquest was held before Simon Read, the coroner, by four neighbouring townships . . . who said that what has been reported, and that the malefactors were unknown. . . .

It happened at Eaton on Thursday next after the feast of the Apostles Peter and Paul in the fiftieth year that Reginald Stead of Eaton, reaper of John Francis, went into the meadows of Eaton to guard the meadow of his lord and, being taken with falling sickness, collapsed and died forthwith by misadventure. Alice, his wife, was the first to discover him, and she finds pledges. . . . Inquest was held before Simon Read, the coroner, by four neighbouring townships . . . who say that he died by misadventure of the aforesaid disease and they know nothing beyond that.

Select Cases from Coroners' Rolls, edited by C. Gross, translation by C. Stephenson and F. G. Marcham

REGULATIONS FOR PEOPLE'S SAFETY

. . . And for the greater security of the country the king has commanded that in the great towns, which are enclosed, the gates be shut from sunset until sunrise; and that no man lodge in the suburbs, or on any foreign part of the town save only in the daytime, nor yet in the daytime if the host will not answer for him. . . . And it commanded that from henceforth watches be kept, as has been used in times past . . . . in every city by six men at every gate; in every borough by twelve men; in every town by six men or four, according to the number of the inhabitants . . . and that they keep watch continually all night, from sunset to sunrise. And if any stranger pass by them, he shall be arrested until morning and if no suspicion be found, he shall go quit; and if they find cause of suspicion, he shall be delivered to the sheriff forthwith. . . . And if they will not suffer themselves to be arrested, hue and cry shall be levied against them, and those who keep watch shall follow with all the town, with the towns near, with hue and cry from town to town, until they be taken and delivered to the sheriff. . . .

And further, it is commanded, that highways from one market town to another be enlarged, where there are woods, hedges or ditches, so that there be neither ditches, underwood, nor bushes, wherein a man may lurk to do hurt, near the road, within two hundred feet on the one side, and two hundred feet on the other side, provided that this . . . extend not to oaks, or to great woods, so as it be clear underneath. . . .

And if, perchance, a park be near the highway, it is requisite that the lord of the park diminish his park, so that there be a space of two hundred feet from the highway, as before said, or that he make such a wall ditch or hedge, that evil doers will not be able to pass or return to do evil.

From the Statute of Westminster, 1285

PIEPOWDER COURT

From the end of the eleventh century the royal grant of licence to hold a fair carried also the licence to hold a court to try offences committed at the fair itself. The suitors often appeared in travel-stained clothes. The word 'piepoudreux', meaning 'dusty-feet', was used in the name, Piepowder Court. Here a jury of merchants gave judgment.

Below are examples from the records of St. Ives Fair, Huntingdonshire, which belonged to the Abbot of Ramsey.

1288. William of Houghton complains of Joan of Earith, for that whereas the said William was in front of his gate near the waterside on Thursday last, the said Joan came there and assaulted him with vile words, (saying that all his life he had lived by knavery and that the measures of the said Joan had been seized by the contrivance of the said William) to his dishonour to the amount of 2s.

1291. John, son of William, son of Agnes of Lynn, who is ten years of age, was found in the vill of St. Ives near the foot of the bridge of the said vill stealing a purse during the fair; but because he is not old enough to sustain the judgment which is ordained and provided for such evil-doers, it is awarded that he abjure the vill of St. Ives and the fair thereof.

1300. Ives Vickery [and five others] who were appointed to watch in Cross Lane near the canvas booth on the night of Thursday before the feast of St. Dunstan, withdrew from their vigil and watched badly, so that the canvas booth was broken into by robbers, and the greater part of the canvas and other goods were carried. Therefore let them be attached to answer etc., and they are in mercy 3s. for the contempt.

TRIAL BY COMBAT, c. 1290

Then let them both be brought to a place appointed for that purpose, where they must swear thus. 'Hear this, ye Justices, that

I John (or I Peter) have neither eaten or drunk anything, nor done or caused to be done any other thing, whereby the law of God may be abased, and the law of the devil advanced or exalted.' And thus let it be done in all battles in appeals of felony. And let proclamation be immediately made, that no one, except the combatants, whatever thing he see or hear, be so bold as to stir, or cry aloud, whereby the battle may be disturbed; and whosoever disobeys the proclamation shall be imprisoned a year and a day.

Next, let them go to combat, armed without iron and without the slightest armour, their heads uncovered, their hands and feet bare, with two staves tipped with horn of equal length, and each of them a target of four corners, without any other arms, whereby either of them may annoy the other; and if either of them have any other arms concealed about him, and therewith annoy or offer to annoy his adversary, let it be done as shall be mentioned in treating of battle in a plea of land.

If the defendant can defend himself until the stars can be seen in the firmament, and demands judgment whether he ought to combat any longer, our will is, that judgment pass for the defendant, and so in all battles between champions; and in the case of felony the appellor shall be committed to prison. . . .

And if the defendant be vanquished, let the judgment be this, that he be drawn and hanged, or put to such other painful death as we shall direct, and that all his movable goods be ours, and his heirs disinherited; and his children shall be incapable of ever holding land in our realm. And let not any, unless they would be suspected themselves of the felony, presume to intercede for him; and let the accuser, who without delay shall prosecute such felony with good effect, receive from us a notable reward. Appeals may likewise be sued for us in the same manner for counterfeiting our seal and our coin, and also for violating our consort, or our daughters, or the nurses of our children; and in such cases, the judgment is, to be drawn and hanged. . . .

Britton, the French Text carefully revised with an English translation, introduction and notes by Francis Morgan Nichols,
Clarendon Press

PARISH OFFICERS, 1297

It was ordered that every bedel [parish officer] shall make summons by day in his own Ward, upon view of two good men, for setting watch at the Gates; and that those so summoned shall come to the Gates in the day-time, and in the morning, at day-light, shall depart therefrom. And such persons are to be

82. Medieval monks set in the stocks for robbing a church.

properly armed with two pieces; namely, with haketon [a buff-coat] and gambeson [quilted coat], or else with haketon and corset, or with haketon and plates. And if they neglect to come so armed, or make default in coming, the bedel shall forthwith hire another person, at the rate of twelve pence, in the place of him who makes such default; such sum to be levied on the morrow upon the person so making default.

In like manner, if any person shall be summoned to watch within the Ward, and shall make default, the bedel shall substitute another in his place, and on the morrow shall take from him three pence, to the use of such substitute.

H. T. Riley, *Memorials of London*

GREAT LOSS BY WRESTLINGS AND PLAYS, 1301

Edward by the grace of God King of England Lord of Ireland and Duke of Aquitaine to the Mayor and sheriffs of London greeting. Whereas we have learnt by the earnest complaint of the Prioress of Clerkenwell, our beloved in Christ, that men of the said city on horse and on foot in great number come to the fields, meadows and pastures of the said prioress at Clerkenwell with their followers and make wrestlings and other plays there; and flatten the enclosures, hedges and ditches that are around the corn, the meadows and the pastures of the said prioress; and crush and trample the corn and grass in many ways and this is to the great loss of the said prioress and a grievance; We therefore wish to attend to the redress of the said prioress in this matter and do order you with a firm injunction that if it is thus in the said city you do have ordered.and proclaimed publicly on our behalf that they do not dare in future exercise such wrestlings and plays in the fields, meadows and pastures of the said prioress whereby she can receive hurt and loss. In this we hold you that no repeated complaint reach us whereby we have to attend to this matter further.. Witnessed by me at Fakenham, 8 April in the twenty-ninth year of our reign [1301].

Cartulary of St. Mary, Clerkenwell, British Museum

PLAYING IN THE STREET, 1301

On Tuesday the feast of Sts. Philip and James [4 May] a certain Hugh Picard was riding a white horse after the hour of vespers, when Petronilla, daughter of William de Wyntonia, aged three years, was playing in the street; and the horse, being strong, quickly carried Hugh against his will over Petronilla so that it struck her on her right side with its right forefoot. Petronilla lingered until the next day, when she died, at the hour of vespers, from the blow. Being asked who were present, the jurors know only of those mentioned. The corpse viewed, the right side of which appeared blue and badly bruised, and no other hurt. The horse valued at a mark, for which Richard de Caumpes, the sheriff, will answer. Hugh fled and has no chattels; he afterwards surrendered to John de Boreford (or Burford), sheriff.

London, Coroner, *Calendar of the Coroners Rolls*

THE KEEPING OF THE PEACE IN THE CITY OF LONDON, c. 1309

Articles confirmed by the lord the King touching the state of the City and the strict observance of the peace, which articles are sealed with the Great Seal of the King [Edward II].

These are the articles which our lord the King commands to be kept in his city of London for the preservation of his peace. Firstly, that whereas murders, robberies, and homicides have in times past been committed in the city by night and day, it is forbidden that any one walk the streets after curfew tolled at St. Martin le Grand with sword, buckler, or other arm unless he be a great lord, or other respectable person of note, or their acknowledged retainer, bearing a light; and if any be found doing the contrary they are to be committed to the Tower, and the next day brought before the Warden or Mayor and Aldermen, and punished accordingly.

No taverner to keep his tavern open for wine or beer after curfew, nor admit any one into his tavern, nor into his house, unless he is willing to answer for the King's peace, under penalties named.

No one to keep a fencing school by night or day, under pain of imprisonment for forty days. And whereas murderers who have been arrested are often treated too leniently, to the encouragement of others, it is ordained that no prisoner be released by a Sheriff or his officer without the cognisance of the Warden or Mayor and the Aldermen; and that each Alderman, make diligent search in his Ward for misdoers, and if any such be found, to bring them before the Warden or Mayor and the Aldermen for due punishment if proved guilty of the charges brought against them.

No foreigner nor stranger to keep hostel within the City, but only those who are freemen of the City, or who can produce a good character from the place whence they have come, and are ready to find sureties for good behaviour.
Calendar of Letter Books of the City of London. Edited by Sharpe

MISDOERS AND COMMON BRUISERS, 1310

The Mayor, Sheriffs, and Aldermen proceeded to make inquisition.
John de Lorymer attached, for that he is indicted in the Ward of Bradestreet as a misdoer and a common bruiser, wandering about by night to attack freemen and strangers, contrary to the peace of the lord the King. Also, because he is indicted in the Ward of Bassieshaw as a disturber of the King's peace, and as a doer of many evil things, contrary to the peace. He appeared, and being asked how he would acquit himself thereof, he says he is no way guilty, and puts himself upon the country. And the jury, by Adam Rugge and others, come and say on their oath that the said John de Lorymer is guilty of the trespass aforesaid. Therefore he is committed to prison.

Oliver de 'Maltone' attached because indicted in the Wards of Chepe, Tower, and Creplegate for similar practices, as well as for enticing men to taverns for gambling purposes. Found guilty and committed to prison.

Master Roger le Skirmisour attached because indicted for holding a school for fencing and drawing young men together, sons of respectable parents, to the wasting of their property and the injury of their characters. Pleads not guilty . . . Found guilty and committed.

John Baroun attached because indicted in the Ward of Bassieshaw for keeping open house at night, and receiving night walkers and dice players; and John Vantort attached because indicted in the same Ward as being of ill fame. Pleads not guilty . . . Found not guilty, therefore, let them be therefore quit.

Henry de Kirkelly attached because indicted in the Ward of Bishopsgate as a receiver of strangers who wound men and afterwards return home. Pleads not guilty . . . Found not guilty.

Calendar of Letter Books of the City of London. Edited by Sharpe

LEAVING THE SOLAR TO GET SOME FIRE, 1321

When on Sunday [December 29] at dusk, Elena Scot, a servant, left the solar of the house to get some fire, she slipped from the top step of the entrance of the solar and fell backwards down the steps upon a stone at the bottom and broke her neck and forthwith died in consequence of that and from no other felony. Being asked who were present when this happened, the jurors say Margaret de Sandwich, her mistress, and one Christina Lovel, and Margaret first discovered the corpse and raised the cry, so that the country came; nor do they suspect any man or woman of the death, but only mischance. The corpse was viewed, on which the broken neck appeared and no other hurt.

London, Coroner, *Calendar of the Coroners Rolls*

A BOY THIEF, 1324

On Monday [in April 1324] at the hour of vespers John, son of William de Burgh, a boy five years old, was in the house of Richard le Latthere and had taken a parcel of wool and placed it in his cap. Emma, the wife of Richard, chastising him, struck him with her right hand under his left ear so that he cried. On hearing this, Isabella, his mother, raised the hue and carried him thence. He lingered until the hour of curfew of the same day, when he died of the blow and not of any felony. Emma forthwith fled, but where she went or who received her the jurors knew not. Afterwards she surrendered herself to the prison of Newgate.

London, Coroner, *Calendar of the Coroners Rolls*

THE FALL OF A LIGHTED CANDLE, 1326

On Monday, the Feast of the Nativity [25 December], John Rynet and Alice his wife were alarmed at midnight by a fire which had been caused by the fall of a lighted candle, as they were going to sleep, and hurriedly left the burning shop. Immediately afterward John, blaming Alice for causing the disaster, violently pushed her back into the shop and fled, but whither the jurors knew not. Alice was thus injured by the fire and again leaving the shop lingered until the following Tuesday, when she had her ecclesiastical rights and died of burns.

London, Coroner, *Calendar of the Coroners Rolls*

A HIT AND RUN CARTER, 1337

On Thursday [13 February], about the hour of vespers, two carters taking two empty carts out of the city were urging their horses apace, when the wheels of one of the carts collapsed opposite the rent of the hospital of St. Mary, Bishopsgate, so that the cart fell on Agnes de Cicestre, who immediately died. The carter thereupon left his cart and three horses and took flight in fear, although he was not suspected of malicious intent. The cart and its trappings were appraised by jurors of the ward of Bishopsgate at 6s. 8d.; the first horse, of a dun colour, at 10s., the second, a gray, and blind of both eyes, at 4s., and the third, a black, at 6s.; also five old sacks and five pounds of candles of 'coton' [with cotton wicks] which were in the cart at the time of the accident at 16½d. Total 28s. ½d., for which John de Northhalle, one of the sheriffs, will answer.

London, Coroner, *Calendar of the Coroners Rolls*

JUSTICES OF THE PEACE, 1361

These are the measures which our lord the king, the prelates, the lords, and the commons have ordained in this present parliament, held at Westminster on Sunday next before the feast of the Conversion of St. Paul, to be observed and publicly proclaimed throughout the kingdom, to wit:

First, that for the keeping of the peace, there shall be assigned in each county of England one lord, and with him three or four of the most worthy men of the county together with certain men skilled in the law, and they shall have power to restrain evil-doers, rioters, and all other miscreants; to pursue, arrest, capture, and chastise them according to their trespass or offence; to have them imprisoned and duly punished according to the law and custom of the kingdom, and according to what the justices may think best to do at their discretion and good advisement. Also they shall have power to inform themselves and to make inquiry concerning all those who have been pillagers and robbers in the regions beyond the sea, and who have now returned to become vagrants, refusing to work as they used to in times past; and to take and arrest all whom they can find on indictment or suspicion, and to put them in prison. . . . Also they shall have power to hear and determine, at the king's suit, all manner of felonies and trespasses committed in the same county, according to the laws and customs aforesaid. . . . And the fine to be assessed before the justices, because of trespass committed by any person, shall be just and reasonable, according to the gravity of the offence and as the causes leading to it are taken into account. . . .

Item, it is agreed that the men assigned to keep the peace shall have power to make inquiry concerning measures and also weights, according to the statute thereupon made in the twenty-fifth year of our lord the king's reign. . . .

Statutes of the Realm (1810-28),
translated by C. Stephenson and F. G. Marcham

FRENCH LANGUAGE DISCONTINUED IN COURTS, 1362

Item, because it is often showed to the king by the prelates, dukes, earls, barons, and all the commonalty, of the great mischiefs which have happened to divers of the realm, because the laws, customs and statutes of this realm be not commonly known in the same realm, for that they be pleaded, showed and judged in the French tongue, which is much unknown in the said realm; so that the people which do implead, or be impleaded, in the king's court, and in the courts of other have no knowledge nor understanding of that which is said for them or against them by their sergeants and other pleaders; and that reasonably the said laws and customs shall be the more learned and known, and better understood in the tongue used in the said realm, and by so much every man of the said realm may the better govern himself without offending of the law, and the better keep, save and defend his heritage and possessions; and in divers regions and countries where the king, the nobles, and other of the said realm have been, good governance and full right is done to every person, because that their laws and customs be learned and used in the tongue of the country, the king desiring the good governance and tranquillity of his people, and to put out and eschew the harms and mischiefs which do or may happen in this behalf by the occasions aforesaid, hath ordained and established by the assent aforesaid, that all pleas which shall be pleaded in his court whatsoever, before any of his justices whatsoever, or in his other places, or before any of his other ministers whatsoever, or in the courts and places of any other lords whatsoever within the realm, shall be pleaded, showed, defended, answered, debated, and judged in the English tongue, and that they be entered and inrolled in Latin, and that the laws and customs of the said realm, terms, and processes, be holden and kept as they be and have been before this time; and that by the ancient terms and form of pleaders no man be prejudiced, so that the matter of the action be fully showed in the declaration and in the writ: and it accorded by the assent aforesaid, that this ordinance and satute of pleading begin and hold place at the fifteenth of Saint Hilary next coming.

Statutes of the Realm (1810-1828),
translated by C. Stephenson and F. G. Marcham

CORRUPT WINE, 1364

John de Brykelesworthe, who prosecuted for the King and the Commonalty of the City of London, said that the same John Ryghtwys and John Penrose sold red wine to all who came there, unsound and unwholesome for man, in deceit of the common people, and in contempt of our Lord the King, and to the shameful disgrace of the officers of the City; to the grievous damage of the Commonalty. [The judgment was] that the said John Penrose shall drink a draught of the same wine which he sold to the common people; and the remainder of such wine shall then be poured on the head of the same John; and that he shall forswear the calling of a vintner in the City of London for ever, unless he can obtain the favour of our Lord the King as to the same.

H. T. Riley, *Memorials of London*

WAITING FOR THE TIDE, 1367

On Wednesday [15 September 1367], at dusk, John Farnaham entered a boat belonging to John Sevar of Portsoken, which boat lay in the Thames near Botolph's Wharf, in the ward of Billingsgate, desiring to voyage in her to the village of North Wokyngdon. While he and his fellow travellers lay asleep waiting for the tide, a great storm of wind and rain arose and overturned the boat, so that John fell into the water and was drowned. His corpse was carried hither and thither until Wednesday after the Feast of St. Michael [29 September], when it was found cast by the water in the Fleet [a river west of St. Paul's], at 'le Lymhostes' [Lime Hurst]. The vessel and its belongings were appraised by the jury at 20s. Having been asked what became of the boat, they said that John Sevar the same night took it and sailed away. Precept was sent to the sheriff to attach the boat, etc., when found in their bailiwick.

London, Coroner, *Calendar of the Coroners Rolls*

DECEIT IN A PENNY LOAF, 1387

Robert Porter, servant of John Gibbe, baker of Stratforde, was brought here, into the Guildhall of London, before Nicholas Extone, Mayor of the said city, John Hadle, and other Aldermen, and questioned for that, when the same Mayor on that day went into Chepe, to make assay there of bread, according to the custom of the City, he, the said Robert, knowing that the bread of his master, in a certain cart there, was not of full weight, took a penny loaf, and in it falsely and fraudulently inserted a piece of iron, weighing about 6s. 8d. [about one-third of a pound. Coin, then, was known by weight of metal. Often pound-weight was expressed in shillings and pence.]; with intent to make the said loaf weigh more, in deceit of the people etc.

Wherefore, enquiry was made of the same Robert, how he would acquit himself thereof; upon which, he acknowledged that he had done in manner aforesaid. And for this said falsity and deceit, it was adjudged that he should be taken from thence to Cornhulle, and be put upon the pillory there, to remain upon the same for one hour of the day, the said loaf and piece of iron being hung about his neck. And precept was given to the Sheriffs, to have the reason for such punishment publicly proclaimed.

H. T. Riley, *Memorials of London*

TRADE-UNIONS, 1387

John Clerk, Henry Duntone, and John Hychene, were attached on the 17th day of August, in the 11th year etc., at the suit of Robert de York, Thomas Bryel, Thomas Gloucestre, and William Mildenhale, overseers of the trade of Cordwainers, and other reputable men of the same trade, appearing before Nicholas Extone, Mayor, and the Aldermen in the Chamber of the Guildhall of London; and were charged by the said prosecutors, for that—whereas it was enacted and proclaimed in the said city, on behalf of our Lord the King, that no person should make congregations, alliances, or compacts of the people, privily or openly; and that those belonging to the trades, more than other men, should not, without leave of the Mayor, make alliances, confederacies, or conspiracies—the aforesaid John Clerk, Henry

Duntone, and John Hychene, serving-men of the said trade of Cordwainers, together with other their accomplices, on the Feast of the Assumption of the Blessed Virgin [15 August] last past, at the Friars Preachers in the said city, brought together a great congregation of men like unto themselves, and there did conspire and confederate to hold together; to the damage of the commonalty, and the prejudice of the trade before mentioned, and in rebellion against the overseers aforesaid; and there, because that Richard Bonet, of the trade aforesaid, would not agree with them, made assault upon him, so that he hardly escaped with his life; to the great disturbance of the peace of our Lord the King, and to the alarm of the neighbours there, and against the oath by which they had before been bound, not to make such congregations, or unions, or sects, for avoiding the dangers resulting therefrom.

And the said persons, being examined and interrogated thereon, could not deny the same. But they further confessed that a certain Friar Preacher, 'Brother William Bartone' by name, had made an agreement with their companions, and had given security to them, that he would make suit in the Court of Rome for confirmation of that fraternity by the Pope; so that, on pain of excommunication, and of still more grievous sentence afterwards to be fulminated, no man should dare to interfere with the well-being of the fraternity. For doing the which, he had received a certain sum of money, which had been collected among their said companions: a deed which notoriously redounds to the weakening of the liberties of the said city, and of the power of the officers of the same. Wherefore, by award of the said Mayor and Aldermen, it was determined that the said John Clark, Henry Duntone, and John Hychene, should be confined in the Prison of Newgate, until they should have been better advised what further ought to be done with them.

H. T. Riley, *Memorials of London*

CHARMS FAIL TO SAVE A CHIEF JUSTICE FROM EXECUTION FOR TREASON, 1388

The wretched [Sir Robert] Tresilian was discovered above the gutter of a certain house next the palace wall [at Westminster] lurking among the tiles to watch the people coming and going to Parliament. And when certain esquires entered the house and, looking about, found no one, one esquire, advancing threateningly upon the master of the house, throttled him by the hood, with dagger drawn, and said: 'Show us where Tresilian is hid, or your days are short.' At once, the trembling man said, 'Lo, this is the place where he always is.' And strange to say, the unhappy Tresilian was revealed under a round table which for his sake was covered at that time with cloths. His tunic of old russet reached to mid-shin, like an old man's; he had a thick, stiff beard; and was clad in red hose with Joseph's shoes, so that he resembled rather a pilgrim or beggar than the King's chief justice. Straightway this came to the hearing of the lords, and as soon as they heard it, the five appellants hurried from Parliament without saying why they withdrew. All their adherents in Parliament were amazed, and many followed them in alarm; and when they had arrested Tresilian at the gate of the Palace, bringing him to Parliament, they cried out loud, 'We have him! We have him!'. . .

At length Tresilian was bound hand and foot to a hurdle and, with an innumerable crowd of lords and commoners, as well on horseback as on foot, was drawn behind horses through the city, resting at times throughout the length of the journey, out of charity, in case he should repent. But, alas, he made no public confession; yet what he said to his friar confessor is unknown, nor is it for us to inquire. . . . And when he came to the gallows to be executed, he would not climb the ladder; but he was encouraged to climb by blows from fists and whips, and he said: 'So long as I wear certain things about me, I cannot die.' Immediately they stripped him and found certain charms and certain signs painted upon them, after the fashion of the signs of the Zodiac, and one demon's head painted, and many names of demons were written. These were taken away, and he was hanged naked, and to be more sure of his death, they cut his throat. And night fell, and he hung until the morrow; and, leave having been begged and obtained by his wife from the King, he was carried to the Friars Minor and there buried.

Thomas Favent, *Historia . . . mirabilis parliamenti*,
edited by May McKisack

JUSTICE IMPROVES UNDER RICHARD II

Item, it is agreed and established that no man of law shall henceforth be justice of assize or of common jail delivery in his own country, and that the chief justice of the common bench, among others, shall be assigned to hold assizes of this sort and to deliver jails; but with regard to the chief justice of the king's bench, let such action be taken as has been customary for the greater part of the past hundred years.

Item, . . . after the said ordinance [of Edward III] had been recited in parliament, it was agreed and established that no justice of the king's bench or of the common bench, or any baron of the exchequer, so long as he held the office of justice or baron, should henceforth take, either by himself or through others, whether openly or in secret, any robe, fief, pension, gift, or reward from anybody except the king; nor should he take any present from anybody except one of food and drink which is not of great value. And it is established that henceforth such justices and barons shall not give counsel to any one, whether great or small, in causes or concerns to which the king is a party or which in any way touch the king; and that they are not to be of counsel to any one in any case, plea, or dispute pending before themselves or in any other great court or tribunal of the king, on penalty of forfeiting office and of paying fine and ransom to the king.

Statutes of the Realm (1810-1828),
translated by C. Stephenson and F. G. Marcham

JUDGMENT OF PILLORY, 1419

Judgment of Pillory for selling a peck of stinking eels

Judgment of Pillory for enhancing the price of corn

Judgment of Pillory for selling oats, good on the outside and the rest bad

Judgment of Pillory for making false deeds. . . .

Judgment of Pillory for deficiency of coal in sacks. . . .

Judgment of Pillory for rings and buckles made of latten [brass] plated with gold and silver, and sold for gold and silver

Judgment of Pillory upon certain Bakers, who had holes in their tables, called '*moldyngbordes*', by means whereof they stole their neighbours' dough. . . .

Judgment of Pillory for cutting a certain purse. . . .

Judgment of Pillory upon a person for taking away a child, to go begging with him. . . .

Judgment of Pillory upon a person for false dice, with which he played and deceived people. . . .

Judgment of Pillory for a false obligation [forged bond]. . . .

Judgment of Pillory for a certain false and counterfeit letter

Judgment of Pillory for a deception committed, namely, counters [jettons or Nuremberg tokens made of brass] passed as gold. . . .

Judgment of Pillory for lies uttered against the Mayor and Aldermen. . . .

Judgment of Pillory for selling a stinking partridge. . . .

Liber Albus, the White Book of the City of London compiled in
A.D. 1419 by John Carpenter and Richard Whittington,
translated by H. T. Riley

THE MURDER OF WILLIAM TRESHAM
His enemies gathered and assembled with them divers misdoers
and murderers of men to the number of 160 persons and more,
arrayed in form of war with cuirasses, light helmets, long
swords . . ., and all other unmerciful and forbidden weapons. In
the night next following [these men came] to a place called
Thorplandclose [in Multon, Northants.], and there lodged them
under a large hedge adjoining to the highway . . . and thence lay
in wait for the said William Tresham in order to execute their
malicious purpose, from the hour of midnight till the hour of six
before noon, at the which hour the said William Tresham, riding
in the highway to the said long hedge towards the said Duke [of
York] saying the Matins of Our Lady, the said William King who
was sent by the misdoers to await and give them perfect knowledge
of his coming, made to them a sign accorded between them,
whereby they knew the person of William Tresham, the day being
then dark. Whereupon, the said misdoers feloniously issued out
upon the said William Tresham and smote him through the body
a foot or more, whereof he died, and gave him many and great
deadly wounds, and cut his throat.

The Rolls of Parliament, 1450

CORONER'S INQUEST AT MARSTON, STAFFS.
Report on view of the body of John Swale, by the oath of
twelve jurors of four neighbouring townships. They say on their
oaths, that on Monday next [after the feast of the Holy Trinity],
Nicholas of Cheddleton was going along the King's highway with
linen and woollen cloths and other goods, when he was met by
certain thieves who tried to kill and rob him. And the said
Nicholas, in self defence, struck one of the robbers named John
Swale, right over the head with a staff worth a penny, of which
blow he died forthwith.

Coroners Rolls, 1450

DANGERS IN NORFOLK
William Paston, a sergeant at law, was in so 'great and intolerable
dread and fear of any enemy of his that he durst not go nor
ride about such occupation as he used [to do]'.

A great multitude of misruled people . . . sometime six,

sometime twelve, sometime thirty or more, armed with cuirasses and helmets, with bows, arrows, spears, and bills, override the country and oppress the people, and do many horrible and abominable deeds like to be the destruction of the shire of Norfolk.

Paston Letters, 1452

LAWLESS STATE OF AFFAIRS

[The faithful Commons tell of] great and lamentable complaints of your true poor subjects, universally throughout every part of this your realm, of robberies, ravishments, extortions, oppressions, riots, unlawful assemblies, wrongful imprisonments done unto them, unto such time as your said true subjects have made, as well for their enlarging as for the sureties of their lives, fine and ransom at the will of such misdoers. And forasmuch as the said misdoers be so favoured and assisted by persons of great might, having towards them of their livery, expressly against your laws, such multitude of robbers, rioters and mischievous persons, which in riotous and forcible manner disturb and hinder as well your Justices of Assize as of Peace in every part of this your realm, that no execution of your law may be had.

Rolls of Parliament, 1459

HOW SANCTUARY WAS CLAIMED, 1477

Let it be remembered that on October 6th, 1477, William Rome and William Nicholson of the parish of Forsgate fled to the cathedral church of St. Cuthbert at Durham, where, on account of a felony, amongst other things, committed and publicly confessed by them, namely, the murder by them some time before of William Aliand, they besought from the venerable and holy men, Thomas Haughton, sacristan of the said church, and William Cuthbert, master of the Galilee there, both brothers and monks of the same church, that the sanctuary of the church should be favourably extended to them in accordance with the liberties and privileges conceded to the most glorious confessor Saint Cuthbert of old; and by the ringing of a single bell, as is the custom, this boon was granted them. As witnesses called and summoned specially for the occasion there were present to see and hear those discreet men, William Heghyngton, Thomas Hudson, John Wrangham and Thomas Strynger.

Sanctuarium Dunelmense, V. Surtees Society

83. Court of the King's Bench in the fifteenth cesntury. The judges sit at the top. On the left the jury is being sworn in. Facing the judges, stands the chained prisoner guarded by a sergeant at law. Six more prisoners stand below.

THE PILLORY

The said John shall come out of Newgate without hood or girdle, barefoot and unshod, with a whetstone hung by a chain from his neck, and lying on his breast, it being marked with the words, 'A false liar', and there shall be a pair of trumpets, trumpeting before him on his way to the pillory; and there the cause of his punishment shall be solemnly proclaimed. And the said John shall remain on the pillory for three hours of the day, and from thence shall be taken back to Newgate in the same manner.

Memorials, fifteenth century

WIDESPREAD CRIME IN THE FIFTEENTH CENTURY

It is the easiest thing in the world to get a person thrown into prison in this country; for every officer of justice, both civil and criminal, has the power of arresting anyone, at the request of a private individual, and the accused person cannot be liberated without giving security, unless he be acquitted by the judgment of a jury of twelve men; nor is there any punishment awarded for making a slanderous accusation. Such severe measures against criminals ought to keep the English in check, but, for all this, there is no country in the world where there are so many thieves and robbers as in England; insomuch, that few venture to go alone in the country, excepting in the middle of the day, and fewer still in the towns at night, and least of all in London.

. . . people are taken up every day by dozens, like birds in a covey, and especially in London; yet for all this, they never cease to rob and murder in the streets.

Italian Relation of England, translation by Camden Society Editor

CLOSING TIMES OF TAVERNS, 1419

And whereas such [disreputable] persons going about by night do commonly have their resort and hold their common meetings in taverns more than elsewhere, and do there seek shelter, and lie in wait and watch their time to do ill—it is forbidden that any person shall keep a tavern for wine or for ale open after the hour of curfew aforesaid; but they shall keep their taverns closed after such hour. Nor shall they have persons therein, sleeping or sitting up; nor shall any one receive persons into his house from out of a common tavern, by night or by day, except those for whom he shall be willing to be answerable unto the peace of the King.

And if it shall be found that any taverner does otherwise, he shall be put on his surety, the first time by the hanap [a two-handled drinking cup often of silver] of the tavern, or by some other good pledge therein found; and he shall be amerced [fined] in the sum of half a mark; and the third time, in ten shillings. The fourth time he shall pay the whole penalty double, that is to say, twenty shillings. And the fifth time, he shall forswear such trade in the City for ever. And if any taverner shall receive any bad character, knowing that he has been a transgressor, he shall have the imprisonment that is provided for all receivers of felons.

Liber Albus, the White Book of the City of London compiled in 1419 by John Carpenter and Richard Whittington, translated by H. T. Riley.

INNS OF COURT, Early Fifteenth Century

There belong to it [the study of the law] ten lesser inns, and sometimes more, which are called the Inns of Chancery: in each of which there are an hundred students at the least; and in some of them a far greater number, though not constantly residing. The students are, for the most part, young men; here they study the nature of original and judicial writs, which are the very first principles of the law: after they have made some progress here, and are more advanced in years, they are admitted into the Inns of Court, properly so called; of these there are four in number. In that which is the least frequented there are about two hundred students. In these greater inns a student cannot well be maintained under eight and twenty pounds a year; and, if he have servants to wait on him, as for the most part they have, the expense is proportionately more: for this reason, the students are sons to persons of quality; those of an inferior rank not being able to bear the expenses of maintaining and educating their children in this way. As to the merchants, they seldom care to lessen their stock in trade by being at such large yearly expenses. So that there is scarce to be found, throughout the kingdom, an eminent lawyer, who is not a gentleman by birth and fortune; consequently they have a greater regard for their character and honour than those who are bred in another way. There is both in the Inns of Court, and the Inns of Chancery, a sort of academy, or gymnasium, fit for persons of their station; where they learn singing, and all kinds of music, dancing and such other accomplishments and diversions, which are called revels, as are suitable to their quality, and such as are usually practised at court. At other times, out of term, the greater part apply themselves to the study of the law. Upon festival days, and after the offices of the church are over, they employ themselves in the study of sacred and profane history: here everything which is good and virtuous is to be learned: all vice is discouraged and banished. So that knights, barons, and the greatest nobility of their kingdom, often place their children in those Inns of Court; not so much to make the laws their study, much less to live by the profession, having large patrimonies of their own, but to form their manners and to preserve them from the contagion of vice The discipline is so excellent, that there is scarce ever known to be any piques or differences, any bickerings or disturbances amongst them. The only way they have of punishing delinquents is by expelling them the society: which punishment they dread more than criminals do imprisonment and irons: for he who is expelled out of one society is never taken in by any of the other. Whence it happens that there is a constant harmony amongst them, the greatest friendship and a general freedom of conversation. I need not be particular in describing the manner and method how the laws are studied in those places, since your highness is never like to be a student there. But, I may say in the general, that it is pleasant, excellently well adapted for proficiency, and every way worthy of your esteem and encouragement.

In Praise of the Laws of England, written by Sir John Fortescue between 1464 and 1470 for Edward, Prince of Wales. Fortescue was Chief Justice in 1442. This work was translated by Francis Gregor in 1737

JUDGES, Fifteenth Century

. . . from thenceforth [after appointment], he changes his habit in some few particulars, but not in all: for when only a Serjeant-at-Law, he is clothed in a long robe, not unlike the sacerdotal habit, with a furred cape about his shoulders, and an hood over it with two labels or tippets; such as the Doctors of Law use in some universities, with a coif, . . . But after he is made a Judge, instead of the hood he shall be habited with a cloak, fastened upon his right shoulder; he still retains the other ornaments of a Serjeant, with this exception, that a Judge should not use a party-coloured habit, as the Serjeants do, and his cape is furred with minever, whereas the Serjeant's cape is always furred with white lamb; which sort of habit, when you [Prince Edward, son of Henry VI] come in power, I could wish your highness would make a little more ornamental, in honour of the laws, and also of your Government. You are to know further, that the Judges of England do not sit in the King's Courts above three hours in the day, that is, from eight in the morning till

eleven. The courts are not open in the afternoon. The suiters of
the court betake themselves to the pervise, and other places,
to advise with the Serjeants-at-Law, and other their counsel, about
their affairs. The Judges, when they have taken their refreshments,
spend the rest of the day in the study of the laws, reading of the
Holy Scriptures, and other innocent amusements, at their
pleasure; it seems rather a life of contemplation than of much
action: their time is spent in this manner, free from care and
wordly avocations. Nor was it ever found that any of them has
been corrupted with gifts or bribes. And it has been observed,
as an especial dispensation of Providence, that they have been
happy in leaving behind them immediate descendants in a right
line. . . . And I think it is no less a peculiar blessing, that from
amongst the Judges and their offspring, more Peers and great
men of the realm have risen, than from any other profession or
estate of men, whatsoever who have rendered themselves wealthy,
illustrious, and noble by their own applications, parts, and
industry. Although the merchants are more in number by some
thousands and some of them excel in riches all the Judges put
together. . . .

Sir John Fortescue, *On the Laws of England*,
translated by Francis Gregor, 1737

Famous People

THOMAS à BECKET, 1118-1170

Thomas was handsome and pleasing of countenance, tall of stature, with a prominent and slightly aquiline nose, nimble and active in his movements, gifted with eloquence of speech and an acute intelligence, high-spirited, ever pursuing the path of highest virtue, amiable to all men. . . .

In his consecration as archbishop he was anointed with the visible unction of God's mercy. Putting off the secular man, he now put on Jesus Christ. . . . Clad in a hair shirt of the roughest kind, which reached to his knees and swarmed with vermin, he mortified his flesh with the sparest diet, and his accustomed drink was water used for cooking of hay . . . He often exposed his naked back to the lash of discipline. Immediately over his hair-shirt he wore the habit of a monk, as being abbot of the monks of Canterbury; above this he wore the garb of a canon so as to conform to the custom of clerks. But the stole, the emblem of the sweet yoke of Christ, was ever day and night about his neck. His outward visage was like to that of ordinary men, but within all was different.

William Fitzstephen, *Materials for the History of Thomas Becket,
Archbishop of Canterbury*

ABBOT SAMSON, 1135-1211

Abbot Samson was below the average height, almost bald; his face was neither round nor oblong; his nose was prominent and his lips thick; his eyes were clear and his glance penetrating; his hearing was excellent; his eyebrows arched, and frequently shaved; and a little cold soon made him hoarse. On the day of his election he was forty-seven, and had been a monk for seventeen years. In his ruddy beard there was a few grey hairs, and still fewer in his black and curling hair. But in the course of the first fourteen years after his election all his hair became white as snow.

He was an exceedingly temperate man; he possessed great energy and a strong constitution, and was fond of riding and walking, until old age prevailed upon him and moderated his ardour in these respects. When he heard the news of the capture of the cross and the fall of Jerusalem, he began to wear undergarments made of horsehair, and a horsehair shirt, and gave up the use of flesh and meat. None the less, he willed that flesh should be placed before him as he sat at table, that the alms might be increased. He ate sweet milk, honey, and similar sweet things, far more readily than any other food.

He hated liars, drunkards, and talkative persons; for virtue ever loves itself and .spurns that which is contrary to it. He blamed those who grumbled about their meat and drink, and especially monks who so grumbled, and personally kept to the same manners which he had observed when he was a cloistered monk. Moreover, he had this virtue in himself that he never desired to change the dish which was placed before him. When I was a novice, I wished to prove whether this was really true, and as I happened to serve in the refectory, I thought to place before him food which would have offended any other man, in a very dirty and broken dish. But when he saw this, he was as it were blind to it. Then, as there was some delay, I repented of what I had done and straightway seized the dish, changed the food and dish for better, and carried it to him. He, however, was angry at the change, and disturbed.

He was an eloquent man, speaking both French and Latin, but rather careful of the good sense of that which he had to say than of the style of his words. He could read books written in English very well, and was wont to preach to the people in English, but in the dialect of Norfolk where he was born and bred. It was for this reason that he ordered a pulpit to be placed in the church, for the sake of those who heard him and for purposes of ornament.

The abbot further appeared to prefer the active to the contemplative life, and praised good officials more than good monks. He rarely commended anyone solely .on account of his knowledge of letters, unless the man happened to have knowledge of secular affairs, and if he chanced to hear of any prelate who had given up his pastoral work and become a hermit, he did not praise him for it. He would not praise men who were too kindly, saying, 'He who strives to please all men, deserves to please none. . . .'

When news reached London of the capture of King Richard [1193], and of his imprisonment in Germany, and the barons had met to take counsel on the matter, the abbot stood forth in their presence, and said that he was ready to seek his lord the king. He said that he would search for him in disguise or in any other way, until he found him and had certain knowledge of him. And from this speech he gained great praise for himself. . . .

When the abbot had purchased the favour and grace of King Richard with gifts and money, so that he believed that he could carry through all his affairs according to his desire, King Richard died, and the abbot lost his labour and expenditure. But King John after his coronation [1199], laying aside all his other work, at once came to St. Edmunds, being led to do so by his vow and devotion. And we thought that he would have made some great offering, but he offered a silken cloth, which his servants borrowed from our sacristan and have not yet paid for.

He enjoyed the hospitality of St. Edmund, which involved great expenses, and when he left he gave nothing at all honourable or beneficial to the saint, except thirteen pence sterling, which he paid for a mass for himself, on the day on which he departed from us.

The Chronicle of Jocelin of Brakelond, monk of St. Edmundsbury,
c. 1200. Translated by L. C. Jane, The King's Classics

GERALD THE WELSHMAN, 1147-1222

Therefore let those know who envy me, that I have hitherto led no idle nor easy life, nor with God's grace will I ever lead such a life while strength remains to me. Wherefore let the envious call me at their pleasure a foolish and mad old man; let them gnaw and rend and cease not to bark at me; for I, according to the warnings and salutary precepts of the holy man whom I have often cited, will not relinquish that grace of style which God hath given me from on high. Truly it is my desire unweariedly to exercise my studious mind in the study of literature, theology, philosophy and history, even as it hath always been my past custom, and not only to linger over these things in zealous charity for the erudition of posterity, but even so to die, and thus to breathe out my vital breath when my hour shall come. Yet to write books, and especially to strike out new thoughts, is a perilous thing to-day as in the past; and it exposeth us on all sides to the calumnious detraction of the envious.

Here therefore, in my studies and in my books, elaborated with much toil for the profit of posterity, is matter to burst the sides of our envious rivals, matter for the present time to tear to pieces in wrath, and for posterity to praise. Let the present rend them, and posterity read them. Let the present loathe them, and posterity love them. Let the present reprove, let posterity approve.

ROBERT GROSSETESTE, 1175-1253

He was a manifest confuter of the pope and the king, the blamer of prelates, the corrector of monks, the director of priests, the instructor of clerks, the support of scholars, the preacher to the people, the persecutor of the incontinent, the sedulous student of all scripture, the hammer and the despiser of the Romans. At the table of bodily refreshment he was hospitable, eloquent, courteous, pleasant, and affable, At the spiritual table, devout, tearful, and contrite. In his episcopal office he was sedulous, venerable, and indefatigable.

Matthew Paris, as translated in the
Dictionary of National Biography

MATTHEW PARIS, 1200-1259

In his time [Abbot John II, 1235-60] flourished and died Dom Matthew Paris, monk of St. Albans, a man of eloquence and renown, fulfilled of innumerable virtues, a magnificent historiographer and chronographer, a most excellent composer in the Latin tongue, and one who kept saying in his heart: 'idleness is the enemy of the soul'. This man's fame was so spread abroad that it had recommended him even to men of remote parts who had never seen his face. He collected from ancient time even unto the end of his own life, and wrote down fully in his books, the deeds of great men in Church and State, with sundry and marvellous chances and events, whereby he bequeathed to posterity a marvellous knowledge of the past. Moreover he was so subtle a workman in gold and silver and other metals, in carving and in painting, that he is believed to have left no equal in this world of the West. Let us therefore take him for our pattern, and labour without ceasing at wholesome works, that we may share with him in the rewards of heaven.

Thomas Walsingham, *Deeds of the Abbots*, translation by G. G. Coulton, *Social Life in Britain from the Conquest to the Reformation*

SIMON DE MONTFORT, 1208-1265

Thus ended the labours of that noble man Earl Simon, who gave up not only his property, but also his person, to defend the poor from oppression, and for the maintenance of justice and the rights of the kingdom. He was distinguished for his learning; to

84. Matthew Paris at the feet of the Virgin from his own drawing.

him an assiduous attention to divine duties was a pleasure; he
was moderate and frugal; and it was a usual practice of his to
watch by night in preference to sleeping. He was bold in speech,
and of severe aspect; he put great confidence in the prayers of
religious men, and always paid great respect to ecclesiastics. He
endeavoured to adhere to the counsels of St Robert, surnamed
Grosseteste, Bishop of Lincoln, and intrusted his children to him
to be brought up, when very young. On that prelate's counsel
he relied when arranging matters of difficulty, when attempting
dubious enterprises, and in finishing what he had begun,
especially in those matters by which he hoped to increase
his merits. It was reported that the same bishop had enjoined
on him, in order to obtain remission of his sins, to take
up this cause, for which he fought even to the death;
declaring that the peace of the church in England could
not be firmly established except by the sword, and positively
assuring him that all who died for it would be crowned with
martyrdom. Some persons, moreover, stated that on one occasion,
the bishop placed his hand on the head of the earl's eldest
son, and said to him, 'My well-beloved child, both thou and
thy father shall die on one day, and by one kind of death;
but it will be in the cause of justice and truth.' Report
goes, that Simon, after his death, was distinguished by the working
of many miracles, which, however, were not made publicly
known, for fear of kings.

Matthew Paris, *Historia Anglorum,* translated by J. A. Giles

SIR JAMES DOUGLAS 'THE GOOD', 1286-1330

In visage he was some deal gray,
And had black hair, as I heard say,
But then of limbs, he was well made,
With bones great, and shoulders braid.
His body well made and lenzie,
As they that saw him said to me.
When he was blyth, he was lovely
And meek, and sweet in company;
But who in battle might him see,
Another countenance had he;
And in his speech he lispt some deal,
But that set him right wonder well.

John Barbour, *The Bruce*

CATHERINE, COUNTESS OF SALISBURY, 1301-1344

The countess of Salisbury, who was esteemed one of the most beautiful and virtuous women in England, was in this castle [Wark], which belonged to the earl of Salisbury, who had been taken prisoner, with the earl of Suffolk, near Lisle, and was still in prison at the Chatelet in Paris. . . .

The countess comforted much those within the castle; and from the sweetness of her looks, and the charm of being encouraged by such a beautiful lady, one man in time of need ought to be worth two . . .

That same day that the Scots had decamped from before the castle of Wark, king Edward, and his whole army, arrived there about mid-day, and took up their position on the ground which the Scots had occupied. When he found that they were returned home, he was much enraged; for he had come there with so much speed, that both his men and horses were sadly fatigued.

He ordered his men to take up their quarters where they were, as he wished to go to the castle to see the noble dame within, whom he had never seen since her marriage . . . and the king, as soon as he was disarmed, taking ten or twelve knights with him, went to the castle, to salute the countess of Salisbury, and to examine what damage the attacks of the Scots had done, and the manner in which those within had defended themselves.

The moment the countess heard of the king's approach, she ordered all the gates to be thrown open, and went to meet him, most richly dressed; insomuch that no one could look at her but with wonder and admiration at her noble deportment, great beauty and affability of behaviour. When she came near the king, she made her reverence to the ground, and gave him her thanks for coming to her assistance, and then conducted him into the castle, to entertain and honour him, as she was very capable of doing.

Jean Froissart, Chronicles

GEOFFREY CHAUCER, 1340-1400

   . . . mine host began to jest
And for the first time looked on me
And spake he thus: 'What man are you?' said he.
'You look as if you hope to find a hare
For always on the ground I see you stare.

85. Chaucer reading his poetry to an audience from the court, c. 1390.

'Come nearer now and look up merrily,
Beware you, sirs, and let this man have place.
He is as shapely round the waist as I—
He'd be a poppet, small and fair of face
For any woman in her arm to embrace.
There's something elfish in his countenance,
And with no fellow does he dalliance.'
Geoffrey Chaucer, *The Rime of Sir Thopas, Canterbury Tales*

JOHN LYDGATE DESCRIBES HIMSELF, 1370-1451
I had in custom to come to school late
    Not for to learn but for appearance sake,
With my fellows ready to debate,
    To quarrel or joke was set all my pleasure;
    Whereof rebuked, this was my device,
To forge a lie, and thereupon to muse,
When I did wrong, myself to excuse.

To my betters did no reverence,
    Paid no attention to those over me,
Became obstinate by disobedience,
    Ran into gardens, apples there I stole;
    To gather fruits, spared neither hedge nor wall,
To pick grapes on other people's vines
Was more ready than for to say matins.

86.   John Lydgate at work in his study.

My pleasure was all to scorn folk and joke,
    Shrewd tricks ever among [them] to use,
To scoff and make faces like a wanton ape,
    When I did wrong, others I could accuse.
    My wits five in waste I did all use,
Rather cherry-stones for to tell [play]
Than to go to church, or hear the holy bell.

Loath to rise, loather to bed at eve,
    With unwashed hands ready to dinner,
My pater noster, my creed, or my belief
    Cast at the cock, lo, this was my manner!
    Waved with each wind, as doth a reed,
Chidden by my friends who would such faults amend,
Made deaf ear, would not to them attend.
John Lýdgate, 'The Testament', *Minor Poems* from Harl. MS.
                           British Museum

Historic Events

THOMAS à BECKET, CHANCELLOR, TO PARIS, 1158, TO ASK IN MARRIAGE THE FRENCH KING'S DAUGHTER FOR HENRY II's SON

He had above two hundred on horseback, of his own household, knights, clerks, butlers, serving men, esquires, sons of the nobles trained by him in arms, all in fit order. These and all their following shone in new holiday attire, each according to his rank. For he had four-and-twenty changes of raiment 'whose texture mocks the purple dyes of Tyre', many garments entirely of silk— almost all to be given away and left over sea—and every sort of material, griese and furs, of robes also and carpets, such as those with which the chamber and bed of a bishop are wont to be adorned. He had with him hounds, and birds of all kinds, such as kings and nobles keep. He had also in his company eight carriages, each drawn by five horses, in size and strength like destriers, for each one being set apart a strong young man, girt in a new tunic, walking by the carriage; and each carriage had its driver and guard. Two carriages bore nothing but beer, made by a decoction of water from the strength of corn, in iron-hooped barrels—to be given to the Franks who admire that sort of drink, which is wholesome, clear, of the colour of wine and of a better taste. One carriage was used for the chancellor's chapel furniture, one for his chamber, one his bursary, one his kitchen. Others carried different kinds of meat and drink; some had the hangings, bags with his nightgowns, packs and baggage. He had twelve sumpter-horses, and eight chests containing the chancellor's plate, of gold and silver; vessels, cups, platters, goblets, pitchers, basons, saltcellars, tankards, salvers, dishes. Other coffers and packs contained the chancellor's money—coin enough for daily expenses and presents—his clothes, books, and such-like. One sumpter-horse going before the others bore the sacred vessels of the chapel, the ornaments and books of the altar. Each of the sumpter-horses had its own groom provided as was meet. Each wagon had a dog chained above or below, great, strong and terrible, which seemed able to subdue a bear or a lion. And on the back of each sumpter-horse was a tailed monkey, or 'the ape that mocked the human face.' At this entry of the French villages and castles first came footboys, 'born to eat up the land' [Horace] —about two hundred and fifty—going six or ten or even more abreast, singing something in their own tongue, after the fashion of their land. There followed at some distance hounds in couples, and greyhounds in leash, with huntsmen and keepers. Then there rattled over the stones of the streets the iron-bound wagons covered with great hides sewn together. Then at a little distance the sumpter-horses, their grooms riding on them, with their knees on the flanks of the horses. Some of the Franks rushing forth from their houses at this great noise asked who this was, and whose the train? They answered that it was the chancellor of the king of the English going on an embassy to the king of the Franks. Then said the Franks, 'Marvellous is the king of the English whose chancellor goeth thus and so grandly.' Then the squires carrying the shields of the knights and leading their destriers; then other squires, of fresh youth, and those who carried hawks on their wrist; after them the butlers, and masters, and servants of the chancellor's house; then the knights and clerks, riding all two and two; last, the chancellor and some of his nearest friends.

William FitzSteven, *Materials for the History of Becket*. Translated by W. H. Hutton, S. *Thomas from the Contemporary Biographers*

THE MURDER OF THOMAS à BECKET, 29 DECEMBER 1170

. . . When the monks had entered the church, already the four knights followed behind with rapid strides. With them was a certain subdeacon, armed with malice like their own, Hugh, fitly surnamed for his wickedness Mauclerc, who showed no reverence for God or the saint, as the result showed. When the holy archbishop entered the church, the monks stopped vespers which they had begun and ran to him, glorifying God that they saw their father, whom they had heard was dead, alive and safe. They hastened, by bolting the doors of the church, to protect their shepherd from the slaughter. But the champion, turning to them, ordered the church doors to be thrown open, saying, 'It is not meet to make a fortress of the house of prayer, the church of Christ: though it be not shut up it is able to protect its own; and we shall triumph over the enemy rather in suffering than in

87. The murder of Thomas à Becket, Archbishop of Canterbury, in Canterbury
Cathedral, 1170.

fighting, for we came to suffer, not to resist.' And straightway they entered the house of prayer and reconciliation with swords sacrilegiously drawn, causing horror to the beholders by their very look and the clanging of their arms.

All who were present were in tumult and fright, for those who had been singing vespers now ran hither to the dreadful sight.

Inspired by fury the knights called out, 'Where is Thomas Becket, traitor to the king and realm?' As he answered not, they cried out the more furiously, 'Where is the archbishop?' At this, intrepid and fearless, as it is written, 'The just, like a bold lion, shall be without fear,' he descended from the stair where he had been dragged by the monks in fear of the knights, and in a clear voice answered 'I am here, no traitor to the king, but a priest. Why do ye seek me?' And whereas he had already said that he feared them not, he added, 'So I am ready to suffer in His name, Who redeemed me by His Blood: be it far from me to flee from your swords, or to depart from justice.' Having thus said, he turned to the right, under a pillar, having on one side the altar of the blessed Mother of God and ever Virgin Mary, on the other that of S. Benedict the confessor: by whose example and prayers, having crucified the world with its lusts, he bore all that the murderers could do with such constancy of soul as if he had been no longer in the flesh. The murderers followed him; 'Absolve,' they cried, 'and restore to communion those whom you have excommunicated, and restore their powers to those whom you have suspended.' He answered: 'There has been no satisfaction, and I will not absolve them.' 'Then you shall die,' they cried, 'and receive what you deserve.' 'I am ready,' he replied, 'to die for my Lord, that in my blood the Church may obtain liberty and peace. But in the name of Almighty God, I forbid you to hurt my people whether clerk or lay.' Thus piously and thoughtfully, did the noble martyr provide that no one near him should be hurt or the innocent be brought to death, whereby his glory should be dimmed as he hastened to Christ. Thus did it become the martyr-knight to follow in the footsteps of his Captain and Saviour Who when the wicked sought Him said: 'If ye seek Me, let these go their way.' Then they laid sacrilegious hands on him, pulling and dragging him that they might kill him outside the Church, or carry him away a prisoner, as they afterwards confessed. But when he could not be forced away from the pillar, one of them pressed on him and clung to him more closely. Him he pushed off calling him 'pander', and saying, 'Touch me not, Reginald; you owe me fealty and subjection; you and your accomplices act like madmen.' The knight, fired with terrible rage at this severe repulse, waved his sword over the sacred head. 'No faith', he cried, 'nor subjection do I owe you against my fealty to my lord the king.' Then the unconquered martyr seeing the hour at hand which should put an end to this miserable life and give him straightway the crown of immortality promised by the Lord, inclined his neck as one who prays and joining his hands he lifted them up, and commended his cause and that of the Church of God, to S. Mary, and to the blessed martyr Denys. Scarce had he said the words than the wicked knight fearing lest he should be rescued by the people and escape alive, leapt upon him suddenly and wounded this lamb, who was sacrificed to God, on the head, cutting off the top of the crown which the sacred unction of chrism had dedicated to God; and by the same blow he wounded the arm of him who tells this. For he, when the others, both monks and clerks, fled, stuck close to the sainted archbishop and held him in his arms till the one he interposed was almost severed. . . .

Then he received a second blow on the head but still stood firm. At the third blow he fell on his knees and elbows, offering himself a living victim, and saying in a low voice, 'For the Name of Jesus and the protection of the Church I am ready to embrace death.' Then the third knight inflicted a terrible wound as he lay, by which the sword was broken against the pavement, and the crown which was large was separated from the head; so that the blood white with the brain and the brain red with blood, dyed the surface of the virgin mother Church with the life and death of the confessor and martyr in the colours of the lily and the rose. The fourth knight prevented any from interfering so that the others might freely perpetrate the murder. As to the fifth, no knight but that clerk who had entered with the knights, that a fifth blow might not be wanting to the martyr who was in other things like to Christ, he put his foot on the neck of the holy priest and precious martyr, and, horrible to say, scattered his brains and blood over the pavement, calling out to the others, 'Let us away, knights; he will rise no more.'

Edward Grim tried to prevent the murder and was wounded in the arm. His account above appeared in William FitzStephen's *Materials for the History of Becket,* translated by W. H. Hutton

S. Thomas from the Contemporary Biographers

AFTER THE MURDER OF THOMAS à BECKET

While the body still lay on the pavement, some of them [Canterbury townsfolk] smeared their eyes with blood. Others brought bottles and carried off secretly as much of it as they could. Others cut off shreds of clothing and dipped them in the blood. At a later time no one was thought happy who had not carried off something from the precious treasure of the martyr's body. And indeed with everything in such a state of confusion and tumult, each man could do as he pleased. Some of the blood left over was carefully and cleanly collected and poured into a clean vessel and treasured up in the church. The archbishop's pallium and outer vesture, stained with blood, were with indiscreet piety given to the poor to pray for his soul, and happy would it have been for them, if they had not with inconsiderate haste sold them for a paltry sum of money. . . . [The monks prepare a burial.] They therefore stripped him of his outer garments to put on him his pontifical vestments; in so doing they discovered that the body was covered in a hairshirt, no less painful from its stiffness than from other causes and—a circumstance of which we have neither read nor heard of an example in the case of any other saint—they found the body covered in sackcloth, even from the thighs down to the knees, beneath the cowl and robe of the Cistercian habit. At this sight the monks gazed at one another, astounded at this proof of a hidden piety greater than would have been credited the archbishop. . . .

Benedict of Peterborough, translated in *English Historical Documents*, 1042-1189, by D. C. Douglas and G. W. Greenaway

HENRY II's PENANCE, 12 JULY 1174

So then, the king returned to England at the beginning of July [1174]. Taught by good advice he postponed dealing with nearly every matter of State, and immediately on landing set out with a penitent heart to the tomb of St. Thomas of Canterbury. Accordingly on Saturday, 12 July, he left the church of St. Dunstan, which is sited a good distance outside the city, and walked barefoot and clad in a woollen smock all the way to the martyr's tomb. There he lay prostrate for a great while and in devout humility, and of his own free will was scourged by all the bishops and abbots there present and each individual monk of the church of Canterbury. There he remained, constant in prayer before the holy martyr all that day and night. He neither took food nor went out to relieve nature, but, as he had come, so he remained, and would not permit a rug or anything of the kind to be provided for him. After lauds he made a tour of the altars in the choir of the church and the bodies of the saints interred there, and then returned to the tomb of St. Thomas in the crypt. At dawn on Sunday he heard Mass. Last of all he drank of water [from the well] of the holy martyr and was honoured with the gift of a phial. So he departed from Canterbury rejoicing, reaching London on the Sunday.

Gervase of Canterbury, *Chronicles,* translated by D. C. Douglas and G. W. Greenaway, *English Historial Documents,* 1042-1189

MAGNA CARTA, 1215

In 1215; which was the seventeenth year of the reign of King John; he held his court at Winchester at Christmas for one day, after which he hurried to London, and took up his abode at the New Temple; and at that place . . . nobles came to him in gay military array, and demanded the confirmation of the liberties and laws of King Edward, with other liberties granted to them and to the kingdom and Church of England, as were contained in the Charter, and above-mentioned laws of Henry the First, they also asserted that, at the time of his absolution at Winchester, he had promised to restore those laws and ancient liberties, and was bound by his own oath to observe them.

King John, when he saw that he was deserted by almost all, so that out of his regal superabundance of followers he scarcely retained seven knights, was much alarmed lest the barons would attack his castles and reduce them without difficulty, as they would find no obstacle to their so doing; and he deceitfully pretended to make peace for a time with the foresaid barons, and sent William Marshall, Earl of Pembroke, with other trustworthy messengers, to them, and told them that, for the sake of peace he would willingly grant them the laws and liberties they required; he also sent word to the barons by the same messengers, to appoint a fitting day and place to meet and carry all these matters into effect. The king's messengers then came in all haste to London, and without deceit reported to the barons all that had been deceitfully imposed on them; they in their great joy appointed the fifteenth of June for the king to meet them, and a field lying between Staines and Windsor. Accordingly at the time and place pre-agreed on, the king and nobles came to the appointed conference, and, when each party had stationed themselves apart from the other, they began a long discussion about terms of peace

88. Part of the Magna Carta, 15 June 1215. There are only four copies in existence. Two are in the British Museum, one in Lincoln Cathedral, one in Salisbury Cathedral.

89. Eleanor of Castile died in 1290 at Hardby in Lincolnshire; Edward I,
her husband, marked the stopping-places of her body on the way to London
with memorial ꜩ crosses. This is the Eleanor Cross at Hardingstone,
Northamptonshire.

and the aforesaid liberties. . . . At length after various points on both sides had been discussed, King John, seeing that he was inferior in strength to the barons, without raising any difficulty granted the underwritten laws and liberties, and confirmed them by his Charter. . . .

Roger of Wendover, *Flores Historiarum,* translated by J. A. Giles

THE GREAT CHARTER

1. In the first place we have granted to God and by this our present charter have confirmed, for us and our heirs forever, that the English church shall be free, and shall have its rights undiminished and its liberties unimpaired; and it is our will that it be thus observed, which is evident from the fact that, before the quarrel between us and our barons began, we willingly and spontaneously conceded and confirmed by our charter, and got confirmed by the lord pope Innocent III, freedom of elections, which is held most important and very essential to the English church; the which we shall observe and wish our heirs to observe in good faith for ever. We have also granted to all the freemen of our kingdom, for ourselves and our heirs for ever, all the liberties written below, to be had and held by them and their heirs from us and our heirs.

12. No scutage or aid shall be imposed in our realm except with the common counsel of the realm, except it be to ransom our person, to make our eldest son a knight or for once marrying our eldest daughter; and for these only a reasonable aid shall be levied. And this shall also apply to aids from the city of London.

13. And the city of London shall have all its ancient liberties and free customs both by land and by water. Furthermore we will and grant that all other cities, boroughs, towns and ports shall have all their liberties and free customs.

14. And to obtain the common counsel of the realm about levying an aid (except in the three cases aforesaid) or a scutage, we will cause to be summoned archbishops, bishops, abbots, earls and greater barons separately by our letters; and, in addition, we shall cause to be summoned generally through our sheriffs and bailiffs all those holding of us in chief, for a fixed date, to be after the expiry of at least forty days [from the date of summons], and to a fixed place; and in all letters of such summons we will specify the reason for the summons. And when the summons has thus been made, the business shall go forward on the day assigned according to the counsel of those present, even if not all those summoned have come.

15. Henceforth we will not grant anyone the right to take an aid from his freemen tenants, except to ransom his own person, to make his eldest son a knight and to marry his eldest daughter once; and for these [purposes] only a reasonable aid shall be levied.

16. No one shall be compelled to perform greater service for a knight's fee or for any other free tenancy than is due therefrom.

17. Common pleas shall not follow our court but shall be held in some fixed place.

18. Inquests of Novel Disseisin, of Mort d'Ancestor, and of Darrein Presentment shall not be held elsewhere than in the court of the county in which they arise, and in this manner—we, or if we are out of the realm, our chief justiciar, shall send two judges through each county four times a year who, with four knights of each county elected by the county [court] shall hold the said assises in the county court on the day and in the place of meeting of [that] county court.

39. No freeman shall be arrested or imprisoned or deprived of his freehold or outlawed or banished or in any way ruined, nor will we take or order action against him, except by the lawful judgment of his equals and according to the law of the land.

40. To no one will we sell, to no one will we refuse or delay right or justice.

61. Since, moreover, we have conceded all the above things for God, for the reform of our kingdom and the better quietening of the discord that has sprung up between us and our barons, and since we wish these things to flourish unimpaired and unshaken for ever, we constitute and concede to them the following guarantee:—namely that the barons shall choose any twenty-five barons of the kingdom they wish, who with all their might are to observe, maintain and secure the observance of the peace and rights which we have conceded and confirmed to them by this present charter of ours; in this manner, that if we, or our [chief] justiciar or our bailiffs, or any of our servants in any way do wrong to anyone, or transgress any of the articles of peace or security, and the wrongdoing has been demonstrated to four of the aforesaid twenty-five barons, those four barons shall come to us or our [chief] justiciar, if we are out of the kingdom, and laying before us the grievance, shall ask that we will have it redressed without delay.

J. C. Dickinson, *The Great Charter*, Historical Association pamphlet G. 31

WILLIAM WALLACE EXECUTED AT SMITHFIELD, 1305

Wilielmus Waleis, a man void of pity, a robber given to sacrilege, arson and homicide, more hardened in cruelty than Herod, more raging in madness than Nero . . . was condemned to a most cruel but justly deserved death. He was drawn through the streets of London at the tails of horses, until he reached a gallows of unusual height, especially prepared for him; there he was suspended by a halter; but taken down while yet alive, he was mutilated, his bowels torn out and burned in a fire, his head then cut off, his body divided into four, and his quarters transmitted to four principal parts of Scotland. Behold the end of the merciless man, who himself perishes without mercy.

Roger of Wendover, *Flores Historiarum*

THE STONE OF SCONE

The Scots also demanded that the royal stone should be restored to them, which Edward I had long ago taken from Scotland and placed at Westminster by the tomb of St. Edward. This stone was of famous memory amongst the Scots, because upon it the kings of Scotland used to receive the symbols of authority and the Sceptre. Scota, daughter of Pharaoh, brought this stone with her from the borders of Egypt when she landed in Scotland and subdued the land. For Moses had prophesied that whoever bore that stone with him should bring broad lands under the yoke of his lordship. Whence from Scota the land is called Scotland which was formerly called Albany from Albanactus.

Life of Edward II, edited by N. Denholm-Young

THE PEASANTS' REVOLT, ST ALBANS, 1381

Appalling threats forced all to rally regardless of ploughing and sowing . . . some lads had sticks, others rusty swords, axes, or smoke-stained bows . . . they slew lawyers old and young . . . and decided to burn all court rolls and old muniments. . . . During Matins on Friday [14 June 1381] hasty messengers from Barnet to St. Albans said the Commons bade speed to London with the Barnet and St. Albans men with their best arms, or else 20,000 would burn the vills and coerce them. Informed at once, the abbot dreaded the damage of such a raid and quickly summoned the servants and villeins of his court to bid them speed to London to appease and stop them. So they hurried off enthusiastically. They found a mob of 2000 yokels burning the valuable farm of the Hospitallers at Highbury and busy pulling down the ruins. The

90. Edward the Confessor's Chair, the Coronation Chair, in Westminster
Abbey. Under it rests the Stone of Destiny (*Lia Fail*), brought by Edward I
from Scotland to London in 1296.

ringleader John [Jack] Straw made them swear loyalty to 'King Richard and the Commons'. Other mobs were at Mile End and at Tower Hill where they killed Archbishop Sudbury, who worked miracles posthumously. Richard II gave them charters dated 15 June granting freedom to the serfs of various counties.

On reaching London the Abbey villeins and servants separated. The former in St. Mary Arches church debated services to the Abbey and how to achieve ancient aspirations, like new town boundaries, free pastures and fisheries, revival of lost sporting rights, freedom to establish hand mills, the exclusion of the liberty's bailiff from the town limits, and the return of bonds made by their sires to the late abbot Richard of Wallingford. . . .

They decided both to hurry home with authority from [Wat] Tyler, the Kentish vagabond king, making demands with threats of fire and slaughter, and to extort an order under royal privy seal to the abbot to restore their rights as in Henry's reign. William Gryndecobbe, the biggest debtor of the monastery, reared there, a neighbour and relation of the monks, was so forward in the business that the mob saw him kneel to the king six times to get that order, and he was chief spokesman with Walter, the rustic idol. Walter did not want to leave London or send a party but Gryndecobbe and other rascals swore loyalty to him so he promised to come with 20,000 if necessary to shave the beards of abbot, prior and monks [i.e. to behead them]. An abbey servant got home before them by a dashing ride to say the treasurer and many others were murdered, the Commons were merciless executioners and the prior would be beheaded and the other monks imperilled if they stayed. The prior, four monks and various associates fled on horse and on foot the dangerous trail to Tynemouth. Soon the villeins were back, led by William Gryndecobbe and William Cadyndon, baker, who coveted some obvious success before their comrades arrived, longing to get extra credit so as to seem important afterwards. They reported good progress. They would be masters not slaves, and that very night they would break the abbot's folds in Falcon and other woods and demolish the gates of Eye and other woods with the sub-cellarer's house, opposite the street where fish was sold, as it spoilt the townsman's view and damaged prestige. The fools took rapid action. . . . Thus ended Friday at St. Albans with its train of evil.

On Saturday morning [15 June] the St. Albans men arose to review their crimes. A monster procession marched to Falcon wood, calling out all of military age on pain of death or destruction of their house or goods; threats united the decent and criminal.

Our William Gryndecobbe and William Cadyndon led. At the rendezvous the mob plotted its demands, actions and threats. They decided to finish off the folds and coppice gates, and did so. Back in town they awaited peasants from surrounding villages and the home farm. They had summoned with menaces 2000 or more rascals to rally about freedom from St. Albans. They would gain any demands and not let any gentlemen linger at home but bring them as supporters. From Wat Tyler they learnt the trick of executing the hesitant or wrecking their homes.

The sight of the mob they had conjured up raised their spirits, clasping hands and swearing oaths. An arrogant rush to the abbey gates showed Walter's power. The gates were opened and they contemptuously told the porter to open the prison. Some godly villeins had told the abbot and he had told the porter the plan, so he obeyed. They freed the captives in return for unswerving support except for one whom they judged and butchered in the space before the gate, yelling diabolically as they had learnt at the archbishop's murder in London and setting the head on the pillory. Soon allies from Barnet arrived and Richard de Wallingford, a substantial St. Albans villein, briskly rode up from London with the royal letter Gryndecobbe had kept demanding, bearing the banner of St. George like the criminals in London.

They swarmed round him as he dismounted and planted his standard where they should stand until he brought the abbot's answer. The leaders entered the church with him and sent word to the abbot's chamber to answer the Commons. The monks convinced the abbot that the death which he would have preferred would not save the abbey's rights so he went down to them like a beaten man. Wallingford showed him the letter extracted from the king by Gryndecobbe dated 15 June about certain charters from King Henry concerning common, pasture and fishing rights. The abbot raised legal objections but Wallingford said the Commons did not expect excuses, would turn on him if kept waiting, and would summon Wat Tyler and 20,000 men. The abbot complained that he had befriended them for 32 years. Admitting this, they said they had hoped to get their demands from his successor. He yielded everything to the lesser evil. They burnt many charters by the market cross and also demanded a certain old charter about the liberties of the villeins 'with gold and blue capital letters'. He said he had never seen this but would hunt for it. The leaders reported a promise of a new charter, and the rascals went into the cloister with the deeds and ripped up millstones set in the parlour floor to commemorate an old suit between the villeins and the late abbot Richard. Smashing these, they distributed fragments like holy bread in a parish church. Meal time was granted and allowed sad reflection on slaves become masters and life and death in the hands of merciless countrymen. London had lain at their will a day and a night, the archbishop and treasurer were executed, the king was captive, his soldiery powerless. . . .

At the ninth hour the villeins came back for their charter, or else 2000 of them would destroy the gate. The abbot prepared a charter to be read and then sealed, but they sent a squire for clerk with ink and parchment to write at their dictation. They insisted that there was another charter of old liberties which they would have or wreck the abbey. He offered to swear at the morrow's mass that he withheld nothing, but they scorned his oaths, keener to destroy the abbey than get charters. Ale and a great basket of bread were put at the gate for all as a sop, which did not work, until the chief townsmen risked telling them to be quiet. They then left the gate to join another mob sacking houses on Walter's London pattern.

Under the royal colours they dared to set watches round the town against any help and to execute any monks going in or out. On the morrow they invited any with financial claims on the abbey to appear, and one demanded 100 marks damages, threatening to burn St. Peter's Grange and Kyngebury manor, which he had leased until he fled for debt. He had 2000 Commons near to avenge his wrongs and would rather make payment on the prior's body than recover his cash.

The monks had a sleepless night because of the impossible demand of the villeins to produce the unfindable charter, but Sunday [16 June] brought hopeful rumours of Tyler's death and London's rally to the king. A royal messenger enjoined peace, bringing a letter of royal protection for the abbey. Mobs summoned from Luton, Watford, Barnet, Rickmansworth and Tring arrived and the townsmen did not wish to seem disheartened or obedient to the king. Regardless of the future they would get their charters, but with a more conciliatory air. . . . The chief townsmen entered the abbot's chamber, stood over the clerk, inserting their requirements about liberties in the charter, and made the abbot seal a bond in £1000 to produce the non-existent charter, if found. Sir Hugh Segrave, royal steward, and Thomas Percy wrote advising every concession as it would never be held valid, so the abbot gave his bond. They acted as lords, not servants, in the abbot's chamber and chapel, present at the engrossing, dictating words and superintending the sealing.

The seal which showed St. Alban holding a palm was properly applied to their charter but miraculously it thrice stuck to the wax to show that the martyr did not want them for masters but would keep his lordship over them. They departed gleefully to publish the new charter at the cross with the royal pardon and manumission. They even published the royal charter of protection to show goodwill, but with malice at heart as appears.

On Monday and Tuesday villeins from all the abbey's vills came urgently requiring charters of manumission pursuant to the royal charter. These were made in a standard form. Then the villagers thought themselves gentry of royal blood who need not even pay rent. . . . They made grammar-school masters swear never to teach boys grammar. . . . They tried to burn all records and killed all who could record past or current events. It was dangerous to be known as a clerk and worse still to be found carrying an inkhorn. . . .

The abbot then sent some villeins to swell the royal army, but they claimed to have come on their own authority. Richard Peeres recognised some as ringleaders at St. Albans, imprisoned them and would have executed them—on the vigil of the passion of St. Alban, the eighth day after the Friday. During matins the chief townsmen went to enlist the abbot's help. In distress he despatched a monk to London to see the prisoners released, which he did. . . .

The king proposed to come to do justice at St. Albans, but Sir Walter Atte Lee, a local man, feared the damage done by such a host and persuaded the king to commission him to make peace between villeins and abbot. William Gryndecobbe persuaded them not to bolt but to meet him and if he did not come as a friend to drive him away. They greeted him and he made the people collect in the shape of a rainbow, while he with his armed guard about him explained that he came with a commission to prevent the damage threatened by the proposed arrival of the royal army. He adjured them to give up the ringleaders and make peace with the abbey. Some applauded but the jury said nobody should be indicted. When told to give up the charters they prevaricated, alleging intimidation, and ignorance as to who held them. The abbot said he trusted their consciences and mollified the knight by saying he needed no intermediary. The knight called a meeting at Barnet Wood but did little for fear of the villeins there—about 300 stood round with bows, especially Barnet and Berkhamstead men, and if he had tried to do justice they would probably have made a riot and his soldiers have joined them. He secretly told the bailiffs and constables, when the mob dispersed, to compass the capture of William Gryndecobbe, William Cadyndon, John the Barber who had removed the millstones from the pavement, with other notorieties. He hastened to Hertford whither he wanted them brought. Richard Peeres, John Chival, Thomas Eydon and William Eccleshale, admirable squires of the abbot, captured the three with the unwilling help of the bailiffs and put them in the gate. Next morning they were taken to Hertford with the chief townsmen of St. Albans and all the abbot's squires and varlets to reinforce the knight in doing justice. On their departure the town seethed with hot air and empty oaths—a hundred would die if one neighbour fell. Mobs gathered in fields and woods outside the town and, with the defenders away, the abbey looked like getting burnt, so the abbot in alarm summoned some local gentry for protection. Hearing his squires were gone executing the prisoners he wrote for them to hurry back to dispel this new danger. The trial was on and they grieved to go for otherwise they would have seen them executed, but they hurried home. . . . Two stopped in gaol but William Gryndecobbe was released, on three neighbours going bail for £300 each, to return to prison next Saturday.

The villeins wavered between violence and conciliation, now incited by Gryndecobbe, now depressed by the reported approach of the Earl of Warwick and Thomas Percy, now elated by the diversion of Warwick, now dismayed by the approach of the king himself. The abbot asked Hugh Segrave in London to divert the king because of the damage threatened by the royal entourage to crops, though the villeins alleged that the abbot spent £1,000 to ruin them. They hired an expensive lawyer to compromise with the abbot, repairing damage, replacing as many millstones as were removed, and returning extorted charters. The abbot met the king at the west gate with bells ringing. He had thousands of tenants in chief, soldiers and Robert Tresilian the justiciar. The ringleaders were kept prisoner until Monday while John Ball was brought to St. Albans tried [14 July] and hanged [15 July]. . . .

The jury refused to indict, but Tresilian produced a list of ringleaders, forcing the jury to indict and getting assent from second and third juries. William Gryndecobbe, William Cadyndon, John the Barber and other criminals to the number of 15 were drawn and hanged for riot. Some leading townsmen like Richard, John Garlick, William Berewill and Thomas the Stink, were imprisoned, the 80 others whom royal clemency later released. Meanwhile the villeins spitefully accused the abbot, who had risked royal displeasure by his intercessions, of forcing them to join the London mob. Such malice shocked the justiciar who silenced them by asking why the abbot did so. Other slanders about the abbot's reduction of freemen to villeinage, compulsion to use his mill instead of grinding at home, and bribing the king were shaking most of the abbey's friends, despite penalties for slander, against the abbot, of hanging for men and burning for women. After 8 days the king met the obvious perversity of the abbey's dependents by sending a commission to see that the abbey's dues were rendered—for the royal chancery was being held in the chapter-house so that the abbot could manage things better.

On St. Margaret's Day after eating, the king was to go to Berkhampstead Castle. In the great abbey hall he first took an oath of fealty from the men of Hertfordshire between 15 and 60 years old. They swore to prefer death to obedience to agitators, to seize agitators and render their dues . . . the king was amazed to hear that the bodies of those hanged at St. Albans had been audaciously taken from the gallows so he sent a writ dated 3 August to the bailiffs, bidding them be replaced in chains to hang as long as they lasted. This reduced to a revolting slavery the freedom-loving revolutionaries of St. Albans, for none would do the work for them and with their own hands they had to hang up their fellow citizens whose decomposing bodies were full of maggots and stank. It was just for men who usurped the name 'citizen' to have the disgusting task whereby they earned the apt name of 'hangmen' to their lasting shame. . . .

Thomas Walsingham, Historia Anglicana

DEATH OF WAT TYLER, 1381

Among the most wondrous and hitherto unheard-of prodigies that ever happened in the City of London, that which took place there on the Feast of Corpus Christi, the 13th day of June, in the 4th year of the reign of King Richard the Second, seems deserving to be committed to writing, that it may not be unknown to those to come.

For on that day, while the King was holding his Council in the Tower of London, countless companies of the commoners and persons of the lowest grade from Kent and Essex suddenly approached the said City, the one body coming to the town of Southwark, and the other to the place called 'Mileende', without Algate. By the aid also of perfidious commoners within the City, of their own condition, who rose in countless numbers there, they suddenly entered the City together, and, passing straight through it, went to the mansion of Sir John [of Gaunt], Duke of Lancaster, called 'le Savoye', and completely levelled the same

91. Two scenes are depicted here at Smithfield. Walworth, the Mayor of London, strikes Wat Tyler down, who is then killed by a squire, Standish. The King, Richard II, on the right, has moved over to the rebels, and proceeds to lead them out of London.

with the ground, and burned it. From hence they turned to the Church of the Hospital of St. John of Jerusalem, without Smethefeld, and burnt and levelled nearly all the houses there, the church excepted.

On the next morning, all the men from Kent and Essex met at the said place called 'Mileende', together with some of perfidious persons of the City aforesaid; whose numbers in all were past reckoning. And there the King came to them from the Tower, accompanied by many knights and esquires, and citizens on horseback, the lady his mother following him also in a chariot. Where, at the prayer of the infuriated rout, our Lord the King granted that they might take those who were traitors against him, and slay them, wheresoever they might be found. And from thence the King rode to his Wardrobe, which is situate near to Castle Baynard; while the whole of the infuriated rout took its way towards the Tower of London; entering which by force, they dragged forth from it Sir Simon [of Sudbury], Archbishop of Canterbury, Chancellor of our Lord the King, and Brother Robert Hales, Prior of the said Hospital of St. John of Jerusalem, the King's Treasurer; and, together with them, Brother William Appeltone, of the Order of Friars Minors, and John Leg, Serjeant-at-arms to the King, and also, one Richard Somenour, of the Parish of Stebenhuthe [Stepney]; all of whom they beheaded in the place called 'Tourhille', without the said Tower; and then carrying their heads through the City upon lances, they set them up on London Bridge, fixing them there on stakes.

Upon the same day there was also no little slaughter within the City, as well of natives as of aliens. Richard Lions, citizen and vintner of the said City, and many others, were beheaded in Chepe. In the Vintry also, there was a very great massacre of Flemings, and in one heap there were lying about forty headless bodies of persons who had been dragged forth from the churches and their houses; and hardly was there a street in the City in which there were not bodies lying of those who had been slain. Some of the houses also in the said City were pulled down, and others in the suburbs destroyed, and some too, burnt.

Such tribulation as this, greater and more horrible than could be believed by those who had not seen it, lasted down to the hour of Vespers on the following day, which was Saturday, the 15th of June; on which day God sent remedy for the same, and His own gracious aid, by the hand of the most renowned man, Sir William Walworthe, the then Mayor; who in Smethefelde, in presence of our Lord the King and those standing by him, lords, knights, esquires, and citizens on horseback, on the one side, and the whole of this infuriated rout on the other, most manfully, by himself, rushed upon the captain of the said multitude, 'Walter Tylere' by name, and, as he was altercating with the King and the nobles, first wounded him in the neck with his sword and then hurled him from his horse, mortally pierced in the breast; and further, by favour of the divine grace, so defended himself from those who had come with him, both on foot and horseback, that he departed from thence unhurt, and rode on with our Lord the King and his people, towards a field near to the spring that is called 'Whitewellebeche' [in Clerkenwell]; in which place, while the whole of the infuriated multitude in warlike manner was making ready against our Lord the King and his people, refusing to treat of peace except on condition that they should first have the head of the said

Mayor, the Mayor himself, who had gone into the City at the instance of our Lord the King, in the space of half an hour sent and led forth therefrom so great a force of citizen warriors in aid of our Lord the King, that the whole multitude of madmen was surrounded and hemmed in; and not one of them would have escaped, if our Lord the King had not commended them to be gone.

Therefore our Lord the King returned into the City of London with the greatest of glory and honour, and the whole of this profane multitude in confusion fled forthwith for concealment, in their affright.

For this same deed our Lord the King, beneath his standard, in the field, with his own hands decorated with the order of knighthood the said Mayor, and Sir Nicholas Brembre, and Sir John Phelipot, who had already been Mayors of the said City; as also, Sir Robert Launde.

City Letter Book, in H. T. Riley, *Memorials of London*

THE EXECUTION OF SIR JOHN OLDCASTLE, 1413

In this same year, thanked be Almighty God, the general council was ended and union made in holy church: and a pope chosen at Constance upon St. Martin's Day by the assent of all the general council, and he is called Martin V. Also in the same year was Sir John Oldcastle, called the Lord Cobham, taken in the Marches of Wales and brought to the City of London, the which was chief lord maintainer of all the Lollards in this realm, and ever about to destroy to his power holy church. And therefore he was first drawn, and afterwards hanged, and burnt hanging on the new gallows besides St. Giles with an iron chain about his neck, because that he was a lord of name. And so there he made an end of his cursed life.

London Chronicle Julius B.11, quoted in J. J. Bagley, *Historical Interpretation*

DICK WHITTINGTON LORD MAYOR FOR THE THIRD TIME, 1419

On Friday, the Feast of St. Edward the King and Confessor [13 October] . . . after the Mass of the Holy Spirit devoutly and becomingly celebrated with solemn music in the Chapel of the Guildhall of the City of London, according to the Ordinance made thereon in the time of John Wodecok . . . in presence of William Sevenok, Mayor [with the Recorder, Aldermen and

Sheriffs] and an immense number of the Commonalty of the citizens of the said city, summoned to the Guildhall of London for the election of a Mayor for the ensuing year, by their common assent, consent, and desire, Richard Whitingtone was chosen Mayor for the ensuing year; and on the morrow of the said Feast was presented before the Barons of the Exchequer of our Lord the King, at Westminster, admitted, and accepted as such.

London, Letter Book I, translated by H. T. Riley,
Memorials of London

LIMITATION OF THE FRANCHISE, 1429

. . . whereas in many counties the elections of knights of the shires, those chosen to attend the king's parliaments, have of late been carried out by too great and excessive a number of people dwelling within those same counties, of whom the larger part have been people of little substance or of no worth, each pretending to have the same voice in such elections as the most worthy knights or squires dwelling in the same counties, whereby homicides, riots, assaults, and feuds are very likely to arise among the gentlefolk and other people of the same counties unless a suitable remedy is provided in this connection; [therefore] our lord the king considering the premises, has provided and ordained by the authority of this parliament that knights of the shires, elected to attend parliaments hereafter to be held in the kingdom of England, shall be chosen in each county by persons dwelling and resident therein, each of whom shall have a freehold to the value of at least 40s. a year beyond the charges . . .; and that every sheriff of England shall, by the aforesaid authority, have power to examine on the Holy Gospels each such elector, how much he is able to spend annually. . . .

Statutes of the Realm (1810-28),
translated by C. Stephenson and F. G. Marcham

ON 26 SEPTEMBER 1470, WARWICK, 'THE KINGMAKER', FORCES EDWARD IV TO ESCAPE TO FLANDERS

Five or six daies after the Earles arrival his power was so great, that he encamped within three leagues of King Edward. Notwithstanding the Kings force was greater than his, if all his men had been faithfull and true, and lay also in campe to fight with him. Further you shall understand that the King lodged (as himselfe told me) in a strong village—at the least a strong house into the which no man could enter but by a draw bridge,

which was a happy chance for him: the rest of his army lay in
other villages round about. But as hee sat at dinner, suddenly
one came running in, and brought newes that the Marques of
Montague the Earles brother and certaine other were mounted
on horsebacke, and had caused all their men to crie, God save
King Henry. Which message at the first the King beleeved not,
but in all hast sent other messengers forth, and armed himselfe,
and set men also at the barriers of his lodging to defend it. He
was accompanied with the Lord Hastings Lord Chamberlain of
England, a wise Knight and of the greatest authoritie about him,
who was   maried   to   the   Earle   of Warwickes sister, yet
notwithstanding was true and faithfull to his Master, and had
three thousand horse under his charge in the Kings armie as
himselfe told me. With the King was also the Lord Scales the
Queene of Englands brother, and divers other valiant Knights
and Esquiers, who all perceived that this busines went not well:
for the messengers brought word that the report was true, and
that the enimies assembled to assault the King.

But God so provided for the King that he lodged hard by
the sea side, neere to a place where a little ship laden with victuals
that followed his armie, and two hulks of Holland fraughted
with merchandise lay at anchor: he had no other shift but to
run to save himselfe in one of them. The Lord Chamberlaine
staied a while behind him, and talked with the lieutenant of his
band and divers other particular men in the Kings armie, willing
them to go to the enemies, and to beare true and faithfull hearts
to the King and him which talke ended: he went aboord to the
rest being ready to depart. Now you shall understand that the
custome in England is, after the victory obtained, neither to kill
nor ransome any man, especially of the vulgar sort: knowing all
men then to be readie to obey them, because of their good
successe. Wherefore these soldiers after the Kings departure
received no harme. Notwithstanding King Edward himselfe told
me, that in all battels that he wan, so soone as he had obtained
victorie he used to mount on horsebacke, and crie to Save the
people and kil the nobles: for of them few or none escaped.
Thus fled King Edward the yeere 1470 with two hulkes and a
little bote of his owne countrie, accompanied with seven or eight
hundred persons, having none other apparell than that they ware
in the wars, utterly unfurnished of money, and hardly knowing
whether they went. Strange it was to see this poore King (for
so might he now well be called) to flie after this sort pursued
by his owne servants, and the rather, for that he had by the space

of twelve or thirteene yeeres lived in greater pleasures and delicacies than any Prince in his time: for he had wholy given himselfe to dames, hunting, hawking, and banketting, in such sort that he used when he went hunting in the sommer season, to cause many pavilions to be pitched to solace himeselfe there with the Ladies. And to say the truth his personage served aswel to make court as any mans that ever I knew: for he was yonge, and as goodly a gentleman as lived in our age, I meane in this time of his adversitie: for afterward he grew marvellous grosse. But behold now how he fell into the troubles and misfortunes of the world. He sailed straight towards Holland, and at that time the Easterlings were enemies both to the English men and the French, and had many ships of war upon the sea, wherefore they were much feared of the English men, and not without cause. . . . The King had not one peny about him, but gave the Master of the ship for his passage a goodly gown furred with martins, promising one day to do him a good turne: and as touching his traine never so poore a company was seene. But the Lord of Gruteuse dealt very honorably with them: for he gave much apparell among them, and defraied the King to La Hay in Holland whither himself also waited upon him. Afterward he advertised the Duke of Burgundie of this adventure, who was marvellously abashed at the newes, and had much rather have heard of the Kings death: for he feared the Earle of Warwicke, who was his mortall enemy, and bare now the sway in England. The sayd Earle soone after he was landed, found infinite numbers to take his part. For the army that King Edward left behind him, what for love, what for feare yeelded to him, in such sort that every day his forces encreased. And in this estate went hee to London, where a great number of Knights and Esquiers (who afterward did King Edward good service), tooke sanctuary, as also did the Queene his wife, who was there delivered of a sonne in very poore estate.

Philip de Comines, *Memoirs of His Own Times*, translated by Thomas Danett, 1614

HENRY TUDOR, EARL OF RICHMOND, LANDS AT MILFORD HAVEN, 7 AUGUST 1485. THE DUKE OF NORFOLK WRITES TO JOHN PASTON

To my well-beloved friend John Paston, be this bill delivered in haste.

Well-beloved friend, I commend me to you; letting you to understand that the king's enemies be a-land, and that the king would have set forth as upon Monday, but only for our Lady-day, but for certain he goeth forward as upon Tuesday, for a servant of mine brought to me the certainty.

Wherefore I pray you that you meet with me at Bury, for, by the grace of God, I purpose to lie at Bury as upon Tuesday night; and that ye bring with you such company of tall men as ye may goodly make at my cost and charge, besides that which ye have promised the king; and I pray you, ordain them jackets of my livery, and I shall content you at your meeting with me.

Your lover,
J. Norfolk.

[August, 1485]

Paston Letters, edited by J. Fenn

Warfare

WAR IN THE MARCHES OF WALES, 1188

In this, as well as in every other military expedition, either in
Ireland or in Wales, the natives of the marches, from the constant
state of warfare in which they are engaged, and whose manners
are formed from the habits of war, are bold and active, skilful
on horseback, quick on foot, not nice as to their diet, and ever
prepared when necessity required to abstain both from corn and
wine. By such men were the first hostile attacks made upon
Wales as well as Ireland and by such men alone can their final
conquest be accomplished . . . but the Gallic soldiery is known
to differ much from the Welsh and Irish. In their country
[Normandy, Flanders etc.] the battle is on level, here on rough
ground; there in an open field, here in forests; there they consider
their armour as honour, here as a burden; there soldiers are
taken prisoners, here they are beheaded; there they are ransomed
here they are put to death. Where, therefore, the armies engage
in a flat country, a heavy and complex armour, made of cloth
and iron, both protects and decorates the soldier; but when the
engagement is in narrow defiles, in woods and marches, where
infantry have the advantage over cavalry, a light armour is
preferable. For light arms afford sufficient protection against
unarmed men, by whom victory is either lost or won at the first
onset; where it is necessary that an active and retreating enemy
should be overcome by a certain proportional quantity of
moderate armour; whereas with a more complex sort, and with
high and curved saddles, it is difficult to dismount, more so to
mount, and with the greatest difficulty can such troops march, if
required, with the infantry. . . .

Gerald the Welshman, Description of Wales,
translated by Sir R. C. Hoare

SIEGE OF ACRE, 1191

The king of France first recovered from his sickness, and turned
his attention to the construction of machines and petrariae

[artillery for throwing stones], suitable for attacks, and which he determined to ply night and day, and he had one of superior quality, to which they gave the name of 'Bad Neighbour'. The Turks also had one they called 'Bad Kinsman', which by its violent casts, often broke 'Bad Neighbour' in pieces; but the king of France rebuilt it, until by constant blows, he broke down part of the principal city wall, and shook the tower Maledictum. On one side, the petraria of the duke of Burgundy plied; on the other that of the Templars did severe execution; while that of the Hospitallers never ceased to cast terror amongst the Turks. Besides these, there was one petraria, erected at the common expense, which they were in the habit of calling the 'petraria of God'. Near it, there constantly preached a priest, a man of great probity, who collected money to restore it at their joint expense, and to hire persons to bring stones for casting. By means of this engine, a part of the wall of the tower Maledictum was at length shaken down, for about two poles' length. The count of Flanders had a very choice petraria of large size, which after

92. A crusader paying homage.

his death, King Richard possessed; besides a smaller one, equally good. These two were plied incessantly, close by a gate the Turks used to frequent, until part of the tower was knocked down. In addition to these two King Richard had constructed two others of choice workmanship and material, which would strike at a place at an incalculable distance. He had also built one put together very compactly, which the people called 'Berefred', with steps to mount it, fitting most tightly to it; covered wih raw hides and ropes, and having layers of most solid wood, not to be destroyed by any blows, nor open to injury from the pouring thereon of Greek fire, or any other material. He also prepared two mangonels, one of which was of such violence and rapidity, that what it hurled reached the inner rows of the city market-place. These engines were plied day and night, and it is well known that a stone sent from one of them killed twelve men with its blow; the stone was afterwards carried to Saladin for inspection; and King Richard had brought it from Messina, which city he had taken. Such stones and flinty pieces of rock, of the smoothest kind, nothing could withstand; but they either shattered in pieces the object they struck, or ground it to powder. The king was confined to his bed by a severe attack of fever, which discouraged him; for he saw the Turks constantly challenging our men, and pressing on them importunately, and he was prevented by sickness from meeting them, and he was more tormented by the importunate attack of the Turks than by the severity of the fever that scorched him.

Itinerary of Richard I from *Chronicles of the Crusades being contemporary narratives of the Crusade of Richard Coeur de Lion, by Richard of Devizes and Geoffrey de Vinsauf; and of the Crusade of Saint Louis by Lord John de Joinville*

BOWS IN CLOSE FIGHT, Twelfth Century

It seems worthy of remark, that the people of what is called Venta [Gwent or Monmouthshire] are more accustomed to war, more famous for valour, and more expert in archery, than those of any other part of Wales. The following examples prove the truth of this assertion. In the last capture of the aforesaid castle, which happened in our days, two soldiers passing over a bridge to take refuge in a tower built on a mound of earth, the Welsh, taking them in the rear, penetrated with their arrows the oaken portal of the tower, which was four fingers thick; in memory of which circumstance, the arrows were preserved in the gate. William de Braose also testifies that one of his soldiers, in a conflct

93. Guido Rex seizing the cross held by Saladin.

with the Welsh, was wounded by an arrow, which passed through
his thigh and the armour with which it was cased on both sides,
and through that part of the saddle which is called the *alva*,
mortally wounded his horse. Another soldier had his hip, equally
sheathed in armour, penetrated by an arrow quite to the saddle,
and on turning his horse round, received a similar wound on
the opposite hip, which fixed him on both sides of his seat. What
more could be expected from a balista? Yet the bows used by
this people are not made of horn, ivory, or yew, but of wild elm;
unpolished, rude, and uncouth, but stout; not calculated to
shoot an arrow to a great distance, but to inflict very severe
wounds in close fight.

Gerald the Welshman, Description of Wales,
translated by Sir R. C. Hoare

MANORBIER CASTLE, Late Twelfth Century
Manorbier near Pembroke is excellently well defended by turrets
and bulwarks, and is situated on the summit of a hill extending
on the western side towards the sea-port, having on the northern
and southern sides a fine fish-pond under its walls, as conspicuous
for its grand appearance, as for the depth of its waters, and a
beautiful orchard on the same side, inclosed on one part by a
vineyard, and on the other by a wood, remarkable for the
projection of its rocks, and the height of its hazel trees. On the
right hand of the promontory, between the castle and the church,
near the site of a very large lake and mill, a rivulet of

never-failing water flows through a valley, rendered sandy by the violence of the winds. Towards the west, the Severn sea, bending its course to Ireland, enters a hollow bay at some distance from the castle; and the southern rocks, if extended a little further towards the north, would render it a most excellent harbour for shipping. From this point of sight, you will see almost all the ships from Great Britain, which the east wind drives upon the Irish coast, daringly brave'the inconstant waves and raging sea. This country is well supplied with corn, sea-fish, and imported wines; and what is preferable to every other advantage, from its vicinity to Ireland, it is tempered by a salubrious air. . . . It is evident, therefore, that Maenor Pirr is the pleasantest spot in Wales; and the author may be pardoned for having thus extolled his native soil, his genial territory, with a profusion of praise and admiration

Gerald the Welshman, Itinerary through Wales,
translated by Sir R. C. Hoare

SCORCHED EARTH IN 1257

About the same time the King [Henry III] issued his warrants throughout all England, calling on each and every one who owed knightly service to their lord and king to be ready and prepared, provided with horses and arms, to follow him into Wales, on the feast of St. Mary Magdalen, whither he was about to proceed on an expedition to check their violence; as they were roving about at will, seizing the castles of the frontier nobles, and even those of the English, with impunity, putting the garrisons to death, and spreading fire, slaughter, and incendiarism in all directions. The Welsh, thereon, learning that the king intended to take the field against them with his army, prudently sent away their wives, children, and flocks into the interior of the country, about Snowdon and other mountainous places inaccessible to the English, ploughed up their fields, destroyed the mills in the road which the English would take, carried away all kinds of provisions, broke down the bridges, and rendered the fords impassable by digging holes, in order that, if the enemy attempted to cross, they might be drowned. Fortune favoured them in this war; for their cause appeared, even to their enemies, to be just; and what chiefly supported and encouraged them was the thought that, like the Trojans, from whom they were descended, they were struggling, with a firmness worthy of their descent, for their ancestral laws and liberty.

Matthew Paris, *Historia Anglorum*

94.   A knight was made by robing, girding on a sword, and fixing a pair of spurs.

ASSESSED AND SWORN TO ARMOUR, 1285

And further it is commanded that every man have in his house
harneis for to kepe the peace after the auncient assise that is for
to saye every man betwixt fiftene yeres of age and 40 yeres shall
be assessed and sworne to armour accordinge to the quantitie of
their lands and goods, that is to wit from £15 lands and goodes
40 markes, that is to witte an hawberke, a brest plate of yron,
a swode, a knife, and an horse. And from £10 of landes and 20
markes goods, a hawberke, a brest plate of yron, swode and a
knyfe, and from £5 landes, a doublet, a brest plate of yron, a
swode, and knyfe, and from 40s. lande and more unto 100s.
of lande, a swode, a bowe and arrowes and a knyfe. And he that
hath lesse than 40s. yerely, shall bee sworne to kepe gisarmes
[halberds with hooks], knives and other lesse weapons. And he
that hath lesse than 20 markes in goodes shall have swordes,
knives, and other lesse weapons, and all other that maye shal
have bowes and arrowes out of the foreste, and in the foreste
bowes and boltes. And that viewe of armour be made every yere
two times. And in al hundredes and fraunchises two constables
shal be chosen to make the view of armour, and the constables
aforesaid shal present before Justices assigned : such defautes as
they doe see in the countrey aboute armour. . . .

                        Statute of Winchester, 13 Edward I, cap 6
                            (translated as in 1577 edition)

WELSH TROOPS OF EDWARD I, 1297

There you saw the peculiar habits of the Welsh. In the very depth of winter they were running about bare-legged. They wore a red robe. They could not have been warm. The money they received from the king was spent in milk and butter. They would eat and drink anywhere. I never saw them wearing armour. I studied them very closely and walked among them to find out what defensive armour they carried when going into battle. Their weapons were bows, arrows and swords. They had also jardins. They wore linen clothing. They were great drinkers. They endamaged the Flemings very much. Their pay was too small and so it came about that they took what did not belong to them.

Lodewyk van Veltham, translation of the Cymmrodorion
Society (1925-6)

THE BATTLE OF BANNOCKBURN, 1314

On the morrow—an evil, miserable and calamitous day for the English—when both sides had made themselves ready for battle, the English archers were thrown forward before the line, and the Scottish archers engaged them, a few being killed or wounded on either side; but the King of England's archers quickly put the others to flight. Now when the two armies had approached very near each other, all the Scots fell on their knees to repeat *Pater-Noster*, commending themselves to God and seeking help from heaven; after which they advanced boldly against the English. They had so arranged their army that two columns went abreast in advance of the third, so that neither should be in advance of the other; and the third followed, in which was Robert [Bruce]. Of a truth, when both armies engaged each other, and the great horses of the English charged the pikes of the Scots, as it were into a dense forest, there arose a great and terrible crash of spears broken and of destriers wounded to the death; and so they remained without movement for a while. Now the English in the rear could not reach the Scots because the leading division was in the way, nor could they do anything to help themselves, wherefore there was nothing for it but to take to flight. This account I have heard from a trustworthy person who was present as eyewitness.

In the leading division were killed the Earl of Gloucester, Sir John Comyn, Sir Pagan de Typtoft, Sir Edmund de Mauley and many other nobles, besides foot soldiers who fell in great numbers. Another calamity which befell the English was that, whereas they

95. Battle of Bannockburn in 1314, from John Fordun's *Scotichronicon;* fifteenth century.

had shortly before crossed a great ditch called Bannockburn, into which the tide flows, and now wanted to recross it in confusion, many nobles and others fell into it with their horses in the crush, while others escaped with much difficulty, and many were never able to extricate themselves from the ditch; thus Bannockburn was spoken about for many years in English throats.

The Chronicle of Lanercost, translated by Herbert Maxwell

THE BATTLE OF CRECY, 1346

Next morning [Saturday 26 August] they left Abbeville with banners unfurled, and it was a great sight to see these lords finely dressed and nobly mounted, with pennons fluttering in the breeze—an army estimated at twenty thousand men-at-arms on horseback, and more than a hundred thousand on foot, of whom twelve thousand were pikemen or Genoese. The King of England had no more than four thousand horsemen, ten thousand archers and ten thousand Welsh and foot-soldiers.

King Philip urged his men on to follow the English, and sent a party of knights and squires to spy out where they were, for he

96.   The Feat of Arms at St. Inglebert's.

believed they could not be far off. When they had gone four leagues they returned with the report that the English could not be more than another few leagues away. He then gave orders for a valiant and experienced knight to go ahead with few others and find out the disposition of the English forces. These brave knights gladly undertook their mission, and on their return found some of their own banners had advanced to within a league of the English; they made these halt to await the others, then went back to the king and said they had seen the English less than a league away, drawn up in three divisions. The king therefore held a council to decide on their action, and asked this valiant knight, Le Moine de Bazeilles, to give them his opinion. He replied that he was unwilling to speak in front of the great lords, but that it was his duty to do so. 'My lord,' he said, 'your army is widely scattered, and it will be late before it can be all assembled. I would advise you to camp for the night, and then after mass in the morning to draw up your battle array and advance on your enemy in the name of God and Saint Denis, for I am certain from what I have seen that they will not flee, but will await your coming.'

The king was pleased with this advice, and would gladly have followed it. But when he gave orders that everyone should retreat with his banner—for the English were arrayed very close to them—none would do so unless those in the van came back first, and those in the van refused to retreat because they thought it shameful to do so; meanwhile those at the rear continued to advance and thus the valiant knight's advice was wasted through the pride and envy of the lords. They still rode proudly ahead, one in front of the other without any order, and came within sight of the English, who were waiting for them in careful array, and now it was even more shameful to turn back.

Then the commanders of the pikemen and the Genoese crossbowmen ordered their men forward in front of the companies of the lords so as to shoot first at the English, and they advanced close enough to loose their arrows on the enemy. But very soon pikemen and Genoese were routed by the English archers and would have taken to flight if the companies of the chief lords had not been so fired with envy of each other that they did not wait to make a concerted attack, but rushed forward in such disorder that the pikemen and the Genoese were trapped between them and the English. The weaker horses fell on top of them, and the others trampled them and fell on top of each other like a litter of piglets. The arrows of the English were directed with such marvellous skill at the horsemen that their mounts refused to advance a step; some leapt backwards stung to madness, some reared hideously, some turned their rear quarters towards the enemy, others merely let themselves fall to the ground and their riders could do nothing about it, The English lords, who were on foot, advanced among them striking at their will, because they could not help themselves on their horses.

The misfortunes of the French lasted until midnight, for it was nearly dark when the battle began, and the King of France and his company never came near to the fighting. At the end it was necessary for the king to withdraw from where he was, and Comte Jean de Hainault, who had been detailed as the king's personal bodyguard, took his bridle, conducted him sadly and unwillingly from the field, and rode with him through the night to Labroye, where the king took some rest, very sick at heart. Next day he continued to Amiens to await those that remained of his men. This sorry remnant of the French—lords, knights and others—who were left behind, withdrew like routed men, uncertain where to go, for it was pitch dark, not knowing of any town or village, and not having eaten all day. They went off in groups of three or four like lost men, and did not know whether their leaders or brothers or cousins were dead or had escaped. Never did a greater disaster befall any christian men than happened then to King Philip and his army. . . .

I have recorded the truth as exactly as I could, as I heard it from the mouth of my lord and friend Comte Jean de Hainault, whom may God absolve, and from ten or a dozen knights of his household, who were in the thick of the fight with the valiant and noble King of Bohemia, and who had their horses killed under them. I have also heard similar accounts from several knights of England and Germany who were engaged on the other side.   ,

The Chronicles of Jean le Bel, translated by P. E. Thompson

BATTLE OF POITIERS, 1356

Truly this battle which was near Poitiers in the fields of Beaumanoir and Maupertuis was right great and perilous, and many deeds of arms were done there which all came not to knowledge, and the fighters on both sides endured much pain. King John (*John II of France*) with his own hands did that day marvels in arms; he had an axe in his hands wherewith he defended himself. In the breaking of the press there were taken near to him the Earl of Tankarville, Sir Jacques of Bourbon, count of Ponthieu . . . and many other knights. The chase endured

97. Soldiers looting a house; late fourteenth century.

to the gates of Poitiers; there were many slain and beaten
down, horse and man, for they of Poitiers closed their gates and
would suffer none to enter. Wherefore in the street before the
gate was horrible murder, men hurt and beaten down. The
Frenchmen yielded themselves up as far off as they could see an
Englishman; and there were many English archers that had four,
five, or six prisoners. . . .

Then the Prince (*Black Prince*) had his banner set high up on
a bush and trumpets and clarions began to sound; the Prince
took off his basinet . . . and a little red pavilion was put up
wherein he entered, and drink was brought to the Prince and
to the lords who were with him, the which still increased as
they came from the chase, for they tarried there and their
prisoners with them.

Jean Froissart, Chronicles

JOHN, KING OF FRANCE, PRISONER IN THE TOWER
The battle of Poitiers brought a second monarch, and the chief
nobility of a second kingdom, prisoners to the Tower. John, King
of France, and his son Philip, together with four other princes,
eight earls, and many lords of France, who were destined to grace
the triumph of an English prince, were conducted into England by
the hero of that memorable day. Prince Edward landed with
his train of captives on the 5th of May, 1357, and on the 24th
of the same month entered London.

Most of the French princes and nobility were at first placed in the Tower, but the captive monarch with his son was lodged at the Savoy, the stately palace of the duke of Lancaster; where he 'kept his house a long season', and was frequently visited by the king and queen who 'made him great feast and cheer'. About the middle of the following year he was removed, together with his son, to the castle of Windsor, where he experienced the same marks of kindness and attention: he was allowed his liberty; enjoyed the sports of the field.

But when King Edward prepared to carry his victorious arms again into France, all the French prisoners were placed in the Tower and other fortresses, and his royal captive was removed first to Hereford, and thence to the castle of Somerton in Lincolnshire, under charge of Sir William Deyncourt and four other knights, with a retinue of twenty-two men at arms and twenty archers. He was attended by his own physician, chaplains, a painter, falconer, and a variety of other officers and servants of his household from France. He remained at Somerton for several months, till the formidable appearance of a French fleet on the seas excited apprehensions of an invasion, and rendered it advisable that he should be removed to a place of greater security. He was then conducted by easy journeys to the Tower of London, where apartments were fitted for his reception, and where he remained with his captive son, till the famous treaty of Bretigny restored him to his liberty and his throne.

From *The History and Antiquities of the Tower of London from Records, State-Papers, and Manuscripts*

QUITE SIX THOUSAND CARTS, 1360
EDWARD III MARCHES FROM RHEIMS TO PARIS

You ought to know that the King of England and the rich brought with them on their carts tents, pavilions, mills, cooking ovens, horse smithies and everything needful. And to furnish this they brought along quite six thousand carts, each with four good strong carthorses brought out of England. And on the carts they had many boats, so cleverly made of boiled leather that it was surprising to see them. They could carry three men so as to float on even the biggest lake or fishpond and fish at will. Thus they were quite comfortable in Lent—that is to say the Lords and people of standing. But the common folk had to make do with what they could get. Furthermore the king personally had thirty mounted falconers with birds and sixty couples of strong hounds and the same number of greyhounds. With these

98.   Battle at the gates of the city; late fourteenth century.

he went hunting or fishing every day according to his fancy. Many of the noble and wealthy also had their dogs and birds like the king. They were arranged in three columns.

Jean Froissart, *Chronicles*

THE KNIGHT

There was a Knight, a most distinguished man,
Who from the day on which he first began
To ride abroad had followed chivalry,
Truth, honour, generous thought and courtesy.
He had done nobly in his sovereign's war
And ridden into battle, no man more,
As well in christian as in heathen places,
And ever honoured for his noble graces.

99. Woodcut by Richard Pynson, *c.* 1490, of the Knight from Chaucer's *Canterbury Tales.*

He saw the town of Alexandria fall;
Often, at feasts, the highest place of all
Among the nations fell to him in Prussia.
In Lithuania he had fought, and Russia,
No christian man so often, of his rank,
And he was in Granada when they sank
The town of Algeciras, also in
North Africa, right through Benamarin;
And in Armenia he had been as well
And fought when Ayas and Attalia fell,
For all along the Mediterranean coast
He had embarked with many a noble host.
In fifteen mortal battles he had been
And jousted for our faith at Tramissene
Thrice in the lists, and always killed his man.
This same distinguished knight had led the van
Once with the Bey of Balat, doing work
For him against another heathen Turk;
He was of sovereign value in all eyes.
And though so much distinguished, he was wise
And in his bearing modest as a maid.
He never yet a boorish thing had said
In all his life to any, come what might;
He was a true, a perfect gentle-knight.
　　Speaking of his appearance, he possessed
Fine horses, but he was not gaily dressed.
He wore a fustian tunic stained and dark
With smudges where his armour had left mark;
Just home from service, he had joined our ranks
To do his pilgrimage and render thanks.
Geoffrey Chaucer, Canterbury Tales, Prologue,
translated by Nevill Coghill

THE SQUIRE

He had his son with him, a fine young Squire,
A lover and cadet, a lad of fire
With curly locks, as if they had been pressed.
He was some twenty years of age, I guessed.
In stature he was of a moderate length,
With wonderful agility and strength.
He'd seen some service with the cavalry
In Flanders and Artois and Picardy
And had done valiantly in little space

Of time, in hope to win his lady's grace.
He was embroidered like a meadow bright
And full of freshest flowers, red and white.
Singing he was, or fluting all the day;
He was as fresh as is the month of May.
Short was his gown, the sleeves were long and wide;
He knew the way to sit a horse and ride.
He could make songs and poems and recite,
Knew how to joust and dance, to draw and write.
He loved so hotly that till dawn grew pale
He slept as little as a nightingale.
Courteous he was, lowly and serviceable,
And carved to serve his father at the table.

Geoffrey Chaucer, Canterbury Tales, Prologue,
translated by Nevill Coghill

THE BATTLE OF AGINCOURT, 1415

Of the mortal battle of Azincourt, in which the King of England discomfitted the French.

It is true that the French had arranged their battalions between two small thickets, one lying close to Azincourt, and the other to Tramecourt. The place was narrow, and very advantageous for the English, and, on the contrary, very ruinous for the French, for the said French had been all night on horseback, and it rained, and the pages, grooms, and others, in leading about the horses, had broken up the ground, which was so soft that the horses could with difficulty step out of the soil. And also the said French were so loaded with armour that they could not support themselves or move forward. In the first place they were armed with long coats of steel, reaching to the knees or lower, and very heavy, over the leg harness; wherefore this weight of armour, with the softness of the wet ground, as has been said, kept them as if immovable, so that they could raise their clubs only with great difficulty, and with all these mischiefs there was this, that most of them were troubled with hunger and want of sleep. There was a marvellous number of banners, and it was ordered that some of them should be furled. Also it was settled among the said French that everyone should shorten his lance, in order that they might be stiffer when it came to fighting at close quarters. They had archers and cross-bowmen enough, but they would not let them shoot, for the plain was so narrow that there was no room except for the men-at-arms.

Now let us return to the English. After the parley between the two armies was finished, as we have said, and the delegates had returned, each to their own people, the King of England, who had appointed a knight called Sir Thomas Erpingham to place his archers in front in two wings, trusted entirely to him, and Sir Thomas, to do his part, exhorted every one to do well in the name of the king, begging them to fight vigorously against the French in order to secure and save their own lives. And thus the knight, who rode with two others only in front of the battalion, seeing that the hour was come, for all things were well arranged, threw up a baton which he held in his hand, saying 'now strike', which was the signal for attack; then dismounted and joined the king, who was also on foot in the midst of his men, with his banner before him. Then the English, seeing this signal, began suddenly to march, uttering a very loud cry, which greatly surprised the French. And when the English saw that the French did not approach them, they marched dashingly towards them in very fine order, and again raised a loud cry as they stopped to take breath.

Then the English archers, who, as I have said, were in the wings, saw that they were near enough, and began to send their arrows on the French with great vigour. The said archers were for the most part in their doublets, without armour, their stockings rolled up to their knees, and having hatchets and battle-axes or great swords hanging at their girdles; some were bare-footed and bare-headed, others had caps of boiled leather, and others of osier, covered with harpoy [skins] or leather.

Then the French, seeing the English come towards them in this fashion, placed themselves in order, every one under his banner, their helmets on their heads. The constable, the marshal, the admirals, and the other princes earnestly exhorted their men to fight the English well and bravely; and when it came to the approach the trumpets and clarions resounded everywhere; but the French began to hold down their heads, especially those who had no bucklers, for the impetuosity of the English arrows, which fell so heavily that no one durst uncover or look up. Thus they went forward a little, then made a little retreat, but before they could come to close quarters, many of the French were disabled and wounded by the arrows; and when they came quite up to the English, they were, as has been said, so closely pressed one against another that none of them could lift their arms to strike against their enemies, except some that were in front, and these fiercely pricked with the lances which they had shortened to be more stiff, and to get nearer their enemies.

The company under Sir Clugnet de Brabant who were detailed to break the line of the English archers were reduced from eight hundred to seven score before the attempt was made. Sir Guillaume de Saveuses, who was also in this company, rushed ahead of his own men, thinking they would follow him, but before he had dealt many blows among the archers he was pulled from his horse and killed. Most of the others and all their horses were driven back among the vanguard by fear of the English archers, and there they did much damage, breaking the line in several places; so many of the horses were wounded by the English arrows that their riders could not control them, and they caused many more knights to fall and so disordered their ranks that some fled behind the enemy in fear of their lives, and others were forced to withdraw into some newly-sown land. Their example caused many more French from the main body to flee.

As soon as the English saw this disorder in the vanguard they all entered the fray, and throwing down bows and arrows, they took their swords, axes, mallets, billhooks and staves and struck out at the French, many of whom they killed, until they came up with the main army. The King of England and his bodyguard followed close behind the archers. . . . As they advanced they killed cruelly and without mercy; if a man who was down could be got on his feet by his servant he might escape, because the English were so single-mindedly killing and taking prisoners as they advanced that they had no time to pursue those who fled. When all the rearguard, who had remained on horseback, saw the first two divisions getting the worst of it, they all took to flight with the exception of some of their leaders.

Jehan de Wavrin, *Collection of Chronicles and Ancient Histories of Great Britain,* translated by W. Hardy and E. L. C. P. Hardy,
Rolls Series, 1864-91

TO ARM A MAN, Fifteenth Century

First ye must set on sabbatons [broad-toed foot armour] and tie them upon the shoes with small laces so that they will bend; and then greaves [armour for the legs below the knee]; and then cuisses [armour for the thigh]; and then the breech of mail [short skirt of mail]; and then the tonlets [armour to protect the lumbar regions], then the breastplate; then the vambraces [armour for the forearm]; then the rerebraces [armour above the elbow]; then the gloves. Then hang his dagger upon his side; then his short sword on the left side in a round ring, all naked to pull it out lightly. Then put his coat upon his back, and then his basinet [a lighter helmet] pinned upon two great staples before the breastplate, with a double buckle behind upon the back, in order to make the helmet sit correctly; and then his long sword in his hand; then his pennant in his hand, painted with Saint George or with Our Lady, to bless him as he goes towards the field and in the field.

Viscount Dillon, 'On a MS. Collection of Ordinances of Chivalry of the Fifteenth Century, Belonging to Lord Hastings', *Archaeologia, LVII*

HOW A MAN SHALL BE ARMED AT HIS EASE WHEN HE SHALL FIGHT ON FOOT, Fifteenth Century

He shall have no shirt upon him, but a doublet of fustian lined with satin, cut full of holes. The doublet must be strongly laced where the points are set about the great [chief part] of the arm, and the best before and behind, and the gussets of mail must be sewed to the doublet at the bend of the arm and under the arm. The arming points must be made of fine twine such as men use to make strings for crossbows, and they must be tied small and pointed as points. They must be waxed with shoemaker's wax, and then they will neither stretch nor break. He shall have a pair of hose of worsted cloth, and a pair of short pads of thin blanket to put about his knees to prevent chafing of his leg harness; also a pair of shoes of thick leather, and they must be fastened with small whipcord, three knots upon a cord, and three cords must be fast sewed to the [heel] of the shoe, and fine cords in the middle of the sole of the same shoe, and there must be between the cords of the heel and those of the middle of the shoe the space of three fingers.

Viscount Dillon, 'On a MS. Collection of Ordinances of Chivalry of the Fifteenth Century, Belonging to Lord Hastings', *Archaeologia, LVII*

THE EARL OF WARWICK, THE 'KINGMAKER', AT THE FIRST BATTLE OF ST ALBANS, 1455

The Earle of Warrewyk knowyng ther offe, toke and gadered his men to gedere and ferosly brake in by the gardeyne sydes, betuene the signe of the Keye, and the sygne of the Chekkere in Holwell strete; and anoon as they wer wythinne the toon, sodeynly the[y] blew up Trumpettes, and sette a cry with a shout and a grete voyce, 'a Warrewe, a Warrewyk, a Warrewyk!' . . . And at this same tyme were hurt lordes of name; the Kyng our sovereyne lord in the neck with an arowe, the Duke of

100.   A mêlée, c. 1450

Buckingham with an arrowe in the vysage, the lord of Dudle with
an arowe in the vysage, the lord of Stafford in the hond with an
arowe, the lord of Dorsette sore hurt that he myght not go,
but he was caryede hom in a cart, and Wenlok knyght, in lyke
wyse in a carte sore hurt; and other diverse knyghtes and squyers
sore hurt. The Erle of Wyldshyre, Thorp, and many others,
fflede and left her harneys behynde hem cowardly; and the
substance of the Kyngs partye were dyspoyled of hors and harneys.
This don the seyde lordes, that ys to wote the Duke of Yorke, the
Erle of Salesbury, the Erle of Warrewyk, come to the Kyng our
sovereyne lord, and on here knees besoughte hym of grace, and
for yevenesse of that they hadde doon yn his presence: and
besought hym of hys heynesse to take hem as hys true legemen,
seyng that they never attendyde hurt to his owne persone and
ther fore the kyng oure sovereyne lord toke hem to grace, and so
desyred hem to cesse there peple and that there sshulde no more
harme be doon; and they obeyde hys commaundement, and lote
make a cry on the kyngs name that al maner of pepull shulde
cesse and not so hardy to stryke ony stroke more after the
proclamacyon of the Crye: and so cessed the seyde Batayle.

An Account of the First Battle of St. Albans, from a contemporary manuscript in the possession of Sir William Stonor, Steward of the Abbot of St. Albans, edited by John Bayley in *Archaeologia*, xx, 1824

DEFENCE OF A MANSION DURING THE WARS OF THE ROSES, c. 1458

To my right worshipful husband, John Paston

Right worshipful husband, I recommend me to you, and pray you to get some crossbows and wyndoes [windlasses to draw the bow-string] to bind them with, the quarrels [heavy arrows or bolts], for your houses here be so low that there may none man shoot out with no long bow, though we had never so much need.

I suppose you could have such things of Sir John Fastolf if you would send to him; and also I would you should get two or three short poleaxes to keep within doors, and as many jackets, and you may.

Partrick and his fellowship are sore afraid that you would enter again upon them and they have made great ordinance within the house, and it is told me they have made bars to bar the doors crosswise, and they have made wickets [apertures] on every quarter of the house to shoot out at, both with bows and with hand-guns, and the holes that be made for hand-guns, they be scarce knee high from the plancher [floor], and of such holes be made fire, there can none man shoot out of them with no hand-bows . . .

I pray that you will vouchsafe to do buy for me one pound of almonds, and one pound of sugar and that you will do buy some freise to make of your children's gowns; you shall have best cheap and best choice of Hays's wife, as it is told me. And that you will buy a yard of broad cloth of black for one hood for me of 44d. or four shillings a yard, for there is neither good cloth nor good freise in this town. As for the children's gowns, and I have them I will do them maken.

The Trinity have you in his keeping, and send you good speed in all your matters.

Margaret Paston
Paston Letters

THE BATTLE OF BARNET, 1471

Mother, I recommend me to you, letting you know, that blessed be God, my brother John [Paston] is alive and fareth well, and in no peril of death, nevertheless he is hurt with an arrow on his right arm beneath the elbow; and I have sent him a surgeon, which hath dressed him, and he telleth me that he trusteth that he shall be all whole within right short time.

It is so that John Mylsent is dead, God have mercy on his soul! and William Mylsent is alive, and his other servants all be escaped by all likelihood.

Item, as for me, I am in good case, blessed be God; and in no jeopardy of my life as me list myself; for I am at my liberty if need be.

Item, my lord archbishop is in the Tower; nevertheless I trust to God that he shall do well enough; he hath a safeguard for him and me both; nevertheless we have been troubled since, but now I understand that he hath a pardon; and so we hope well.

There are killed upon the field, half a mile from Barnet, on Easter day, the Earl of Warwick, the Marquis Montagu, Sir William Tyrrell, Sir Lewis Johns, and divers other esquires of our country, Godmerston and Booth.

And on the King Edward's party, the Lord Cromwell, the Lord Say, Sir Humphrey Bourchier of our country, which is a sore mourned man here; and other people of both parties in the number of more than a thousand.

As for other things, [it] is understood here, that the Queen Margaret is verily landed and her son in the west country, and I trow that as to-morrow, or else the next day, the King Edward will depart from hence to her ward to drive her out again.

Item, I beseech you that I may be recommended to my cousin Lomner, and to thank him for his good will to me ward if I had had need, as I understood by the bearer thereof; and I beseech you on my behalf to advise him to be well ware of his dealing or language as yet, for the world I assure you is right queasy, as ye shall know within this month; the people here feareth it sore.

God hath showed himself marvellously like him that made all, and can undo again when he list; and I can think that by all likelihood shall show himself as marvellous again, and that in short time; and as I suppose oftener than once in cases like.

Item, it is so that my brother is unprovided of money, I have helpen him to my power and above; therefore, as it pleaseth you, remember, for [I] cannot purvey for myself in the same case.

Written at London the Thursday in Easter week.

Paston Letters, edited by J. Fenn, letter 311

USE BEACONS TO SOUND THE ALARM, 1485

For the custom of the countries adjoining near the sea is

(especially in the time of war), on every hill or high place to erect a beacon with a great lantern in the top, which may be seen and discerned a great space off. And when the noise is once bruited that the enemies approach near the land, they suddenly put fire in the lanterns, and make shouts and outcries from town to town, and from village to village. Some run in post from place to place, admonishing the people to be ready to resist the jeopardy and defend the peril. And by this policy the fame is soon blown to every city and town, insomuch that as well the citizens as the rural people be in short space assembled and armed to repel and put back the new arrived enemies. (Whereas if the necessary use of this visible warning were neglected, the policy of the enemy might privily so prevail, as that the people should sooner fall into peril irrecoverable, than they could think on (much less provide) means to avoid it.)

Raphael Holinshed, *Chronicle*, III

THE BATTLE OF BOSWORTH, 1485

The report is that king Richerd might have sowght to save himself by flight; for they who wer abowt him, seing the soldiers even from the first stroke to lyft up ther weapons febly and fayntlye, and soome of them to depart the feild pryvyly, suspectyd treason, and exhortyd him to flye, yea and whan the matter began manyfestly to qwaile, they browght him swyft horses; but he, who was not ignorant that the people hatyd him, owt of hope to have any better hap afterward, ys sayd to have awnsweryd, that that very day he wold make end ether of warre or lyfe, suche great fearcenesse and suche huge force of mynd he had: wherfor, knowinge certanely that that day wold ether yeald him a peaceable and quyet realme from hencefurth or els perpetually bereve him the same, he came to the fielde with the crowne uppon his head that therby he might ether make a beginning or ende of his raigne. And so the myserable man had suddaynly suche end as wont ys to happen to them that have right and law both of God and man in lyke estimation, as will, impyeties, and wickednes. Surely these are more vehement examples by muche than ys hable to be utteryd with toong to tereyfy those men which suffer no time to passe free from soome haynous offence, creweltie, or mischief.

Henry, after the victory obtaynyd, gave furthwith thanks unto Almightie God for the same; than after, replenyssyd with joy incredible, he got himself unto the next ·hill, wher, after he had commandyd his soldiers, and commandyd to cure [i.e. attend to] the woundyd, and to bury them that wer slane, he gave unto the nobylytie and gentlemen immortal thankes, promysing that he wold be myndfull of ther benyfyttes, all which meane whyle the soldiers cryed, God save king Henry, God save king Henry! and with hart and hand utteryd all the shew of joy that might be; which whan Thomas Stanley dyd see, he set anon king Richerds crowne, which was fownd among the spoyle in the feilde, uppon his head, as thoughe he had bene already by commandment of the people proclamyd king after the maner of his auncestors, and that was the first signe of prosperytie. After that, commanding to pak upp all bag and baggage, Henry with his victorious army procedyd in the evening to Leycester, wher, for refresshing of soldiers from ther travaile and panes, and to prepare for going to London, he taryed two days. In the meane time the body of king Richerd nakyd of all clothing, and layd uppon an horse bake with the armes and legges hanginge down on both sydes, was browght to thabbay of monks Franciscanes at Leycester, a myserable spectacle in good sooth, but not unwoorthy for the mans lyfe, and there was buryed two days after without any pompe or solemne funerall. He raigned two yeres and so many monethes, and one day over. He was lyttle of stature, deformyd of body, thone showlder being higher than thother, a short and sowre cowntenance, which semyd to savor of mischief, and utter evydently craft and deceyt. The whyle he was thinking of any matter, he dyd contynuolly byte his nether lyppe, as thowgh that crewell nature of his did so rage agaynst yt self in that lytle carkase. Also he was woont to be ever with his right hand pulling out of the sheath to the myddest, and putting in agane, the dagger which he did always were. Trewly he had a sharp witt, provydent and subtyle, apt both to counterfayt and dissemble; his corage also hault and fearce, which faylyd him not in the very death, which, whan his men forsooke him, he rather yealded to take with the swoord, than by fowle flyght to prolong his lyfe, uncertane what death perchance soon after by sicknes or other vyolence to suffer.

Polydore Vergil, *English History,* Camden Society XXIX

England and the Sea

CORACLES MADE OF SKINS, 1188

The boats which they employ in fishing or in crossing the rivers are made of twigs, not oblong nor pointed, but almost round, or rather triangular, covered both within and without with raw hides. When a salmon thrown into one of these boats strikes it hard with his tail, he often oversets it, and endangers both the vessel and its navigator. The fishermen, according to the custom of the country, in going to and from the rivers, carry these boats on their shoulders; on which occasion that famous dealer in fables, Bledherc, who lived a little before our time, thus mysteriously said: 'There is amongst us a people who, when they go out in search of prey, carry their horses on their backs to the place of plunder; in order to catch their prey, they leap upon their horses, and when it is taken carry their horses home again upon their shoulders.

Gerald the Welshman, Description of Wales,
translated by Sir R. C. Hoare

RICHARD I's SHIPS, 1190

The ships that King Richard found ready at the sea-coast numbered one hundred together with 14 busses, vessels of vast size, wonderful speed, and great strength. They were arranged and set in order as follows. The first ship had three rudders, thirteen anchors, 30 oars, two sails, and triple ropes of every kind; moreover, it had everything that a ship can want in pairs— saving only the mast and boat. It had one very skilful captain, and fourteen chosen mariners were under his orders. The ship was laden with forty horses of price, all well trained for war, and with all kinds of arms for as many riders, for forty footmen, and fifteen sailors. Moreover it had a full year's food for all these men and horses. All the ships were laden in the same way; but each buss took double cargo and gear. The king's treasure which was exceedingly great and of inestimable value, was divided amongst the ships and the busses so that if one part was endangered the rest might be saved.

101. Hand-to-hand fighting in the English Channel in the twelfth century.

When everything was thus arranged, the king with a small following, and the chief men of the army with their attendants, put off from the shore, preceding the fleet in galleys. Each day they touched at some sea-coast town and, taking up the larger ships and busses of that sea as they went along, reached Messina without disaster.

Richard of Devizes, *Chronicle of the Acts of Richard I.*
Translated by T. A. Archer, *The Crusade of Richard I, 1189-92*

REGULATIONS REGARDING SEA-FARING MEN, 1190

The King [Richard I] also made the same time certain ordinances to be observed among the sea-faring men which tended to this effect:

(1) First, that if any man chanced to slay another on the shipboard, he should be bound to the dead body and so thrown into the sea.

(2) Secondly, if he killed him on land, he should yet be bound to him as before, and so buried quick together.

(3) Thirdly, if any man should be convicted by lawful witness, that he drew any weapon to strike any other, or chanced by strikng at any man to draw blood of him that˗was smitten, he should lose his hand.

(4) Fourthly, if he gave but a blow with his fist without bloodshedding, he should be plunged several times over head and ears in the water.

(5) Fifthly, if any man reviled another he should for every time so misusing himself, forfeit an ounce of silver.

(6) Sixthly, that if any man were taken with theft or pickery [larceny], and thereof convicted, he should have his head polled, and hot pitch poured upon his pate, and upon that, the feathers of some pillow or cushion shaken aloft, that he might thereby be known for a thief, and at the next arrival of the ship to any land,

he put forth of the company to seek his adventures without all hope of return unto his fellows.

Raphael Holinshed, *Chronicle, I*

THIRTEENTH-CENTURY SALVATION AT SEA

. . . once when he [Edward I, as prince, after a crusading expedition] was on his way back to England and had reached the coast and had been received on board ship in a fitting manner he was sailing to England with a great company. Storms suddenly arose at sea so that imminent destruction threatened the whole structure of he vessel. The sailors could do no more and gave up all hope of rescue, so in terror they prayed loudly to God and the passengers decided each to vow to God whatsoever the Holy Spirit should prompt. All did this devoutly but still the storms did not abate but went on increasing in force. In the face of death everybody on board with one accord begged the prince with tears, as he had not made a vow with the others, to deign to make a vow pleasing to the Lord that he might speedily rescue them from their present peril.

The prince yielded and humbly promised to God and to the Virgin that if the Lord would save him and his and theirs and bring them unharmed to shore, he would then forthwith found a monastery of white monks of the order of the Cistercians in their honour within England. He would endow it so richly that it could support one hundred monks for ever. God's strength in saving his people was at once revealed for hardly had the most Christian prince stopped speaking when the storm was quite dispersed and there was calm. Everyone was amazed at the change. The ship was miraculously brought to land though broken and torn in many places and with many perilous leaks, thanks to the Virgin Mary in whose honour the prince had made his vow. This was done without human aid. All saw this and were amazed with joy and were filled with happy devotion towards the glorious Virgin who had not allowed them to perish. In the same hour a marvel took place which should not be passed over in silence. When all had taken their gear out of the ship the prince remained on board last of all. When the boat was empty and he had disembarked the ship fell in two parts, in the twinkling of an eye. Thus it was shown that the ship was kept whole while the good man was in her. . . .

Vale Royal Cartulary, translated, from W. Dugdale,
Monasticon Anglicanum, A History of the Abbies and other Monasteries, Hospitals, Frieries and Cathedral and Collegiate Churches

BATTLE OF SLUYS, 1340

King Edward [III] kept his Whitsuntide at Ipswich, because he intended from thence to make his passage into Flanders; but, being informed that the French King had sent a great navy of Spanish ships and also the whole fleet of France to stop his passage, he caused his ships of the Cinque Ports and others to be assembled, so that he had in his fleet, great and small, 260 ships.

Wherefore, on the Thursday before the Nativity of Saint John the Baptist, having a favourable wind, he began to sail; and the next day, in the even of the said feast, they descried the French fleet lying in Swinehaven. Wherefore the King caused all his fleet to come to anchor.

The next day, being the Feast of Saint John the Baptist, early in the morning the French fleet divided themselves into three parts, withdrew about a mile, and then approached the King's fleet. When the King saw this, about nine o'clock, having the wind and sun on his back, he set forward and met his enemies as he would have wished; at which the whole fleet gave a terrible shout, and a shower of arrows out of long wooden bows so poured down on the Frenchmen that thousands were slain in that meeting. At length they closed and came to hand blows with pikes, poleaxes, and swords, and some threw stones from the tops of ships, wherewith many were brained. The size and height of the Spanish ships caused many Englishmen to strike many a blow in vain. But, to be short, the first part of the French ships being overcome and all the men spent, the Englishmen entered and took them. The French ships were chained together in such a way that they could not be separated from each other, so that a few Englishmen kept that part of the fleet. They then set upon the second part and with great difficulty made the attack; but when this had been done, the second part was sooner overcome than the first because many of the Frenchmen abandoned their ships and leapt overboard. The Englishmen, having thus overcome the first and second parts of the fleet, and now finding night drawing on, partly for want of light and partly because they were weary, determined to take some rest till the next morning. On this account, during the night thirty ships of the third part fled away, but a large ship called the 'James' of Dieppe, thinking to have carried away a certain ship of Sandwich belonging to the priory of Canterbury, was stopped, for the sailors so stoutly defended themselves by the help of the Earl of Huntingdon that they saved themselves and their ship from the Frenchmen.

The fight continued all night, and in the morning, the Normans

102. Early fourteenth-century illustration shows a ship being built on the stocks. The planks are fastened with trenails (wooden pins).

being overcome and taken, there were found in the ship 400 men slain. Moreover, the King understanding that the ships were fled, sent forty well-equiped ships to follow them. . . . In the first group of ships that were taken they found these conquered ships: the 'Denis', the 'George', the 'Christopher' and the 'Blacke Cocke', all of which had been captured by Frenchmen at Sluys and carried into Normandy. The number of ships of war that were taken was about 230 barges; the number of enemies that were slain and drowned was about 25,000, and of Englishmen about 4,000, among whom were four knights. . . .

Geoffrey le Baker of Swinbrook, translated from E. M. Thompson's edition by E. Rickert, *Chaucer's World*

SEAMAN'S PAY IN REIGN OF EDWARD III, 1375

By ancient custom a mariner is to take for hire from the Pool of London to Lisbon twenty shillings from the portage [carriage] of a ton [nearly one hogshead].

Item, between London and Skone [Scone in Scotland] a mariner used to have eight shillings and four pence wages.

Item, between London and Newcastle-upon-Tyne a mariner shall have four shillings wages and two quarters of coal free of bulk for carriage.

Item, between London and Berwick a mariner shall have eight shillings wages which shall be paid there to the end that he may buy such merchandise as he shall think good, which shall be laden in the same ship wherein he hath the said wages for his carriage.

Black Book of the Admiralty, edited by Sir Travers Twiss.
Rolls Series

SHIPS, Fifteenth Century

Men that sail to St. James may say farewell to all pleasures, for many people suffer they they set sail. For when they have put to sea from Sandwich or Winchelsea or Bristol, or wherever it happens to be, their hearts begin to fail.

Soon the master orders his seamen to hurry up and take their places round the mast for setting sail. Then they cry 'Yo ho, hoist! What ho, mate, you are standing too close, your comrade has not room to haul.' Thus they begin to talk.

A boy or two climb up at once and lie across the yard; the rest cry 'Yo ho, tally [haul]!' and pull with all their might. 'Get the boat stowed, boatswain, for our pilgrims to occupy themselves with it, for some of them will very likely be coughing and groaning before it is midnight'

'Haul the bowline. Now veer the sheet. Cook, make our food ready at once. Our pilgrims have no desire to eat. I pray God to give them rest. Go to the helm. What ho. No closer. Steward fellow, a pot of beer.' 'You shall have, sir, with good cheer, all of the best directly'

'Yo ho, truss! Haul in the brails. You are not hauling; s.' God, you are shirking. Oh, see how well our good ship sai'by And that is how they talk. 'Haul in the wartack [an extra rope].' 'It shall be done.' 'Steward, lay the table at once and put bread and salt on it, and don't take too long about it.'

Then some one comes and says: 'Be merry, you will have a storm or a squall.' 'Be quiet. You never can. You are a sorry meddler.' Meanwhile the pilgrims lie with their bowls close beside them and shout for hot Malvoisie wine to restore their health.

And some ask for salted toast, because they cannot eat either boiled or roast meat. A man could just as well pay for their keep for two days as for one. Some laid their books on their knees and read till they could see no longer. 'Alas, my head will split in three,' so says another, 'I am certain of it.'

Then our owner comes like a lord and speaks many royal words and goes to the high table to see everything is well.

Presently he calls a carpenter and tells him to bring his gear to make cabins here and there and many small compartments.

'A sack of straw would be very good there, for some of them will have to sleep in their cloaks.' 'I would as soon be in the wood without meat or drink; for when we go to bed the pump will be close to the head of our bed, and a man who smells its stink is as good as dead.'

'Men may leve all gamys', a poem describing a voyage by pilgrims to St. James of Compostella in a fifteenth-century MS. at Trinity College, Cambridge, translated by Ramola and R. C. Anderson, *The Sailing-ship, Six Thousand Years of History*

103. A late fifteenth-century carrack, a merchant vessel fitted for war. The illustration shows three cannons, the raised platforms, fore and aft, are for firing catapults.

SELECT BIBLIOGRAPHY

BAGLEY, J. J., *Life in Medieval England* (Batsford)
BAKER, TIMOTHY, *Medieval London* (Cassell)
BENNETT, H. S., *The Pastons and their England* (Cambridge)
BENNETT, H. S., *Life on the English Manor* (Cambridge)
BLOCH, M., *Feudal Society* (Routledge)
BROWN, R. A., *English Medieval Castles* (Batsford)
CHRIMES, S. B. *An Introduction to the Administrative History of Medieval England* (Blackwell)
CLAPHAM, A. W., *English Romanesque Architecture after the Conquest* (Oxford)
CLAPHAM, J. H., and POWER, E. E. (editors) *The Agrarian Life of the Middle Ages* (Cambridge)
COULTON, G. G., *Medieval Panorama* (Collins)
GANSHOF, F. L., *Feudalism* (Longmans)
HALL, D. J., *English Medieval Pilgrimage* (Routledge)
HOLT, J. C., *Magna Carta* (Longmans)
JOLLIFFE, J. E. A., *Angevin Kingship* (Black)
KNOWLES, D., *The Monastic Orders in England* (Cambridge)
LABARGE, M. W., *A Baronial Household in the Thirteenth Century* (Eyre & Spottiswoode)
LENNARD, R., *Rural England* (Oxford)
POOLE, A. L., *Medieval England* (Oxford)
POWER, E. E., *Medieval People* (Methuen)
POWICKE, F. M., *The Thirteenth Century, 1216-1307* (Oxford)
RASHDALL, H., *The Universities of Europe in the Middle Ages* (Oxford)
ROUND, J. H., *Feudal England* (Allen & Unwin)
SOUTHERN, R. W., *The Making of the Middle Ages* (Hutchinson)
STENTON, D. M., *English Society in the Early Middle Ages 1066-1307* (Penguin)
STENTON, D. M., *English Justice between the Norman Conquest and the Great Charter, 1066-1215* (Allen)
TREVELYAN, G. M., *England in the Age of Wycliffe* (Longmans)
WADDELL, H., *The Wandering Scholars* (Penguin)

310

Biographies

ADAM OF USK, wrote *Chronicon Adae de Usk*, which is serviceable for 1377 to 1404.

HENRY ANSTEY, editor of *Munimenta Academica* (1432)

JOHN ARDERNE was born in 1307, and was attached to the households of the Duke of Lancaster and of his son-in-law John of Gaunt. He probably met Chaucer. He is the earliest known of renowned English surgeons. About 1370 he wrote *Treatise on the Fistula*.

ROGER BACON (1214?-1294), philosopher, studied at Oxford and Paris, and by his lectures and writings increased his reputation. He joined the Franciscan order, was under suspicion, and in 1257 was ordered to return to Paris. Under the patronage of Pope Clement IV he produced his *Opus Majus*, Latin treatises on the sciences—logic, mathematics, physics, optics and philosophy. Because of his independence of thought he was regarded as a necromancer, and was considered to have constructed a brass head which could speak. He was imprisoned in 1278. Roger Bacon has been described as the founder of English philosophy.

BARTHOLOMAEUS ANGLICUS (*fl.* 1230-1250), confused with Bartholomew de Glanville, was a Minorite Friar, professor of theology at Paris. His great work *De Proprietatibus Rerum*, written between 1250 and 1260, is an encyclopaedia of the Middle Ages. It was translated into French in 1372, into English by John Trevisa in 1398, and into Spanish and Dutch a century later.

BENEDICT OF PETERBOROUGH, *Benedictus Abbas Petroburgensis de vita et gestis Henrici II et Ricardi I*. This is declared to be 'Indisputably the most important chronicle of the time'.

JOHN BLAKMAN (*or* BLACMAN) was a priest who knew Henry VI. It has been said that his *On the Virtues and Miracles of Henry VI* was written as he knew of the efforts Henry VII made to get Henry VI canonized.

JOHN CAPGRAVE (1393-1464), an Augustinian friar, who lived in the friary at King's Lynn, and became Provincial of his Order in England. He wrote mostly in Latin; his chief patron was Humphrey, Duke of Gloucester. His main works are *Nova Legenda Angliae, De Illustribus Henricis,* and *Vita Humfredi Ducis Glocestriae.* In English he wrote lives of St Gilbert of Sempringham and of St Catharine of Alexandria; also a chronicle of English history.

JOHN CARPENTER (1370?-1441?), town clerk of London 1417-1438. He compiled a collection of records of London, *Liber Albus* (printed in the Rolls Series, 1859, translated by H. T. Riley 1861). The City of London School was founded on land left by Carpenter for educational purposes.

WILLIAM CAXTON (*c.* 1421-1491), the first English printer, also a merchant. He spent thirty years in the Low Countries, was governor of the English merchants in Bruges. He skilfully negotiated commercial treaties with the dukes of Burgundy. He became secretary to the household of Margaret, duchess of Burgundy, who was sister of Edward IV. While translating the *Recuyell of the Historyes of Troye* he worked in a printing house. He set up a press at Westminster in 1476. *The Dictes or Sayengis of the Philosophres,* 1477, is his first dated book. He printed about a hundred books, many of them his own translations from the French.

GEOFFREY CHAUCER (1345-1400), in 1359 was in the army of Edward III invading France. Later he was under the patronage of John of Gaunt. Held various positions at court, was sent on a mission to Genoa and Florence in 1372-3, probably met Boccaccio and Petrarch. He was knight of the shire for Kent in 1386; and went on the pilgrimage to Canterbury in April 1388. He was appointed clerk of the king's works, and later received pensions from Edward III, John of Gaunt, Richard II and Henry IV. Under French influence, 1359-72, he wrote the following: *The Boke of the Duchesse; Romaunt of the Rose.* To the period of Italian influence, notably that of Dante and Boccaccio, 1372-86, belong: *The Hous of Fame; The Parlement of Foules; Troylus and Cryseyde; The Legende of Good Women.* Chaucer used the heroic couplet in his greatest period, 1386-1400, to which belongs the *Canterbury Tales.* Here he depicted the social conditions of the time in a way unrivalled in medieval literature. His prose works include a translation of *Boethius,* and a *Treatise on the Astrolabe.*

THOMAS FAVENT, *Historia . . . mirabilis parliamenti.*

SIR ANTHONY FITZHERBERT (1470-1538) was knighted in 1516, and raised to the Bench in 1523. He wrote a valuable *Book of Husbandry.*

WILLIAM FITZSTEPHEN (*d.* 1190?). Becket, Archdeacon and Chancellor, but not yet Archbishop, was sent in 1158 to demand a French princess in marriage for Prince Henry. His chaplain was William Fitzstephen, author of the *History of Thomas Becket,* which contains a valuable account of twelfth-century London.

SIR JOHN FORTESCUE (1394?-1476?), chief justice of the King's Bench in 1442 under Henry VI, and the earliest English constitutional lawyer. He was a Lancastrian and accompanied Queen Margaret into exile in 1463, returning about 1470. His principal works were a Latin treatise, *De Natura Legis Naturae;* an English treatise, *Monarchia or the Difference between an Absolute and a Limited Monarchy;* and Latin treatise, *De Laudibus Legum Angliae* (written for Prince Edward); and *On the Governance of the Kingdom of England.*

JEAN FROISSART (1337?-1410), a French chronicler, of Hainault, who spent many years at the courts of princes. After the peace of Bretigny, 1360, he visited England, came to the court of Edward III and was welcomed by Queen Philippa, his countrywoman. He travelled to Scotland, Belgium and Italy recording historical events. His *Chroniques* cover other countries in the period 1325 to 1400. He is a splendid guide to an understanding of both sides of knighthood, the political and military power of this instituton was already crumblng in his time. His work was translated into English by John Bourchier, Lord Berners, 1523-5.

GEOFFREY DE VINSAUF (*fl.* 1200), wrote *Poëtria Nova.*

GEOFFREY DE VILLEHARDOUIN was born about 1150; started on the Fourth Crusade in 1202. He was one of the principal captains, and wrote his *Chronicle* only a short time after the events which he records.

GIRALDUS DE BARRI, called CAMBRENSIS (1146?-1220?), of Pembrokeshire and son of Nesta, a Welsh princess. He studied at Paris before 1176, and was later Archdeacon of Brecon. He spent most of his life trying to revive the supposed metropolitan rights of the see of St. David's. He appealed to Rome, sought the help of the Welsh, was outlawed, fled abroad, and was imprisoned at Châtillon. After his release he was reconciled to the king and archbishop. He was a prolific writer. Among his most important works are *Topographia Hibernica, Expugnatio Hibernica, Itinerarium Cambriae, Gemma Ecclesiastica, De Rebus a se gestis* —the history of Wales and Ireland, and on religion, he speaks frankly of Church reform.

JOHN GOWER (1330?-1408), of a good Kentish family, was possibly a merchant, and was well known at court in his later years. He did part of his literary work in a house within the precincts of the priory of St. Mary Overies, Southwark. A friend of Chaucer, who called him 'moral Gower'. His *Speculum Meditantis* or *Mirour de l'Omme,* is written in French; the *Vox Clamantis* in Latin; and the *Confessio Amantis* in English.

EDWARD GRIM, a man who witnessed the murder of Thomas à Becket, and was himself wounded. He wrote *Materials for the History of Archbishop Becket.*

JOHN HARDYNG (1378-1364), at the age of twelve was admitted to the household of Hotspur, Sir Henry Percy, and fought at Homildon Hill and Shrewsbury. He received the royal pardon in 1403, and enlisted under Sir Robert Umfraville, Warden of the Northern Marches, who in 1405 made Hardyng warden of his castle of Warkworth. His rhymed *Chronicle* tells us of events down to 1464.

RANULF (*or* RALPH) HIGDEN (1299?-1364), a Benedictine monk of St. Werburgh's Chester. He wrote, in Latin, *Polychronicon,* a world history, with a geographical introduction, compiled from the standard authors then accessible. A translation of this by John Trevisa, dated 1387, was printed by Caxton in 1482.

RAPHAEL HOLINSHED (*d.* 1580?), his *Chronicles* consist of a description of England followed by a history down to the Conquest; a description of Ireland and a chronicle; a description of Scotland and a history down to 1575; the history of the English kings to 1577. These, known by his name, include the work of other writers.

ITALIAN RELATION OF ENGLAND is a private report drawn up by the Venetian envoy for the information of his government, about 1500.

JOCELIN OF BRAKELOND (*fl.* 1200), a monk of Bury St. Edmunds. His *Chronicle* (1173-1202) gives a picture of monastic life in the twelfth century. Carlyle devoted seventeen chapters of of his *Past and Present* to a study of this work and of Abbot Samson.

JOHANNES DE MIRFIELD, an Austin canon of St. Bartholomew's, Smithfield, c. 1370. He wrote *Florarium Bartholomei.*

JOHN DE BURGO, Chancellor of Cambridge University in 1385 and a strong anti-Wycliffite. He wrote *Pupilla Oculi* to instruct the clergy in the duties of the Church.

JOHN DE GRANDISSON, Bishop of Exeter 1327-1369, was cousin to Sir Otho de Granson. Soon after his elevation he wrote two letters describing his diocese: one to his patron, Pope John XXII, and the other to several friendly cardinals at the Court of Avignon.

MARGERY KEMPE (*b.* c. 1373), a mystic, daughter of John Brunham of Lynn. She married John Kempe about 1393. She travelled extensively—to Italy, Jerusalem, Compostella and Germany, and composed a narrative of her spiritual experiences.

The Book of Margery Kempe was dictated as she was illiterate. A copy was made of the manuscript, and from this Wynkyn de Worde printed extracts in 1501.

HENRY KNIGHTON, a monk of Leicester Abbey, wrote *Chronicon* covering the years 959 to 1395. It is valuable in its later parts on account of the original records it contains.

WILLIAM LANGLAND (1330?-1400?), by origin a Malvern man, probably educated at the monastery of Great Malvern, lived in London most of his life. The great work, *The Vision concerning Piers Plowman,* is attributed to him. It is written in alliterative blank verse derived from Anglo-Saxon poetry. This religious allegory deals with the corruptions of medieval society and religion and expresses the religious seriousness of the age.

HUGH LATIMER (1485?-1555), was educated at Cambridge, where he became a Fellow of Clare College. He became known as a preacher, and having been made Bishop of Worcester in 1535 he devoted his gifts of oratory to further the Reformation. He was committed to the Tower on Mary's accession, condemned as a heretic, and burned at the stake.

JOHN LYDGATE (1370?-1451?) became a Benedictine monk at Bury St. Edmunds. He enjoyed the patronage of Duke Humphrey of Gloucester. Lydgate was a voluminous writer of verse and a devoted pupil of Chaucer. His chief poems are: *Troy Book; The Story of Thebes; Falls of Princes; The Pilgrimage of Man; London Lickpenny.* One prose work, written in 1400, *The Damage and Destruccyon in Realmes,* is said to be by him.

WALTER MAP (*fl.* 1200), a Welshman, was Archdeacon of Oxford under Henry II. He wrote *De nugis curialium,* which included *Dissuasio Valerii ad Rufinum de non decenda uxore.*

MATTHEW OF WESTMINSTER. We are informed by Gross that this is 'an entirely imaginary person'. Work ascribed to him was written by different people at different times. The earlier part is based on *Chronica Majora* of Matthew Paris. The oldest manuscript belonged once to Westminster Abbey. Parts of these two names combined gives us the fictitious Matthew of Westminster.

SIR THOMAS MORE (ST) (1478-1535), succeeded Wolsey as Lord Chancellor under Henry VIII, but fell into disgrace by refusing to take any oaths that should assail the authority of the pope. He was tried for high treason and executed. His famous works include *Utopia,* 1516; *Life of John Picus, Earl of Mirandula,* 1510; *History of Richard III; Supplycacyon of Soulys,* 1529.

ALEXANDER NECKHAM (*d.* 1217), his works include: *De naturis rerum; De laudibus divinae sapientiae; Novus Aesopus; Novus Avianus; Sacerdos ad Altare.*

MATTHEW PARIS (*d.* 1259), historian and Benedictine monk of the monastery of St. Albans. He was a man of great accomplishments, expert in writing, drawing, painting, in working gold and silver. He was a poet, theologian, mathematician, diplomat, especially notable as an historian. His *Chronica Majora,* 1235 to 1259, is the authority for the first half of the thirteenth century, and he stands before every other English chronicler. He also wrote *Historia Minor,* or *Historia Anglorum.*

PASTON, a Norfolk family, named from the village of Paston, whose letters and papers throw much light on family and political affairs. They present a vivid picture of English life in the fifteenth century. The chief members of the family were William Paston (1378-1444), justice of common pleas; his son, John (1421-1466); Clement (*c.* 1515-1597), a sailor; and Sir Robert (1631-1683), Earl of Yarmouth.

PETER OF BLOIS (*d. c.* 1212) was descended from a noble Breton family. He studied in Paris, and was invited to England by Henry II. He held various clerical appointments, was Archdeacon of Bath and became Archdeacon of London. He wrote as a satirist, and his letters emphasize the darker side of politics and customs of the time.

PHILIPPE DE COMMINES, a philosophic historian, one already of the Renaissance. In his *Mémoires* he tells the story of the Wars of the Roses, with their conspiracies and executions.

REGINALD OF DURHAM, a monk of Durham, wrote the *Life of St. Godric* before the saint's death in 1170. He often took notes of St. Godric's words as they were uttered, so we have what is close to an autobiography.

BISHOP RICHARD (*d.* 1198) was Bishop of London and also Treasurer. He wrote the *Dialogue of the Exchequer.*

RICHARD DE BURY came of a good family, was a cleric, and became tutor to Edward III. He rose to be royal clerk, ambassador, papal chaplain, and, in 1333, he became Bishop of Durham. He was a book-lover and a book-collector. His *Philobiblon* is the finest medieval treatise on books.

RICHARD DE MAIDSTONE, *De concordia inter Richardum Secundum at civitatem.*

RICHARD OF DEVIZES, the author of a chronicle of the earliest years of the reign of Richard I.

H. T. RILEY, his *Memorials of London and London Life* (1868) is a valuable collection of translations from the medieval French and Latin documents of the city records, preserved in the Record Room of the Guildhall.

ROBERT OF AVESBURY, *Historia Edwardi Tertii.*

ROGER OF WENDOVER (*d.* 1236), a monk of St. Albans. He wrote *Flores Historiarum,* which deals with history from the Creation to 1235.

RUTEBEUF, born in the first half of the thirteenth century, probably in Paris. His writing covers the years from 1255 to 1285, and includes *Lay of the Poverty of Rutebeuf, The Marriage of Rutebeuf,* and *The Complaint of Rutebeuf.*

THOMAS RYMER (1641-1713), studied at Cambridge and entered Gray's Inn in 1666. He is remembered for his valuable collection of historical records, *Foedera,* extending from the eleventh century to his own time.

SIMEON OF DURHAM, *Simeonis Dunelmensis Opera et Collectanea; Opera omnia* (635-1154).

STAPELDON, BISHOP OF EXETER, 'at episcopal archidiaconal visitations it was required that "sidesmen" should appear from each parish to testify'. Few such testimonies have been preserved. Details of a visitation in 1301 are found in the register of Bishop Stapeldon.

THOMAS DE CABHAM (*d.* 1313), Bishop of Salisbury, compiled a *Penitential,* or guide-book for confessors.

THOMAS DE WALSINGHAM (*d.* 1422) wrote *Gesta Abbatum; Historia Brevis,* 1381, speaking of Wat Tyler and his fellow rebels;

Chronicon Angliae (1328-1388).

THOMAS OF ECCLESTON (*fl.* 1250), an English friar who chronicled the settlement of Franciscan friars in England. His chronicle, *De adventu fratrum minorum in Angliam,* is both clear and detailed.

JOHN OF TREVISA (1326-1412), fellow of Exeter and Queen's Colleges, Oxford. He was expelled in 1379 with the Provost and some others, and became vicar of Berkeley, and chaplain to Lord de Berkeley, for whom his translations were done. These include Higden's *Polychronicon* in 1387, and the *De Proprietatibus Rerum* of Bartholomaeus Anglicus in 1398. He was the most zealous of medieval translators into English.

NICHOLAS TRIVET (*d.* 1328), *Expositio in Leviticum; Annales sex Regum Angliae,* a contemporary source for the reign of Edward I.

POLYDORE VERGIL (1470?-1555?), a native of Urbino. In 1502 he came to England as sub-collector of Peter's pence. He became Archdeacon of Wells from 1508 to 1554. His *Anglicae Historiae Libri XXVI* chronicles effectively the reign Henry VII.

WILLIAM OF MALMESBURY (*d.* 1143?), historian, was educated at Malmesbury Abbey and became librarian. His works include *Gesta Regum Anglorum* (440 to 1127), and its sequel *Historia Novella,* dealing with English history to 1142. He also wrote, in the same lively style, *De Antiguitate Glastoniensis Ecclesiae.*

WILLIAM .OF WYKEHAM (1324-1404), keeper of the privy-seal and secretary to the King in 1364, became Bishop of Winchester and Chancellor of England in 1367. He obtained a papal bull for the endowment of Winchester College in 1378 and founded New College, Oxford, in 1379. He founded his colleges 'first for the glory of God and the promotion of divine service, and secondarily for scholarship'. 'Wykeham's statutes for New College show a definite step forward; King's College was modelled on New College, as Eton was on Winchester.'

INDEX

Figures in **bold** refer to illustrations.

DA
185
.S36

1975